Also by Joe Zeigler

Bible
The Old Testament Retold

Bots
Connecting the Bots
Eliza's Children
Quantum Apocalypse
Tristan

History focused on women.
The Journey

Politics
We Used to be Wise

Trump
The Art of the Lie

PrumpTutin

Standalone

The Breeding

Table of Contents

THE JOURNEY

A Novel

Joe Zeigler

Arrakis Publishing, Inc.

THE JOURNEY

Published by Arrakis Publishing, Inc.
Crystal River, Florida

The Gorge Series, Book Two
Following: The Breeding
ISBN: 979-8-9952539-2-1
ArrakisPublishing.com

Also by Joe Zeigler

Bible

The Old Testament Retold

The New Testament

Bots

Eliza's Children

Connecting the Bots

Quantum Apocalypse

Tristan

The Gorge Series

The Breeding

The Journey

Trump

The Art of the Lie

PrumpTutin

PART ONE: THE JOURNEY

CHAPTER ONE

The watcher

The Lowland had changed.

Two years ago, the canyon people had camped on the outskirts of the Lowlanders' town the way they always had, temporary and seasonal. Now buildings had risen along both banks of the creek, stone foundations and woven-reed walls sealed with clay, roofs of juniper poles cut and stacked so rain ran off them. The Lowlanders' town was still there, six hundred people who farmed and kept livestock. Maxtla's trading hub had grown up on their edge, the way a second city grows beside a first one when there's enough reason. The smell of cooking fires and rendered fat and tanned leather hung permanently in the air.

Maxtla had built most of this by being right at the right time. She had planned a trading hub, not a settlement. The settlement had grown around it the way moss grows around a stone. She had come to the Lowland as a child with nothing and had spent twenty-three years turning that beginning into something that didn't require explaining.

She walked the plaza now in the gray hour before dawn, checking the loads one more time.

The baskets were stacked under oiled hides. Forty-eight of them, each representing weeks of work by the women she had trained and employed. Her best pieces, the picture baskets with their intricate patterns worked in three colors of split reed, were wrapped separately in the softest scraped hide she owned. Those weren't for everyday trade. Those were for the moment when you needed to impress a person who had already seen everything.

The combs were bundled by the gross. Wood, carved from scrap timber, every tooth cut precisely the same width because she had made a gauge and taught the carvers to use it. Light, smooth, consistent, better than most travelers could produce on the road. The Maya, according to Ixchel, set great store by beauty rituals. Good combs would find buyers.

The obsidian mirrors. Six of them, polished to an almost painful clarity by a technique she had developed herself, using progressively finer grades of sand and finally a pad of soft leather and fat. When you held one up, you saw yourself as clearly as a deep pool on a windless day. Nothing like it existed anywhere on the route south that she knew of. The first time you showed a mirror to someone who had never seen one, their face changed. That face was worth more than the mirror.

The medicine kit. Tinga had spent two weeks preparing it, dried herbs and roots packed in small clay pots sealed with beeswax, each marked with a scratch code that Tinga had taught Maxtla to read. The southern people would have their own medicines. But different medicines. Trade in healing was trade in something people would pay nearly anything for.

Maxtla crouched beside the medicine kit and checked the seals one more time. All good.

"You already checked those twice."

She looked up. Ixchel stood in the pre-dawn shadow, her arms folded across her chest, her expression tolerant and amused.

"I'll check them a third time if I want to," Maxtla said.

"Of course you will. I'm merely observing." Ixchel settled herself onto a nearby rock. She was quieter than Maxtla, more internal, though her mind moved faster when it came to numbers and alliances. She had her mother's straight black hair and something in her cheekbones and mouth that spoke of the southern peoples, her mother had traveled north with traders, met a man of the Cliff Dwellers, and stayed. Ixchel had grown up hearing her mother speak two languages and, by some gift or discipline, retained them both.

"Is Lofn ready?" Maxtla asked.

"Lofn will never be ready. She will come anyway."

That was true. Lofn was ready in the ways that mattered, her pack was precise, her weapons were sharp, her instincts in a crisis were unexpectedly sound. She was never emotionally ready. There was always one more thing to grieve or fear or anticipate with dread.

"And Eijá?"

"Eijá has been ready since yesterday morning and has spent the last day finding things to be impatient about."

Maxtla smiled at that.

"And Danijel?"

The question fell between them differently than the others. They had both been surprised when he appeared at the settlement three weeks ago. He had simply walked down the canyon trail one morning as if he had been away a week rather than a year, carrying his pack with the economy of motion that was his alone. He looked at the settlement the way you looked at something you had watched grow for a long time and were not surprised to find changed.

He had asked to come. He hadn't explained why. Maxtla had thought about it for two days, which was more deliberation than she gave most decisions.

She had said yes.

"Danijel," Ixchel said carefully, "will be where he needs to be."

Whatever else Danijel was, and Maxtla had her private theories about what he was, he was reliable the way a good knife was reliable. Without drama, without explanation.

Gedeon was at her side now, having risen at the same time she did, which was his habit. He stood close but not interfering. He knew her moods at dawn.

She had lost two children before Aki. The fever, both times, the third month and the eighth.

She was carrying Aki now. Three months. She had told no one but Gedeon, and Lofn, who had noticed without being told.

Gedeon had stood in the same position both times she had lost them: close, not pressing, present in the way of someone who understood that silence was not absence.

"The horses are ready," he said.

"Thank you."

He put his hand on her arm, briefly. That was all. He was not a man who said things twice, and he had already told her, in the night, what he needed her to know. His hand had been on the back of her neck in the dark. She had leaned into it without meaning to, and neither of them had spoken after that.

She stood and picked up her spear.

"Go wake the others," she said to Ixchel.

Ixchel went.

Maxtla looked up at the red canyon walls, already turning amber as the sky behind them lightened in the east. Somewhere up on the ridge, something had moved three days ago and caught her eye. She wasn't certain it was a threat. She was certain it wasn't nothing.

The man on the ridge had been watching for three days.

He lay flat on the red sandstone shelf, chin on folded arms, watching the settlement below the way a hawk watches a prairie dog hole. Patient. Certain.

His name was Targat, and he was the raid leader for the northern confederation of eleven bands. They had no real name for themselves. Names were for settlements, for people who stayed in one place long enough to need them. His people moved. His people took. That was their economy, simple and ancient, and it had worked for generations.

He counted again. Fourteen women. One man, old or at least moving like old. Seven horses, the four-legged beasts the southern people used for loads. He had seen horses before but never in this number, and never this heavily loaded.

The way they moved, organized, no wasted motion, everyone knowing their role without being told, told him what he needed to know about these women.

The tall one in front was the leader. He could tell by the way the others moved in relation to her, the way their eyes tracked to her when a decision needed making. She wore her black hair loose to her shoulders except for a single braid down the left side, pulled back from her face. She moved like a woman who had never wondered whether she had the right to be in front.

He respected that.

He also planned to take everything she owned and sell her and her companions to the coastal people, who had a use for strong women with sharp eyes. The respect and the plan existed in him without conflict. This was simply how the world worked.

The second scout, Palun, slid up beside him and pressed close enough to whisper.

"They leave at first light tomorrow," Palun said. "I heard it from the man I bribed near the south gate."

"How many days' supplies?"

"Three months. Maybe more."

Targat let out a slow breath. Three months of supplies meant a long journey. A long journey south meant only one thing.

"They're going to the Maya lands."

Palun said nothing. They both understood the implications. Whatever these women brought back from a journey of that length would be worth ten times what they were carrying now.

"We follow," Targat said. "We let them go. We let them make the journey. We let the Maya do the work of stocking their packs. And then, when they are tired and laden and almost home."

Palun smiled.

"Then we take it all."

Below them, the woman with the black braid stopped walking and turned to look up at the ridge. Targat felt a cold finger run up his spine. She could not see them. They were still and dark against the red stone. And yet she looked directly at where they lay, her gaze flat and evaluating for a long three seconds before she turned back to her work.

Targat's jaw tightened.

He would be careful with that one.

Maria came to the gate just as they were leaving.

She was younger than the others, seventeen at most, with a wide, flat face and arms that were roped with muscle from two years of hauling stone and splitting firewood at the south end of the settlement. She carried a pack that suggested she had been planning this longer than one night.

Maxtla stopped.

"No," Maxtla said.

"Yes," Maria said.

"You're not trained."

"I'm trained enough. Eijá taught me her knife work. I've been practicing spear for a year. I can run all day." She met Maxtla's eyes without flinching. "I need to leave. I have reasons I don't want to explain, and you don't need to know them."

Maxtla looked at Eijá.

Eijá shrugged. "She can run all day. That part's true."

Maxtla looked at the girl again. There was something in her eyes Maxtla recognized. The look of someone who had already decided that wherever you were going was safer than where they had been.

"You understand this is not a short journey," Maxtla said.

"I'm counting on it," Maria said.

Danijel stood apart from all of them, watching. He said nothing.

"Keep up," Maxtla said, and turned back to the trail.

Maria fell in behind Eijá.

They walked out of the Lowland as the sun broke over the eastern mesa and painted everything gold.

Gedeon stood at the gate and watched until they rounded the first bend in the canyon trail and were gone.

Behind him, in the settlement, someone's dog was barking at nothing, as dogs do when the balance of a place shifts in a way they can feel but not name.

He turned back to the work of the day.

The work did not help.

He had hauled water and repaired a section of the upper trail and helped the family in the north section reset a fence post that had been leaning since spring. The fence post was straight now. The north family was grateful. He felt exactly as he had felt when Maxtla and the others rounded the bend and were gone from sight, which was a kind of empty that was adjacent to grief.

He had chosen her knowing what she was. The pack weight was heavy, but she had carried heavier. What occupied him was the watcher on the ridge and that she had seen him and filed it without alarm.

He was proud of her and wanted her home. Both were true at once.

He went back to the settlement when the light went and ate the evening meal and reported the fence post to the north family's elder, who nodded the way of someone who had been meaning to fix that for longer than was comfortable to admit. Then he went to the place where the canyon wall curved slightly east and caught the last light, which was her favorite place at that hour, and sat there until the light was fully gone.

Every time she left, the settlement was less itself. The women ran things competently and the work continued. But the quality the settlement had when she was in it, directed energy, things moving toward something, that traveled with her.

He slept and woke and did the work and watched the canyon and did not count the days.

She went back to the camp in the early afternoon and told them they were leaving at first light.

No one questioned this. They had known the departure was coming; the preparations had been complete for two days. The delay had been hers, the watching, the waiting for the feeling of readiness that was less about the packs being right and more about the mind being right.

Gedeon was sitting outside the camp's edge, doing nothing in particular, which for Gedeon was the productive nothing of a person who processed by resting.

"You've been watching him," he said.

"Yes."

She sat down beside him. "He'll hit us at the first natural chokepoint where the load-to-defender ratio looks favorable."

Gedeon was quiet for a while. The late-afternoon canyon light was doing what it did, the red of the walls deepening toward something between red and brown, the shadows filling from the bottom up.

"What do you need from me?" he said.

"What I always need from you," she said. "Be there when it matters."

"I'm always there when it matters."

"I know," she said. "That's why I trust the rest of it."

He smiled, the small smile Gedeon saved for moments that were both difficult and worth being present for. She had known him six years and had learned to read the smile as the indicator it was: not happiness exactly, but recognition.

She had built a settlement. She was now building a route. The route would outlast the journey that established it, would outlast the people who had made the first agreements along it, would become the thing that the next generation inherited and extended the way Aki would inherit and extend the settlement.

"First light," she said, and stood up and went back to the camp.

Behind her, Gedeon watched the western ridge.

On the ridge, the watcher watched back.

The canyon held its breath in the way it always held its breath before something started.

CHAPTER TWO

The size of it

On the second day, they crossed out of the canyon country into the open desert, and the scale of what they were doing became unavoidable.

North of the canyon, you could always see where you had come from. The red walls rose behind you and gave you a frame of reference. Once you cleared the southern lip of the plateau and descended into the flat expanse of the lower desert, all of that was gone. The land was ochre and bone and gray scrub stretching to every horizon, and the sky above it was enormous.

Lofn looked at it and said, "Oh."

"Yes," Maxtla said.

"I had forgotten how big it was."

"I hadn't."

They moved south in a loose column with Maxtla and Danijel in front and Eijá and Maria at the rear, the five loaded horses between them. The pack animals were docile, trained creatures that had reached a philosophical accommodation with their circumstances.

The route they were following was a set of decisions, made by animals and people and water over thousands of years, that tended to go south while avoiding the worst of the terrain. Maxtla had pieces of it from four separate sources, Gedeon's trader knowledge, a drawing scratched on a flat piece of clay by an old woman who had made the journey once as a girl, Ixchel's mother's recalled descriptions, and her own observation of the land. She had assembled these pieces into a route she was mostly confident in, which meant she was prepared for the parts she wasn't confident in.

"The water question," Ixchel said, walking up beside her.

"I know."

"We have three days' supply. The southern springs."

"Are two days away if we move well. One and a half if we push." Maxtla glanced at the horses. "We don't push the horses. We move steadily and we get there with a day to spare."

Ixchel nodded. She had not been asking a question so much as thinking out loud, checking Maxtla's thinking against her own.

Ixchel walked beside her without speaking for a while, processing the open desert quietly, from the outside in.

"The followers," she said finally. "We need them not to know how much we're carrying back."

"Or," Maxtla said, "we need them to become our allies before we're loaded."

Ixchel processed that. "Ambitious."

"Most good solutions are."

Danijel was walking slightly ahead of them. He had said nothing since the departure. What was different now was the quality of his silence, less resting than attending.

She moved up beside him.

"You see them?" she asked without preamble.

"Two, on the ridge. They dropped off our track before the canyon mouth. Picked it back up this morning." He paused. "Three now."

"Three?"

"A third joined them in the night. He came from the east."

She trusted his eyes. They perceived distance and detail and motion at ranges that occasionally made her breath catch.

"Any danger now?"

"No. They're following, not positioning. The patience suggests they're planning something far out."

"The return," Maxtla said.

He nodded.

"Then for now they're just witnesses. Expensive witnesses if you plan to prevent them interfering on the return."

"I'm planning on making them partners," she said.

He glanced at her. There was something in his expression she couldn't quite read, controlled amusement or perhaps respect.

"When?" he asked.

"When they offer. They'll offer at some point. People always offer when you have something they want and they're not sure they can just take it." She watched the horizon. "The key is to make sure they're never quite sure."

He said nothing, but she could feel his attention settle on her fully for a moment before he turned back to the trail.

The desert moved past them.

By midday on the third day they found the springs.

It was more than springs, actually, a series of seeps and pools fed by an underground flow that surfaced in a shallow depression between two rocky ridges, surrounded by willows and cottonwoods that looked wildly out of place in the surrounding desert. The grass around the water was green and thick and the horses put their heads down immediately.

Maxtla let them drink before allowing the women to approach the water.

"Always the horses first?" Maria asked. There was an edge to it.

"The horses carry everything we own," Maxtla said. "Dead horses are not useful."

Maria accepted this.

They set camp in the shade of the cottonwoods, which was better shade than they had had since leaving the canyon. The afternoon heat was genuine now, this far south and this low, the late-summer sun had intent behind it, pressing down with a weight that drained energy from movement and made the shade feel like a gift.

Eijá built a small, nearly smokeless fire and began on the evening meal. This was her domain. She had an understanding with food that the others deferred to completely. Even Danijel, who could presumably have eaten nothing for several days and been fine, sat near her fire without comment.

Maxtla posted the first watch without being asked, assigning the two-hour rotations and giving Maria the second-to-last slot, not the last.

"I could take last," Maria said.

"No."

"I'm perfectly capable."

"Probably. But I don't know that yet." Maxtla met her eyes. "You earn the hard shifts. I'm not withholding them to insult you."

Maria was the kind of person who had to run an objection through several internal filters before she could tell whether it was legitimate or just pride talking. The pause told Maxtla that she was doing that.

"Second-to-last is fine," Maria said finally.

Lofn had been collecting firewood and overheard all of this, which she pretended not to have done. The months since Dewii's death had done something to her, not hardened her exactly, but clarified her. She had learned to feel it quietly. She had been thinking about what it meant to help someone without asking them first. The people who had helped her after Dewii died had done it with kindness. But kindness wasn't the same as asking.

"Do you think the springs will be here on the return?" she asked Maxtla.

"They've been here a thousand years. They'll be here for our return."

Lofn considered this. "Unless it's a drought year."

"It's not a drought year. Look at the grass."

Lofn looked at the grass. "Oh," she said. And then, because she could not help herself: "But what if it becomes a drought year while we're gone?"

Maxtla looked at her. "Lofn."

"Yes."

"We will deal with that problem if it becomes a problem."

"Right." A pause. "But if you wanted to think through contingencies."

"Later," Maxtla said.

Lofn nodded and went back to collecting wood.

Danijel had been watching this exchange from across the camp. After Lofn moved off, he spoke quietly. "She keeps you honest."

"She keeps me irritated," Maxtla said.

"Same thing, often."

That night she lay on her back and looked up at the sky through the cottonwood leaves, which were beginning to turn yellow at the edges. The stars here were brighter than in the canyon, where the walls cut off half the sky. She could see the great river of light that ran from horizon to horizon, the same river she had looked at all her life, dense with stars in ways she had never been able to count.

She thought about Gedeon. She thought about the child that was not yet showing but that she felt the presence of in abstract, tender ways she hadn't expected. She thought about what she was building, not just the trading organization, not just the material wealth, but the other thing, the harder thing.

That idea had enemies at home. She had watched them move back in over the last year, subtle at first, testing what they could get away with, slowly reclaiming the old prerogatives that the old ways had given them. The settlement's growth had attracted people from outside who brought their customs with them. Some of those customs were the ones Maxtla had fought to end.

She couldn't fight them by staying. She could fight them by going. By coming back with wealth and power and allies enough that the old men looked at her and understood something had permanently changed.

She was not naive about this. The wealth and the power didn't guarantee anything.

But it was better than the alternative.

She closed her eyes and matched her breathing to the sound of the creek and slept hard until her watch.

GEDEON: ONE

The weight of it

The settlement had run itself before Maxtla. It would run itself now.

That was what Gedeon told himself on the first morning, walking the creek path at dawn with Aki on his back, the child's weight shifting with each step the way small weights do, adjusting without thought. The trail was familiar. The light was familiar. The smell of cook fires starting in the north section was the same smell it had always been.

What was different was the quality of the quiet.

Not silence. The settlement was not quiet, sixty people going about morning work were not quiet. But there was a directedness missing. The way energy moved when Maxtla was in it: toward something, organized around something that didn't require naming because it was simply present. Without her, the energy was still there. It moved without direction the way water moved when you lifted the channel that had been guiding it.

He noticed it and made no comment. There was no one to comment to.

Aki had his father's habit of watching before deciding. He was eighteen months old and had already learned that the world contained more information than it first appeared to. He watched the creek now, from Gedeon's back, with the serious attention of someone still compiling data.

"Creek," Gedeon said.

Aki considered this.

"Creek," Aki said.

"Yes."

They went on.

The fence post in the north section still needed work. He had repaired it twice; the ground there was soft and it listed back within a week. He set Aki in the shade and began digging.

Danel came past while he was working. A big man, not young, who had come to the settlement the previous summer from the eastern corridor groups. He had a brother in the canyon and had arrived with skills, stone-setting, mostly, and had integrated without difficulty and with not much warmth. He watched Gedeon work.

"The east storage needs assigning," Danel said.

"I know," Gedeon said. He kept digging.

"The woman Peli has been using it for her fiber work. But it's the largest covered space in the north section. There are people who need it for grain storage before the rains."

Gedeon looked up. The east storage had been assigned to Peli by Maxtla before the journey. It was not formally assigned, nothing was formally assigned, which was both the current problem and the coming solution. But Peli had been given the space and had organized her work around it and employed three other women in it, and the economics of that arrangement were not difficult to understand.

"Talk to Peli," he said.

"Peli says it's her space."

"She's right," Gedeon said.

Danel looked at him for a moment with the look of someone who had expected a different response. Not aggressive. Recalculating.

"The grain storage is a real problem," he said. "Before the rains."

"I'll find a solution for the grain storage before the rains," Gedeon said. "The east storage is Peli's."

Danel nodded once and went on.

Gedeon finished with the fence post and tested it and judged it good for three weeks and no more. He would need stone and to pack it properly. He added it to the list he kept in his head, which had grown longer since Maxtla left.

Aki had fallen asleep in the shade. One hand was open and relaxed. The other was gripping a handful of dirt he had picked up and forgotten about.

He picked up the child and stood for a moment with the weight of him, looking north where the canyon trail bent and disappeared. The morning light was still low and red against the upper walls, the shadows long.

She was two days south of the plateau by now. Maybe three.

He carried Aki back to the settlement and began the rest of the morning's work.

CHAPTER THREE

The pass

The first attack came twelve days south of the springs, in a narrow pass between two rocky shoulders where the trail squeezed down to the width of two people walking abreast.

Maxtla had seen the site from half a mile out and had not liked it. There was no way around it, the ridges on either side were sheer and the horses could not manage them, and the raiders who had set up there had done so with enough competence to tell her this wasn't their first attempt.

She counted seven. Possibly eight. Two on the ridge to the east, which she could see. More in the rocks on the west side, which she couldn't see but could feel in the way the pass had gone unnaturally quiet.

She stopped the column fifty yards out.

"Company," she said, loud enough for all of them.

The woman at the rear of the column, Maria, had already seen it. Maxtla could tell by the way she had quietly shifted her pack off her shoulders and set it on the ground to her right, leaving her hands free.

Good.

Danijel moved up beside her. "Eight," he said. "Three on the east ridge, two on the west, three on the ground in the rocks at the pass mouth."

She had miscounted the east ridge. She noted it and kept moving.

"Tribe?" she asked.

He studied the figures on the ridge for a moment. "Lowland people, I think. Not the confederation from the north. Different weapons, different stance."

Different meant unknown. Unknown was harder.

Maxtla cupped her hands around her mouth. "We see you," she called toward the pass. "We are traders. We are willing to pay passage. Come out and speak with us."

Nothing moved for a long breath. Then a figure detached itself from the rocks at the pass mouth and walked toward them. He was a young man, not old enough to have the full authority his swagger was trying to claim, carrying a club with a stone head and a short throwing spear in the other hand.

He stopped twenty yards away and studied them with the contempt of someone who had decided in advance that a group of women with one old man cannot be dangerous.

"Toll," he said. He pointed at the horses. "One horse."

"No," Maxtla said pleasantly.

His expression changed. He had expected either compliance or panic.

"One horse," he said again, louder.

"No. We will give you five packets of dried meat and ten arrowheads. This is fair value for passage through land you don't actually own." She kept her voice conversational. "If you reject this offer, some of your people will die, and the rest will regret it."

He stared at her.

Behind her, she heard rather than saw Eijá and Lofn separate slightly. They had trained for exactly this configuration, spreading the threat across enough space that any attack would have to choose targets rather than swamp them.

Maria, to her left, had not moved, but Maxtla could feel her attention like heat.

The young man turned his head and shouted something in his own language toward the pass. An older voice answered from the rocks, short, sharp, disagreeing. The young man's shoulders set stubbornly. He turned back to Maxtla.

He raised his throwing spear.

What happened next took less time than it took to describe.

Maxtla was already moving as his arm came back. Not toward him, that was what he expected, but to the right, out of his line, while drawing her own spear from its carrier across her back. His throw was good; it passed through the space where she had been standing close enough that she felt the air of it. She completed her turn, found her footing, and put her spear through his upper thigh.

Not the kill shot. The information shot.

He went down with a cry that cut off the battle before it could start.

Danijel had moved on the east ridge. The two figures there were suddenly not in their positions.

Eijá had a figure from the west rocks face-down on the ground with his arm bent behind him. She hadn't needed her spear.

Lofn covered the pass mouth, spear low and ready.

Maria had come forward without being asked, standing over the young raider at the end of her knife's reach. Her face was calm.

The older voice from the rocks spoke again, different in tone now. Maxtla looked toward it.

"Come out," she said. "We're not here to kill anyone who doesn't insist."

A long pause. Then a man emerged from the rocks at the pass mouth, older, gray at his temples, moving with the measured care of someone who had survived enough situations to know that sudden movements were mostly a mistake. He looked at the young man on the ground, at the blood, at the flat-faced women standing over his companions.

"Medicine?" he said. His language and Maxtla's had maybe a quarter of their words in common, just enough.

"If you behave," Maxtla said.

He nodded slowly. He clapped his hands twice and called to the others, who came out of the rocks without weapons raised.

Ixchel was already moving toward the injured man with the medicine kit.

The older man watched her work. He watched all of them for a long time, saying little.

"Who are you?" he said finally, in his language, which Ixchel translated.

"Traders," Maxtla said. "Going south."

"Women traders," he said. Not a question.

"Yes."

He was quiet again. Then: "My son."

"Your son's leg will be fine if the infection doesn't take it," Maxtla said. "Ixchel knows how to prevent infection."

The man looked at his son, who was pale and holding his thigh with both hands, and at Ixchel, who was cleaning the wound with an herbed solution that smelled medicinal and sharp.

"The toll is reduced," the old man said. It cost him something to say it.

"No toll," Maxtla said. "Safe passage only. We are not enemies."

He processed this. "You spear my son."

"Your son threw first," she said without heat.

The young man, listening, said nothing. His jaw was tight with pain and something else, the difficult transition from contempt to revised understanding that young men find hard.

The old man looked at her. “What do you trade?”

"Baskets. Combs. Medicines. Technology that builds things. On the return, things from the south that you've never seen."

He looked at the packed horses. "What do you need?"

"Safe passage through your land. Information about what lies south. And if there are others on this route who might become problems, I'd rather know about them now."

He thought about that. Then he made a decision.

"I will give you a guide," he said. "To the edge of our land."

"What do you want in return?"

He pointed at the pack with the baskets. "To see."

Maxtla nodded to Ixchel, who opened the pack and brought out three of the standard baskets.

The old man took one and turned it in his hands. He looked at the construction, the weave, the colors. He turned it upside down and looked at the bottom. He pressed the sides and felt how they gave and returned. He held it up to the light and looked through the weave.

"These took time," he said.

"Yes."

"Why do this much work for something that carries grain?"

"Because people will pay more for something that is also beautiful," Maxtla said. "And because the woman who made it is worth more than a person who makes only useful things."

He looked at her for a moment. Then he said something in his own language that she didn't catch, but that Ixchel translated softly in her ear later.

It meant: I understand now why you travel without men.

The guide was a young woman, to Maxtla's slight surprise. She was quiet and quick and knew every rock on the route south. She stayed with them for four days and then pointed them down a long valley toward a range of blue mountains and, without ceremony, turned back north.

They watched her go.

"She'll tell others about us," Eijá said.

"I counted on it," Maxtla said.

Three weeks south of the canyon country, the land began to change in earnest.

The dry scrub thinned and then gave way to a different kind of desert, harder and more severe at first, the terrain all sharp edges and pale caliche, and then by degrees more forgiving as they descended and the air held more moisture. Creatures appeared that none of them had seen before, a bird with a long ridiculous tail that ran instead of flew, a lizard the length of Maxtla's arm that turned colors depending on which rock it sat on, a spider the size of a man's fist that Lofn found in her boot one morning and screamed about loud enough to echo from the hills.

"It wasn't poisonous," Eijá noted.

"You don't know that," Lofn said.

"It's still alive and you're still alive, so."

"I'll be watching my boots from now on."

"You should have been watching them before," Maria said, and there was a small surprised silence, because Maria had been mostly quiet for three weeks and this was close enough to a joke that no one knew whether to laugh.

Then Lofn laughed, which decided the matter.

Maria looked faintly startled by her own humor and then something in her face relaxed a little.

Danijel observed all of this from a few steps back. Whatever she was running from, she was running far enough from it now that she could occasionally look at something other than the path behind her.

He was, he knew, doing the same thing.

He had told himself he was coming to observe. That was not entirely false.

But he had come back because he could not think of anywhere else he would rather be. He had watched that fire before, in individuals, in movements. It almost always burned out or got smothered.

Sometimes it didn't.

He was here to see which one this was.

The mountains to the south were getting closer.

CHAPTER FOUR

Three attacks

The second attack came in the night, which was more dangerous and more telling. People who attacked at night were either desperate or experienced, and the group that hit their camp three days into the mountain foothills was experienced. Four men had circled from downwind, used the natural depression of a dry creekbed to approach, and were within twenty yards of the sleeping camp before Danijel moved.

He moved without waking anyone.

By the time Eijá came off watch and found him crouching at the edge of the dark, four men were sitting in a row on the far side of the creekbed, bound with their own bowstrings, looking unhappy. None of them appeared harmed. Maxtla looked at the four men, and then at Danijel, and then back at the men. Four experienced raiders. Downwind. Inside twenty yards. In the dark. The watch hadn't heard them come. The watch hadn't heard Danijel go. She made a note of it the way she made notes of things she didn't yet have a name for.

What nobody had seen, in the dark and the confusion of Danijel's intervention, was the horse.

The third horse from the left had been picketed at the edge of the camp where the creekbed ran closest, and when the four men had come out of the dark it had caught their scent and bolted. The picket line held and then broke, and the horse ran maybe forty yards before the drop-off at the creekbed's edge stopped it. Maria found it standing at the edge in the dark, breathing hard, the picket rope trailing behind it.

The pack was gone.

The lashing had caught on something in the run and torn free. It took twenty minutes to find where it had landed in the dark, and by then they knew from the sound it had made on the way down that the news was going to be bad.

It was the medicine pack.

Lofn went down the creekbed wall on a rope in the dark without being asked. Maxtla stood at the top and held the rope and listened to the sounds from below, careful movement, a low sound that was not quite a word, then silence, then more movement.

When she came back up she was carrying about half of what had gone down. The rest was broken, or scattered in the dark at the creekbed floor in pieces too small to collect by torchlight, or simply gone into the water that ran at the bottom.

She laid it out on the ground in the torchlight. Seven of the sealed clay pots were intact. Four were cracked and their contents compromised. Three were missing entirely. The wound-closure preparation, the one Tinga had spent a week preparing, the most labor-intensive thing in the kit, was gone. The fever treatment that worked on the specific southern fever Tinga had warned them about was reduced to a quarter of what they had started with. The pain preparation was intact. The infection treatment was intact. The bone-setting supplies were intact.

Lofn sat back on her heels and looked at what was left with the expression of someone doing a calculation they do not like the answer to.

"We can manage," she said.

"We can manage if nothing goes badly wrong," Maxtla said.

"Yes," Lofn said. "If nothing goes badly wrong."

The four bound men on the far side of the creekbed had been listening to all of this.

She filed the anger. These were the costs of traveling in the world.

She doubled the watch rotation for the remainder of the night. In the morning, before they broke camp, she went over the picket arrangements with everyone who handled the horses and revised them to account for what she now knew.

Lofn repacked what remained of the medicine kit into a smaller container. The empty space where the rest had been was visible and she did not try to disguise it. She sealed the new pack and strapped it to the horse that had been carrying the baskets, redistributing the load.

She had not cried. Lofn had done the work and repacked the pack and was ready to move when the column moved.

"Scouts for a larger group," Danijel told Maxtla when she came to look.

"How large?"

"Twenty to thirty. They're half a day back. They sent these four ahead to assess the camp."

Twenty to thirty was too many to fight through. It was the right number to negotiate with or avoid.

"Can we go around?"

"Not with the horses. Not on this terrain."

She thought about it while the eastern sky was still black.

"Do any of them have enough language in common with us to talk?"

He had already determined this. "The short one on the left."

She crouched in front of the short one on the left, who looked at her with the focused hatred of a man who has been humiliated. She met it without reacting.

"Your group is behind you," she said. "I know there are more of you. I'm not going to try to fight through. I want to talk. Send for your leader."

The man stared at her.

"We have food," she added. "And something I think your leader will want to see."

CHAPTER FIVE

Teya

The third leader was a tall woman.

Maxtla had not expected this, and she chose not to let the surprise show, though she felt Ixchel stir beside her.

The woman's name, conveyed through the halting chain of shared vocabulary, was something close to Teya. She was perhaps forty, old for the trail life, which meant she was either exceptional or she had people who protected her, or both. She walked into the small clearing where Maxtla had set up for the meeting with the economic confidence of someone who had never once entered a room wondering whether she belonged there.

She looked at the group. She counted. She noted the absence of a male authority figure in any of the positions that would normally hold one. She made no visible reaction to this, which told Maxtla she was intelligent and disciplined.

She spoke. The short man translated, badly.

"She asks what you carry."

"Show her," Maxtla said.

Ixchel laid out the display: two standard baskets, one picture basket, a set of the wood combs arranged by size, two obsidian mirrors face-down until the moment, the medicine kit, and a small wrapped bundle at the end.

Teya looked at the baskets with appreciation but not surprise. She had seen good baskets.

She looked at the combs with more interest. She picked one up, turned it, tested the teeth against her palm. Looked at the regularity of the spacing. Set it down carefully.

She looked at the medicine kit. She picked up one of the sealed pots and smelled the seal. She looked at Ixchel. Something passed between them in that look, professional recognition.

Then Ixchel turned over the mirrors.

The mirrors were always the moment.

Teya picked up the mirror.

She looked into it.

Her expression did not change, she was too controlled for that, but her breathing shifted. She looked for perhaps thirty seconds without moving. Then she set the mirror carefully face-down on the display.

She spoke to the translator. He translated.

"She says: you have come to trade with the southern people."

"Yes."

"She says: they are not honest traders."

"We have heard this. We go anyway."

Teya spoke again, longer.

"She says: we know the routes south from here. We have traded with the coast people for five generations. We do not always stay here. We move."

"Raiders," Lofn said quietly, from behind Maxtla. Not an accusation. An observation.

"When there is nothing else," Teya herself said, in Maxtla's language, not fluently, but clearly. She had been understanding more than she was letting on.

Maxtla let the silence sit for a moment. "How many people in your group?"

"Twenty-six."

"How many fighters?"

"All of them."

"We are going south," Maxtla said. "We will be on the route for two months, perhaps three. The return will be loaded with goods. If you travel with us as protection, I will pay you a fair share of what we bring back."

Teya looked at her for a long time. "You offer partnership? To raiders?"

"I offer partnership to people who know the route and can fight."

Teya sat with this.

"If you move with us," Maxtla continued, "you have a steady income. Reliable food. And when we reach the southern city, you trade on your own account. I will make you proper introductions."

"And if we just take your goods when you return?" Teya said.

"You could try. But I promise you'll find it much more expensive than what I'm offering." She kept her voice even. "And less interesting."

Something happened in Teya's expression then, the smallest possible shift, like a fish turning a fraction in deep water. Interest. Real interest, not tactical.

"What is in the small bundle?" she asked.

Maxtla unwrapped it.

Inside was a knife with a bone handle and an obsidian blade, honed by a technique that Maxtla's craftswomen had developed over the past year, a bevel angle that held an edge three times longer than the standard approach. It was the finest cutting tool currently existing, as far as she knew, anywhere on the route south.

She held it out.

Teya took it. Tested the edge against the pad of her thumb. A thin line of blood appeared, no pressure required. Her eyes widened.

"This is yours," Maxtla said. "Whether we make an agreement or not. It is a gift."

Teya looked at her.

"Why?" she asked.

"Because you deserve to know what is possible," Maxtla said. "And because a person who has been shown something exceptional makes better decisions."

A long silence.

"We will talk more tonight," Teya said.

They talked for three nights. On the second night Teya's second-in-command, a blocky aggressive man named Parruk, made a move on Maria that was interrupted when Maria put her elbow through his nose with a speed that stopped the entire camp for a moment.

In the silence that followed, Maxtla looked at Teya.

Teya looked at Parruk, who was bleeding freely and realizing he had made a serious miscalculation.

"He will apologize," Teya said.

"He will apologize and never do it again," Maxtla said. "To any of us."

Parruk apologized. He was convincing about it, which suggested he had absorbed the lesson. He would prove, later, to be one of the better fighters in Teya's group, and he kept his hands to himself from that night forward.

Maria had not asked permission before responding to the assault. She had not looked to Maxtla, had not waited for direction. She had handled it herself and immediately.

Later, at the edge of the firelight, Maxtla found Maria sitting alone cleaning her blade with more care than necessary.

"Good," Maxtla said.

Maria looked up.

She looked at the fire. Her hands had stopped moving.

"Thank you," she said.

"You were fast," Maxtla said.

"I've been practicing."

"I could see that." Maxtla sat down beside her, not touching, not hovering. Just present. "Where did you learn the elbow strike?"

"Eijá."

"Remind me to thank Eijá."

They sat together for a while without speaking, which Maria found, to her surprise, comfortable.

"What are you running from?" Maxtla asked. Not accusing. Genuinely asking.

Maria was quiet for a moment. Then: "A man who thought I was his to decide about. He was an elder. He had standing in the settlement."

"Ohad's legacy," Maxtla said. It came out tired.

"Not his personally. Just what things are going back to." Maria's jaw tightened. "I watched you build something good. And then I watched it start to unmake itself while you were on the shorter trips. Like water flowing back into a low place."

Maxtla said nothing.

"I'm not running," Maria added. "I'm going somewhere."

"Yes," Maxtla said. "You are."

On the fourth morning, Teya shook hands with Maxtla in the trader fashion, wrist to wrist, and the combined group moved south together.

Twenty-six fighters was a different proposition than six women and one very odd old man.

On the ridge above, Targat counted the new additions to the column below and revised his plans considerably.

CHAPTER SIX

The road south

The jungle announced itself through smell before it was visible.

Maxtla had been told about the south's jungle, Ixchel's mother had described it, and the old woman's clay map had included hatched lines in the lower section with the annotation, in the scratched pictograph system they used, meaning something like "thick and wet and alive in every direction." Neither of these descriptions had prepared her.

The smell reached them two days before the tree line, rotting and growing simultaneously, soil that had never dried out in living memory. Overwhelming and strangely compelling, the nose recognizing, perhaps, that this was what the world smelled like when it had everything it needed.

"That's not nothing," Eijá said, sniffing.

"It's everything," Ixchel said quietly.

She had straightened as the smell intensified, the way a person straightens when they recognize their own home street from a distance. This was her mother's place. Her mother's memory of a place, held in her blood and in the words she had grown up hearing.

Teya's people showed less equanimity. Several of them had never been this far south and didn't try to pretend otherwise. They moved closer together as the vegetation thickened, the desert scrub giving way first to grasses and then to low trees and then, as they dropped into a river valley, to something genuinely lush and intimidating. Birdsong layered on birdsong until the canopy above was a continuous noise, a thousand different announcements and arguments and declarations happening simultaneously.

"Jaguars," Danijel said, not to anyone in particular.

"Here?" Lofn asked.

"Possibly. More likely further south. But possibly here. Larger than mountain lions. Better climbers."

"Why would you say that?" Lofn said.

"So you know. A surprised jaguar is worse than an encountered one. If you hear a deep cough in the dark from above you, don't run."

"What do you do instead?"

"Make yourself larger. Shout. Hold your ground. They generally prefer prey that doesn't complicate itself." He paused. "Generally."

Lofn looked up at the canopy. "I'm going to start having better thoughts than I currently have," she announced.

The river they were following ran east, which was the right direction, Ixchel had told her the great road ran roughly north-south on the east side of the mountains. The road was the key to speed and safety. Without it, a journey through this terrain would take weeks of fighting through undergrowth for every mile gained.

Danijel found it first, as he found most things.

He stopped at the crest of a low ridge and stood looking down, and his expression did something it rarely did. It opened.

"Come see," he said.

They came to the ridge and looked down.

The road was wide enough for four horses abreast, paved in fitted stone that had been leveled and set with a precision that made Maxtla think, with a small shock, of the careful weave of her best baskets, each piece chosen and placed. The edges were defined by low stone curbs. In both directions it ran straight, or nearly straight, cutting through the jungle with the confidence of engineering that didn't negotiate with the terrain but simply overrode it.

It stretched away to the south and was lost in the green dark. It stretched to the north and did the same.

"They built this," Lofn said, as though the fact needed to be stated to be believed.

"They maintain it," Ixchel said. "My mother said there are crews that walk the road continually, repairing and clearing. Merchants pay a fee at toll points. The money pays the crews."

"Like my sharpening stone," Teya said.

Maxtla glanced at her. "Bigger."

Teya studied the road. "Who builds something like this? How many people does it take?"

"Thousands," Ixchel said. "Over generations. It is older than any living person's memory."

They stood at the ridgeline looking at what human beings could make when they stayed in one place long enough. Maxtla felt it land.

"All right," she said. "We go south on the road."

They descended the ridge and stepped onto the stones.

Their footsteps changed. The uncertain sounds of people moving through wilderness became something more definite. The road did not accommodate; you accommodated it.

The surface was white. Pure white, the white of something deliberately made that way and maintained, coated in a plaster that had been applied and renewed across generations until the road glowed in daylight like a thing still warm from the kiln. It would, she understood suddenly, be visible from above. If you looked down from a ridge, the road would appear through the jungle green as a white line, straight, going exactly where it intended to go.

"I understand it now," Maria said, walking beside Maxtla.

"What?"

"Why they matter. The southern people. I thought of them as just far away. Different. But this." She gestured at the road. "This is the same thing you're doing. Just further along."

"Every civilization is the same thing," Danijel said. "Further along or less far."

"Are there others?" Maria asked, looking at him directly. "Other places? Very far away?"

Danijel met her look without blinking. "What makes you ask that?"

"The way you say 'further along.' Like you've seen the whole road." She paused. "Like you've been places we haven't."

A silence. Danijel walked.

"There are other places," he said carefully. "Yes."

"Are they better than this?"

He thought about this honestly. "They are more comfortable. Not necessarily better."

Maria nodded.

Maxtla said nothing. She had been at the edge of this conversation many times, in the space between knowing and asking. She had chosen, each time, not to ask. Some knowledge was best arrived at slowly, in your own time, without having it handed to you before you were ready to carry it.

The road ran south.

They followed it.

On the fourth night Lofn kept the second watch while the others slept. When Maxtla rose for the third rotation, Lofn was standing at the edge of the firelight looking north. "Fire on the ridge," she said. "Small. Consistent." A pause. "It was there last night too." Maxtla looked. The fire was a single point, a long way up and north, not moving, not threatening in any way she could read. Just present. "He's been following since the canyon," she said. Lofn turned to look at her. "Dangerous?" Maxtla watched the distant light for a moment. "Not yet," she said. "Get some sleep."

Two days on the Mayan road taught them several things.

First: the road was genuinely used. They passed three trading parties going north, two small groups and one large caravan of a dozen people with animals carrying loads strapped to their sides. The caravan people were wary and efficient in the way of people who had been moving goods along dangerous roads for a living, and they looked at Maxtla's group with the professional assessment of traders evaluating competition.

Maxtla stopped the larger caravan and offered to trade information for information, what was north of here, from her, for what was ahead to the south, from them. The caravan leader, a squat woman with elaborate tattoos across her cheekbones and forehead, looked at the offer with the same calculating intelligence that Maxtla looked at it.

They sat on the road and talked for an hour.

Second thing learned: the city she was heading for was called Yaxal Nah. The woman described it with the mixture of respect and wariness that people use for things that are powerful and not entirely safe. Large. Prosperous. The lord was named Ix Pakab, a merchant prince. He had multiple wives and advisors and a temple that was not for outsiders to visit.

"They let outsiders trade?" Maxtla asked.

"They want outsiders to trade," the caravan woman said through Ixchel's translation. "The city lives on trade. But outsiders trade in the market, not in the inner precincts. The rules are strict. You learn them or you leave quickly."

"Who do we talk to? Who arranges the introductions?"

The caravan woman described a man at the road's entrance to the city, a fee collector who also sorted arriving traders into the permitted and the not. She gave Maxtla a name and something else: a small token, a carved disk of jade with a specific mark scratched on the back.

"Show him this," the woman said. "He will know you are honest. Somewhat honest, anyway."

Maxtla turned the token in her fingers. "What is the mark?"

"My mark. It says I have dealt with you and you dealt fairly."

A reputation traveling ahead of her. There was a system here, complex and evolved, the product of generations of trade.

Third thing learned: at the road's toll point, they paid a fee per person and a higher fee per loaded horse and received a fired clay token stamped with a mark that would allow them to enter the city without repeat payment.

The toll collector was a small, precise man who had clearly processed ten thousand traders and been surprised by none of them. He counted noses, counted horses, assessed the loads with experienced eyes, named a price.

Maxtla countered. He accepted. She paid.

The gate opened.

"That's it?" Lofn said.

"That's it," Maxtla said. "We have permission to proceed."

"Seems too easy."

"It's organized," Maxtla said, and walked through.

They walked south through the afternoon and into a new world.

CHAPTER SEVEN

Yaxal Nah

Yaxal Nah appeared between the trees like something out of a fever.

They had been following the road through increasingly cultivated land, fields of maize and squash, tended by people who looked at the passing caravan with the mild interest of those accustomed to traffic, when the jungle on both sides simply ended and the city was there.

She heard it before she saw it, not the market specifically, but something: a low pressure of human density, the way a large fire changes the air before you reach the heat. Then smoke. Not wood smoke, not the clean cook-fire smell of camp, but something thicker and older, copal resin and rendered fat. Then, at the tree line, the heat changed. The jungle held its moisture and kept the air close. Outside the trees the sun fell directly on cut stone and the stone gave it back, dry and flat and absolute.

The scale of it was wrong. Not wrong in a bad way, wrong the way the sky is wrong when you first understand that the horizon isn't close. The pyramids were not the tallest things she had ever seen, the canyon walls of the High Country exceeded them by half, but they had been built, and that was the difference. Every stone had been placed by someone's hands, lifted and fitted and mortared into position as part of a deliberate plan. The largest pyramid rose at the center of the city like a statement about what human beings could accomplish when they organized their effort, flat-topped, stepped, with a small temple structure at the summit that looked, from this distance, tiny.

The market was already active when they entered the approach road, flanked by low stone walls and merchants under shade structures of woven reed. The noise hit them before the smell, and the smell hit them before the detail. Voices arguing price in multiple languages. A vendor with a clay pipe producing a steady high note. Dogs working the gaps between stalls. The smell of maize on hot stone. Fish dried to salt and brick. Copal smoke from a small shrine at the road's edge, permanent, its clay bowl blackened with decades of use. Under everything the animal smell of the crowd itself, sweat and tallow and the particular musk of bodies in tropical heat.

Teya's group clustered together instinctively. Most of them had never seen anything like this. A few were holding their weapons with the unconscious tightening of hands that weren't sure whether to be ready.

Danijel stopped walking.

He had seen a hundred cities. He knew what a civilization looked like at this stage. He had watched some reach this threshold and fail to get past it, and others cross it and keep building. He could not tell, standing in the market noise with the pyramid catching the morning light, which kind this was.

"Relax the hands," Maxtla said, not loudly, to no one and everyone. "We are traders. Smile if you can. If you can't, look neutral."

The traders in the market barely glanced at them.

"We don't open our packs yet," Maxtla said to Ixchel.

"I know."

"We find the fee collector first. Get placed. Get established."

"I know."

The fee collector, Ah Kinich, had a station at the junction of the main market road and the road to the inner city precincts, separated from the market by a stone wall and a gate with two very large guards. He was a small, round man with a carefully maintained composure and eyes that had already completed their assessment of Maxtla before she reached his counter.

She showed the jade token.

He looked at it. His expression did something small. Then he looked at her, and then at the group behind her, and then at the loaded horses, and back at her.

"From the north," he said. In her language. Not fluently, but specifically.

"Yes."

"Far north."

"Very far north. We have traveled two months."

He turned the jade token over, read the mark on the back. "You know Chalchih."

The caravan woman's name. "We met her on the road. We traded information."

"She is reliable," he said. Then: "What do you carry?"

"Baskets of unusual quality. Obsidian tools and mirrors. Medicines from the highland plants. And technology for building better things."

"Technology," he repeated. He used the word differently, the way you repeat a word that requires thought before translation.

"Show him," Maxtla said to Ixchel.

Ixchel produced the three items Maxtla had selected: the best picture basket, folded flat; the obsidian knife; one mirror face-down.

Ah Kinich looked at the basket with the eyes of someone who understood craft. He turned the knife and tested its edge. Then he looked at the mirror.

"Turn it," Maxtla said.

Ixchel turned it.

He looked at his own face for about ten seconds. His expression was perfectly controlled. Only his breathing gave him away.

"Your price?" he asked.

"Fair market value plus a finder's payment to you of ten percent, to be paid in whatever form you prefer."

He put the mirror down face-first. "Location in the market is assigned by the first morning's toll. You pay, you get a site. Size depends on what you pay."

"We need a large site. We have five horses of goods and twenty-six people who will need space."

He looked at the group again. Did his own counting. "Your group is mixed."

"Yes."

"Some of these," he said, indicating Teya's people carefully, "are from the hill country."

"They travel with us. They are part of my organization."

He thought about this. "The market has specific rules about fighting. Anyone in your group who violates them loses their market standing and is expelled."

"Understood. My people understand the rules."

"Your people," he repeated, in that same thoughtful tone. Then: "I will give you the best remaining site. The east corner of the central market, near the water."

He named a price.

She offered half.

He came down by twenty percent and held there.

She studied him. He was not negotiating with disrespect, he was negotiating like a man who respected the process. She paid the agreed amount.

He gave her a carved wooden token, larger and more elaborate than the road token. "Show this at the market gate in the morning. Your site will be marked."

Then he said something in his own language. Ixchel translated quietly.

"He says: the lord's third wife, Ix Tunich, has heard of the northern traders who arrive by the road. She asks whether you would visit her at the inner precincts tomorrow at midday."

Maxtla kept her expression neutral. An invitation before she had even opened a pack. "How did she know we were coming?"

Ixchel relayed the question.

"He says: news travels on the road the way water travels downhill. She has known you were coming for two weeks."

The caravan woman, or someone who had spoken to the caravan woman. The reputation-token system worked in both directions.

"Tell him," Maxtla said, "we would be honored."

They made camp outside the city in a designated area for traveling traders, a large flat ground beside a stream, with fire pits already established and wooden structures for shelter. Clean water, shade, and no one bothered them.

That evening, after the camp was arranged and the horses watered and fed, Ixchel and Maxtla sat apart and talked for a long time.

"The lord's wives," Maxtla said.

"My mother explained it. There are three, ranked. Ix Akbal is the first wife. She is the oldest and holds the highest formal status. She is politically influential and dangerous if crossed."

"And the third wife is the one who wants to meet us."

"Yes. Ix Tunich. Third wife means she came last, which means she holds the least formal status. But formal status is not actual power."

"So the third wife is an ally?"

"The third wife is someone who sees a use for us. That is not the same thing." Ixchel paused. "She also may want to acquire goods before the first wife has a chance to, which would be a political move within the household."

"She's using us to score a point against the first wife."

"Possibly. That's useful as long as we're careful not to become weapons in a fight we don't understand."

Maxtla nodded. "Who do we need? First wife or third?"

"Both," Ixchel said. "And neither. We need to appear to be allied with neither while being useful to both. The moment we choose a side in their internal politics, we become the loser's enemy."

"How did you learn this?"

"My mother. She grew up navigating exactly this kind of hierarchy. She said it was like standing in a river, you couldn't choose not to stand in it, so you learned to use the current rather than fight it."

Maxtla was quiet for a while.

"The second wife?" she asked.

"Is the one I would actually watch," Ixchel said. "The second wife in my mother's experience tends to be the most strategic. Not as formally powerful as the first, not as currently favored as the third, so she has had to develop other tools. Information. Alliance networks. The patience of someone who has been waiting a long time."

"And we know nothing about her."

"Not yet."

Neither spoke for a moment.

"We need to know," Maxtla said.

"I know," Ixchel said. "Give me two days in the market. I will find out what the market knows. Market people always know the household politics of anyone worth trading with."

Maxtla looked at her in the firelight. This woman, her friend, her partner, the best political mind she had, was running the domestic intelligence operation of a Mayan city-state's ruling household before they had even set up their market stall.

"What would I do without you?" she said.

Ixchel smiled. "Probably trade well and get killed by something you hadn't mapped out properly."

"Yes. Exactly that."

On the far side of the camp, Danijel sat at the edge of the firelight, writing. Tonight he added a note he would not include in the official record: This one is going to leave a mark that outlasts anything we build here.

Above the jungle, the stars burned.

CHAPTER EIGHT

The north stall

The market opened at dawn with a sound like a river starting.

Maxtla had been at her stall since before first light, arranging and rearranging, while the sky went from black to gray to the deep saturated blue that preceded sunrise in this wet country. The air here was alive with moisture, you breathed it, not just breathed in it.

She had told Teya's people to observe the first morning and not to trade on their own account until she had given them an introduction to the market's rhythms. They had accepted this without enthusiasm. Parruk had accepted it with visible reluctance, but he had accepted it.

The first customer appeared as the light improved.

She was a woman of perhaps thirty with the precise dress and confident bearing of a market professional, a buyer, not a casual browser. She walked the stall without touching, evaluating.

She stopped at the picture basket.

"May I?" she asked, in her own language.

Ixchel translated.

"Please," Maxtla said.

The woman picked up the basket and turned it. The pattern was a hunting scene, deer in red ochre, hunters in black, the long grass rendered in alternating thin lines of yellow and green that created a sense of movement when the basket turned in the light. She studied the execution, her eyes following the weave logic.

"You did this with split reed," she said. Ixchel translated.

"Yes."

"How many colors?"

"Five."

She turned the basket over and looked at the bottom, the most technically demanding part, where the pattern had to originate and would either work or collapse into confusion. It worked.

"This is not from around here," she said.

"No. Very far north. The red canyon country."

"I know no one there."

"You know me," Maxtla said. "I will be back."

The woman put the basket down, looked at Maxtla directly for the first time. "What do you want for it?"

"What are you willing to offer?"

This was where it began.

By midmorning, Maxtla had sold six of the standard baskets, one picture basket, four sets of combs, and one obsidian knife. She had also declined to sell either of the mirrors, which had been looked at with great intensity by four different buyers and which she was holding back for a purpose she had not yet announced.

She had declined politely each time, with the explanation, translated by Ixchel with carefully modulated regret, that the mirrors were intended for a specific important gift. Not for sale this trip.

The mirrors became, as a result, the thing the entire market knew about by midday. The thing that couldn't be bought.

"You're doing that on purpose," Lofn observed.

"Of course," Maxtla said.

"What is the specific important gift for?"

"I don't know yet. I'm waiting to see what presents itself."

Lofn processed this. "So you're lying."

"I'm reserving my options."

"That's." Lofn paused, working through the moral taxonomy. "Provisionally acceptable," she decided.

Eijá found the market fascinating in a purely technical sense. She spent the morning moving between the tool and materials vendors with the focused absorption of an engineer in a parts shop, examining methods of construction she hadn't seen, materials that didn't exist in the canyon country.

She came back to the stall midmorning carrying three things: a small clay pot with a fitted lid sealed with a material that wasn't clay, a length of woven rope made from a fiber she couldn't identify, and a small wedge-shaped stone tool with a handle bound so precisely that the binding itself seemed to be the structural element.

"The rope fiber is stronger than anything I've seen and lighter," she reported. "The pot seal doesn't crack even in heat. And this tool." She held up the wedge. "The handle is the lashing, not the other way around. It's one continuous technique, not two separate steps."

"Replicate?" Maxtla asked.

"I need to see it done. But yes. Eventually."

"Don't buy yet," Maxtla said.

"I wasn't going to. I was looking."

"Good. When we buy, we buy after relationships are established."

Eijá looked faintly insulted. "I know how not to appear interested in something I'm interested in."

"I know you do. I'm reminding myself by saying it out loud."

Maria spent the morning running messages. She had learned, in the first hour, that this was a role that nobody was doing and that needed doing, someone light on their feet who could move between the stall and the other areas of the market without the deliberate purposefulness that marked a committed buyer or seller.

She brought Maxtla a stream of small intelligence: what the two nearest stalls were selling and at what prices, which buyers had come back for second looks, what the large vendor at the western entrance was trading in, and that three men had been observing their stall from a position near the water source for most of the morning without buying or walking away.

"Three men," Maxtla said.

"Not market people. They have the look of people watching someone else's market for someone who sent them."

"Household staff," Ixchel said. "The lord's household, or one of the wives' households. Checking us out before tomorrow."

"Which wife?"

"Can't tell yet." Ixchel glanced toward the water source without making it a glance. "Let me go buy water. I'll pass close."

She bought two clay jugs of water from the water seller, walked back via a route that put her within ten feet of the three observers, and rejoined the stall.

"Third wife," she said. "The tattoo pattern on the eldest one's left forearm. I recognized the family mark from my mother's description."

Maxtla absorbed this. Ix Tunich's people. Scoping the traders before tomorrow's meeting.

"Are they seeing anything that worries us?"

"They're seeing a professional operation with good goods and a controlled demeanor," Ixchel said. "We look like serious traders."

By the end of the day, Maxtla had converted approximately one third of her inventory into local goods that she was already calculating return values for in the canyon country, plus two kinds of currency. The small transactions had been paid in cacao beans, dried and counted out in units that the whole market understood without discussion. The larger sales had been settled in jade tiles, which were accepted by trading parties across a range of five or six weeks' travel from the city. The cacao she had not anticipated. She turned some over in her fingers that evening: a currency you could eat in extremity was different from a currency that held its value only inside the city's system. The canyon country needed something like it.

She tallied it in the early evening, alone in the trader camp.

She was well ahead of the minimum she had needed to justify the journey.

She had not yet shown anyone the mirrors, the best obsidian pieces, or the contents of the two packs she hadn't opened. She had not yet leveraged the lord's wife meeting.

She was not even close to done.

By the end of the third day, the stall had acquired regulars.

The second regular was a craftsman from the weavers' district who had arrived at the stall on the second morning with the professional suspicion of someone who worked in the same material category. He had looked at the baskets with the eye of someone who knew exactly how difficult what he was looking at was to produce.

On the third morning he brought a colleague. On the fourth he came alone and bought a standard basket to establish the transaction relationship. On the fifth morning he said, through a combination of gestures and the few shared words: he wanted to learn how the pictures were made.

Maxtla had been ready for this. "Next trip," she told Ixchel to say. "I'll bring the materials and the teacher." The teacher would be Akua, who had developed the technique herself, who had been told before the expedition departed that this was a possibility. Akua had said yes before the sentence was finished.

"He'll wait," Ixchel said.

"He'll wait," Maxtla agreed. "He's been waiting to see something like this his whole professional life."

Danijel watched this exchange from his position slightly apart from the stall, which was his characteristic position, present but not participatory, available but not intrusive.

"You're building a teaching business," he said.

"A relationship," she said. "The teaching is part of it. A buyer who learned something from us is more invested than one who only bought."

"Part of the route," Danijel said. "Without ever walking it."

"Yes."

By the end of the second week, the stall had developed a personality.

Theirs had become: the north stall. The place with the unusual goods and the women who knew what everything was worth and the old man who sat slightly apart and watched everything and said nothing and somehow made the watching feel like endorsement.

Danijel's silence had turned out to be an asset. He was old, visibly, dramatically old, and he moved with a physical ease that was its own advertisement. People calculated what his presence meant and arrived at conclusions useful to the stall either way.

The standard baskets were gone by the fifth day, replaced with a second cache she had held in reserve. She had planned for this, a stall running out of goods said something different than a stall appearing to have reserves. Running out said: more popular than expected. Reserves said: we know our market.

The combs were selling well. The local artisans made combs too, but not like these, the teeth were uneven, the spacing irregular, the wood rough where it should be smooth. Maxtla's carvers had been working to a gauge for two seasons. The consistency was the product. Buyers noticed. They sold fast and to a broad market, which was important, you needed the broad market to establish the stall's general reputation and the specialized goods to establish its status.

The obsidian tools were a conversation piece more than a volume seller. Each sale required time, the buyer needed to understand what they were getting and why it was worth the premium. But the conversations generated were worth their weight in market intelligence. Every buyer who asked about the obsidian became an informant about their own needs, their own production methods, their own assessment of what the north had that the south lacked.

A woman named Chalchih, the caravan trader whose jade token had opened the gate, arrived at the stall on the ninth day. She had returned from the north, her caravan resupplied and reloaded, and she had come to see in person what the northern trader looked like up close.

She was in her forties, compact and weathered in the way of someone who had been walking trade routes for twenty years. She looked at the stall with the trained eye of a competitor-colleague.

"Better than I expected," she said, without preamble.

"Thank you," Maxtla said.

"The picture basket is not for sale," Chalchih observed. It was still on display.

"Not from this batch," Maxtla said. "We make them in quantity. Next trip."

"How many could you bring?"

"How many do you need?"

They were negotiating. Not yet, that required specifics and terms, but the negotiation was beginning: with the establishing shot of each party's interest.

"I move eight caravans a year between the coast and this city," Chalchih said. "The coastal people want goods from the highlands and the highlands people want goods from the coast. I am the river between them." She looked at the picture basket. "What you have here is better."

"What's on the coast?" Maxtla asked.

Chalchih smiled. It was the smile of someone who has been offered exactly the opening they wanted. "What do you know about the sea?"

She spent the next two hours telling Maxtla about the sea.

Maxtla had heard about the sea in the abstract, a quantity of water so large it had no other shore. Chalchih made it real. She described the coastal cities, a different kind of city from Yaxal Nah, lower and more spread out, oriented toward the water and the boats rather than toward the land and the road. She described the boat traders, people who moved along the coast in wooden vessels, moving goods that couldn't travel overland because of weight or fragility.

"Salt," Chalchih said. "That's what you need to know about the coast. The salt flats produce more than the interior can use, and they produce it more cheaply than any overland route could. The interior needs the coast's salt and the coast needs what the interior makes, the obsidian, the jade, the highland cloth." She looked at Maxtla. "The northern goods fit into this system the same way. You bring what the coast can't produce and the interior can't get overland."

"The coastal route," Maxtla said.

"I'm describing what's there," Chalchih said. "What you do with it is your calculation."

"What do I need to make the extension viable?"

"A relationship with a coastal trading family," Chalchih said. "Someone who knows the boat traders and can make the introductions. Someone who has standing in the coastal market the way you're building standing here." She paused. "I know several families."

She was offering to be the bridge. For a price that they hadn't discussed yet but that Maxtla could already estimate from the way Chalchih was positioning herself.

"On my next trip south," Maxtla said. "We can discuss the terms then."

"Your next trip," Chalchih said, with a precision that was partly question. "When?"

"A year. Maybe a year and a half."

"The coastal families I'm thinking of will be interested in the northern goods," Chalchih said. "I'll keep the conversation warm until you arrive."

"What do you want to keep it warm?"

Chalchih looked at the picture basket again. "One of those," she said. "For my household. Not for trade."

It was a personal request, which was different from a business request, and the difference was the point. She was buying a relationship token, not a commodity.

Maxtla took the basket from its display position and held it out.

"A gift," she said. "For the introduction of the route to the coast."

Chalchih took it. She looked at it for a long moment, the hunting scene, the deer in red and black, the tall grass in alternating lines. She looked up at Maxtla.

"Who made it?" she asked.

"A woman named Akua in the settlement," Maxtla said. "She developed the picture technique herself."

"She's young?"

"Twenty. She started developing it at sixteen."

Chalchih held the basket as someone holds a thing they intend to keep.

"I'll tell the coastal family there's a woman in the north who makes things like this," she said. "I'll tell them what else you carry. And when you arrive." She held up the basket. "I'll show them this."

"Good," Maxtla said. "They'll understand."

GEDEON: TWO

What Kael was building

He heard it first from Ren, who heard it from his sister, who had been present when Kael spoke at the evening fire.

Kael had not called it a challenge. He had called it a question. That was more precise, it was a question, and it was one Gedeon had been expecting since before Maxtla left.

The question was: on whose authority had the land assignments been made?

The answer was: Maxtla's. Which was a real answer. But an answer that generated another question, which was what authority Maxtla had to make them, and that question had no formal answer because the settlement's governance was not formal. It was Maxtla, and her judgment, and the women who worked with her, and the practice that had grown up around all of it without ever being written down.

Kael knew this. He was not a stupid man. The question was not stupid. It was exactly the right question to ask when the person who had been the answer to it was four months south of the canyon.

Gedeon was splitting wood behind the north storage when Merya came to find him. She moved the way she always moved, with the specific economy of a woman who had been managing difficult situations longer than most people in the settlement had been alive. Her hair was gray and she wore it pulled back and she had the kind of face that had been beautiful once and was now more useful.

She sat on the wood pile without asking.

"Kael is building something," she said.

"I know."

"He's talked to the three eastern elders. He's talked to Brak. He's been careful about who he hasn't talked to."

Gedeon set the maul down.

"Who hasn't he talked to?"

"You. Me. The founding women."

That was interesting. Kael was not trying to build a coalition that included the people who had the most standing in the original settlement. He was building one around the newer arrivals, the people who had come after the governance structure was already in place and had benefited from it without having a stake in its creation.

That was smart, in the narrow tactical sense. In the longer sense, it was going to break something.

"What do you want to do?" Gedeon asked.

"Wait," Merya said. "Same as you."

"How long can you wait?"

She looked at the wood pile for a moment. She was the kind of woman who answered questions honestly and without performance, which was one of the reasons Maxtla trusted her.

"Until Brak does what I think he's going to do," she said. "Then I stop waiting."

Gedeon nodded. He picked up the maul again.

"She'll be back in two months," he said. "Maybe less."

"I know," Merya said. She stood. "I'm not saying I'll wait two months."

She left.

He split wood until his shoulders gave out, which took longer than usual. Aki was in the south section with the family that watched him when Gedeon needed both hands.

That evening he sat at the place in the canyon wall where the light came last and thought about what Maxtla would do if she were here. He thought about it the way he thought about structural problems, from the load, working backward to the supports. The challenge was coming. The charter was the answer. The charter was not here yet.

What he had until she returned was time, and the people who had built the settlement, and the fact that even Kael's coalition knew the difference between what the settlement was now and what it had been.

He would use all three.

He did not write to her. There was no way to write to her. But he composed it in his head anyway, the way he sometimes did, the words taking shape in the order he would have said them.

She was going to be angry about Kael. Not surprised. Angry in the specific way she was angry when problems that were preventable had not been prevented.

He had not prevented this one.

He would tell her that honestly and take what came from it.

He went back to the settlement when the light was fully gone and checked the gates and went to sleep in the bed that was half empty in the specific way of a bed built for two people.

CHAPTER NINE

The stone master

Eijá's most significant technical acquisition happened not in the craftspeople's district but in an accident.

She had been examining the road near the toll point, specifically the joint between two paving stones that had been replaced recently, she could tell by the color differential, and had stopped to study how the new stone had been seated into the existing grade. The fitting was exceptionally good. Better than the original, which meant the repair crew had either used a newer technique or a more skilled mason.

She was crouched over the joint, looking at it from an angle, when a voice behind her said something in the local language.

She turned. An older man, seventy, perhaps more, with hands that showed a lifetime of stone work. He was looking at her with an expression she recognized: the expression of a craftsperson who has found another craftsperson studying their work.

"Good?" he said, in her language. One word. He had learned it from the market traffic, probably.

"Very good," she said. She pointed at the joint specifically. "The fit. How?"

He looked at where she was pointing. He thought about whether to answer. He arrived at whatever calculation craftspeople arrive at when they decide to share, if you can see what I did, you deserve to know how.

He sat down on the road beside her.

He talked for an hour, through gestures and the few shared words and increasingly through drawing in the dust beside the road. He showed her the tool, a flat-bladed chisel with a handle design Eijá had never seen, which allowed a sideways rocking cut that produced the flatness required for the zero-gap joint.

She drew the tool in her notation. She drew the cutting angle. She drew the rocking motion, three sequential positions, like a story. She drew the resulting face shape.

He watched her document it. His expression shifted to the look of someone seeing their knowledge preserved in a form that will outlast them.

She held out her own obsidian blade, the folded, beveled one she had developed in the canyon country, the best cutting tool she owned.

He took it. He tested it. He looked at it for a long time.

"Trade?" she asked.

He looked at her. At the blade. At her documentation of his technique.

"Trade," he said.

She gave him the blade.

He gave her the chisel.

She held it for a moment. Turned it. Felt the weight, lighter than she expected, the balance deliberately forward.

"Thank you," she said.

"Thank you," he said.

They sat for a while longer on the road, not talking, in the shared comfort of two people who understand the same things in the same way.

Then she went back to the market and spent the rest of the afternoon and into the night figuring out how to describe the rocking-cut technique in notation precise enough to be replicable by someone who hadn't held the chisel.

When she finished, she held up the drawing and looked at it, and felt the satisfaction of captured knowledge, the moment when something that existed only in one person's hands and one person's understanding became the kind of thing that could be learned by anyone who had access to the record.

CHAPTER TEN

The third wife

The meeting with Ix Tunich required new clothes, which Maxtla did not have.

She had not thought about this until Ixchel raised it the morning before, and then she saw immediately that it was a serious problem. She had brought trading clothes, traveling clothes, and fighting clothes. Not the equivalent of what these people wore to indicate status, which was more elaborate and more carefully made than anything that traveled well in a pack.

"We improvise," she said.

Ixchel raised an eyebrow.

"The market has cloth," Eijá said.

"The market has cloth we can't afford to buy in quantity on one day's notice," Maxtla said. "And even if we could, none of us knows how to dress in this city's style."

A brief pause.

"My mother taught me the basic forms," Ixchel said. "I know the structure of a formal dress. And I know how women of standing carry themselves in that dress."

"If the details are wrong, that makes us northerners who are trying," Maxtla said. "Which we are. That shows respect for their customs without pretending we're what we're not."

Lofn, who had been listening from the corner of the camp, said, "I can sew it if you tell me what to make."

Which was true, Lofn's hands, when they had something precise to do, were steadier and more skilled than anyone else's.

They spent most of the previous evening at the cloth sellers' section of the market, where Ixchel examined options with a deliberateness that made the sellers nervous, and eventually selected three lengths of a cotton cloth dyed in dark red and indigo. Close to the appropriate color range for a woman of trading rank seeking audience with a minor wife. Not so grand as to imply false status. Not so plain as to insult by underestimating. Lofn sewed until the fire burned low. They were dressed by dawn.

The walk to the inner precincts required passing through the gate in the stone wall, where the two large guards looked them over with professional attention and then, apparently finding the criteria satisfied, stepped aside.

Inside the wall was a different city.

Outside had been commerce, noise and movement and the productive disorder of a thousand transactions. Inside was order, the physical expression of hierarchy in stone and water and space. Wide paved plazas, immaculately swept. Low platforms with potted plants precisely arranged. Shade trees at intervals that were clearly deliberate.

The pyramid rose from the center, larger from inside the wall than it had appeared from outside, the stepped stone face casting a hard line of shadow across the plaza. At its summit, the small temple was not small from here, it resolved into a proper structure, painted in ochre and white and green, with a doorway that implied interior space.

The pyramid did something Danijel's technologies didn't do. It was human, people, generation after generation, lifting stones to fulfill a vision no one individual had conceived but everyone had built.

Beside her, Danijel looked at it with an expression she couldn't read. Not awe. Something more careful. The same expression he'd had watching the canyon settlement's first granary go up.

They were being led at a brisk pace by a guide who considered extended pyramid-gazing a rookie characteristic.

Ix Tunich lived in a building on the east side of the plaza, set slightly apart from the main palace complex, close enough to demonstrate her belonging, far enough to suggest a degree of independence. The building was lower than the palace, with a wide covered walkway in front supported by carved wooden posts.

She met them in the walkway.

The third wife was younger than Maxtla had expected. Mid-twenties, perhaps. Compact, with the strong arms and direct bearing of someone who worked at maintaining her own capability regardless of her household status. Her clothing was elaborate, layers of patterned cotton in multiple colors, jade ornaments at her neck and ears, a headdress that was impressive without being ostentatious. Her face was tattooed in a fine geometric pattern across the cheekbones. She looked at Maxtla's group with a directness that was, Maxtla thought, genuine rather than performed.

She spoke. Ixchel translated, quietly.

"She says: I was told that a group of northern women arrived with fine goods and one very old man. She says she is pleased to see you are as interesting as advertised."

Maxtla inclined her head. "We are grateful for the invitation."

Ix Tunich spoke again. Her tone was different from the market professionals they had dealt with, less calculating, more genuinely curious.

"She asks: how far did you travel?"

"Two months' travel to the north. Through the desert country and then the canyon lands."

The wife absorbed this, or the translation of it. "She has never been north of the jungle. She says she has wondered what it looks like."

"Dry," Maxtla said. "And very large. And beautiful in a way that takes time to understand."

A small smile from Ix Tunich at the translation.

"She asks what you brought to trade."

"I brought the best of what my country produces. But I also brought something I've kept from the open market." Maxtla looked at Ixchel, who reached into the folded cloth of her dress and produced a mirror. "I have been saving this for a specific introduction. I would like you to have it."

Ix Tunich looked at the mirror face-down in Ixchel's hands.

"Turn it," Maxtla said.

She did.

Ix Tunich looked at herself. The direct controlled person who had met them in the walkway became, for the duration of those seconds, a young woman who had never seen her own face clearly. She raised one hand and touched her own cheek, watching the reflection do the same. She turned slightly, and the reflection turned with her.

She was quiet for a long time.

Then she said something short, in her own language.

Maxtla waited.

Ix Tunich looked up from the mirror. The evaluation was gone from her face. What had replaced it was something harder to name, the attention of a mind encountering another mind.

"She wants to know if you have enough mirrors for all three wives."

Maxtla had two mirrors. Three wives.

She had anticipated exactly this question and had a planned answer.

"I have two mirrors," she said. "The gift I've given you is one. The second I propose to give to your household collectively, to be decided between the wives how it is placed. I will also explain, in my next trip, how the mirrors are made, so that your own craftspeople can produce them."

The translation. A pause.

"She says: you intend to come back."

"Yes. This is the first trip. I'm establishing the route. On the return, I will organize the next trip, which will carry more goods and offer more things in trade. Including the method for the mirrors."

"She says: you are giving away what you know how to do."

"I am giving it away selectively. The people who receive it can't produce it unless they build the whole technique, which takes time and specific materials. During that time, I will have developed new techniques. I don't compete by hoarding what I know. I compete by knowing more faster."

The translation took longer this time. Ix Tunich was quiet with it.

Then she offered Maxtla a seat in the shade of the walkway, and called for food and drink, and they spent the next two hours talking about trade, about the canyon country, about the road and the jungle and what Ixchel's mother had been like.

When Maxtla rose to leave, the third wife walked with her to the gate.

"My mother would have liked you," Ixchel said, not through translation but directly, in the old southern tongue that she rarely used.

Ix Tunich stopped. Looked at her. Replied in the same language.

"Your mother's accent is in your words," she said. "Where is she now?"

"She died when I was young. She went north and stayed."

"For a man?"

"For love. Which included a man."

Ix Tunich smiled. "Brave."

"Yes," Ixchel said. "She was."

They walked through the gate together, and something had changed in the air between Ixchel and the third wife, something that was not yet friendship but was the groundwork on which friendship could be built, which in some ways mattered more.

CHAPTER ELEVEN

The first wife

The meeting with Ix Akbal happened before the market opened, as the first wife had specified.

The first wife operated differently than the third wife had. Ix Tunich had come to them, had visited their camp, had entered their space on their terms. Ix Akbal sent a staff member at dawn to escort them to the inner precincts, a formal process, a route through the administrative buildings rather than the residential complex, ending in a covered courtyard where Ix Akbal was already seated behind a low working table with two aides flanking her.

The goods Maxtla laid out on the table between them were the same goods she had been selling in the market. She made no special presentation, produced no curated selection, showed no performance of attempting to impress. The first wife had the standing to review the inventory exactly as it existed and the intelligence to understand what she was looking at without staging.

Ix Akbal examined each piece without touching most of them, using the evaluating visual attention of a woman who had been managing a large household's material resources for decades. The baskets she picked up. She turned the picture basket the way the professional buyer on the first morning had turned it, studying the weave logic from the base, following the pattern's origination point.

She put it down and asked a question through Ixchel.

"She asks who made this."

"A woman in our settlement named Akua," Maxtla said. "She developed the technique herself. She's been refining it for four years."

The translation. Ix Akbal looked at the basket again. Then she asked another question.

"She asks what Akua would want in exchange for teaching the technique."

Maxtla had not planned for this question, which meant it was the question she should have planned for. The first wife was interested in the technique, not the product. The technique could be taught in a single trip. The product required ongoing supply. She was choosing the more self-sufficient option.

"I would discuss that with Akua," Maxtla said. "I don't negotiate on her behalf without her knowledge."

The translation. A pause.

"She says: a woman who doesn't negotiate for her people without their knowledge is unusual."

"Or it's what respect looks like," Maxtla said.

Ix Akbal looked at her directly. In the trading plaza, the first wife's attention had been comprehensive but distributed, watching everything. Here it was specific. Here she was deciding something.

"She says: she will consider buying the teaching rights to this basket technique in exchange for consideration on the next trip. She says she will discuss it with her household before committing."

"That's fair," Maxtla said.

They spent another hour in the courtyard. Ix Akbal asked specific questions about the canyon country's production capacity, about the route's reliability, about the protection arrangements. Questions of a woman who was thinking about supply, not novelty, whether this source of goods could be depended on over time, whether the investment of relationship was worth making.

Maxtla answered each question directly and without embellishment. She did not oversell the route's current reliability, it had two successful passages, which was a beginning and not a track record. Ix Akbal absorbed it with the nod of someone who prefers honest assessment to comfortable presentation.

"She says: the third wife spoke well of you," Ixchel translated. A pause. "She says: the third wife speaks well of very few people."

"I understand that's significant," Maxtla said.

"She says: yes."

At the end of the meeting, Ix Akbal walked them to the courtyard gate herself, a gesture the staff member who had received them had not anticipated. The first wife walked guests out when she had decided they were worth walking out.

At the gate, she said something short to Ixchel only, not through the formal translation. Ixchel's expression changed.

Maxtla waited until they were clear of the inner precincts.

"What did she say?"

"She said: my husband is ill. She said: when the succession happens, the northern route should already be established, because new administrations favor arrangements that are already working." Ixchel paused. "She said: you should come back before that happens."

Maxtla walked in silence for a moment.

"How long does the lord have?"

"She didn't say. But she wouldn't have said it at all if it weren't soon."

The market was opening around them, the city resuming its daily commerce with the indifferent momentum of a system that had been running since before anyone currently living was born and would run after all of them were gone.

She filed the information alongside the rest of what the city had given her: the route, the relationships, the knowledge, and now this, a timeline she hadn't known existed and needed to plan around.

"We accelerate the second trip," she said.

"I know," Ixchel said. "I was already thinking that."

CHAPTER TWELVE

The second wife

The meeting with Ix Mam that Maxtla had described to herself as an intelligence-gathering exercise turned out to be more, honest conversations always do.

The second wife's household was the working center of the city in the way that the lord's palace was its ceremonial center and the market was its commercial center. This became apparent in the first hour of the visit, when Maxtla understood that the building she was in was not a residence primarily but an office, a place where work got done. People moved through it with the directed purpose of people who have tasks and the authority to complete them. Ledgers were visible on the storage shelves. Clay tablets were stacked and organized by a system she couldn't immediately read but could tell was systematic.

"She runs this like a business," Ixchel said, very quietly, after fifteen minutes of watching.

"She runs it like a government," Maxtla said.

A business organized around profit. What Ix Mam was running organized around distribution, the movement of surplus to deficit, the maintenance of the relationships that made the movement reliable, the long-term cultivation of the clan networks that were the city's connective tissue. The profit, if there was one, was stability. The stability was the city's margin against bad seasons and conflict and the slow erosion of collective will.

Ix Mam explained this over the course of two hours with the directness of someone who had been explaining it all her life and had perfected the explanation.

"The first wife manages ceremony," she said, through Ixchel. "She maintains the formal relationships, the alliances with other lords, the ritual obligations, the face the city shows to the outside. This requires intelligence and memory and the social skill of someone who never forgets what was promised when and to whom."

"And you manage the inside," Maxtla said.

"I manage the people who don't appear in the ceremony," Ix Mam said. "The stone-cutters who maintain the road. The women who dry and store the grain. The healers who keep the children alive. They exist in the city's life the way foundations exist in a building. Essential. Below the visible surface."

"And the third wife?"

Ix Mam's expression shifted, the movement of a face that has learned to be precise about what it reveals. "The third wife has the lord's favor and uses it to pursue her own ambitions, which are not small. She is intelligent and she builds relationships quickly." A pause that was carefully neutral. "We have different approaches."

"But similar purposes?"

"Entirely different purposes," Ix Mam said, with a precision that was not unkind. "She builds toward her children's futures. I build toward the city's future. These are not the same direction."

Maxtla understood the topology of this immediately. The first wife's children were the succession. The third wife's children were the competition for the succession. The second wife's children occupied the middle ground of a competition they had less standing in, which had either embittered Ix Mam or liberated her from the succession game. Everything Maxtla had seen suggested the latter.

"What do you want?" Maxtla asked her directly.

Ix Mam looked at her. "I want the city to be able to feed its people in a bad year," she said. "I want the distribution network to be redundant enough that one broken link doesn't collapse the system. I want the wall between the inner precincts and the market to be lower than it currently is, because the wall exists to maintain the hierarchy and the hierarchy is becoming less useful than the relationship would be without it."

She had said this before. Many times, from the speed of it. And had been heard and not acted on.

"You need the trade routes to make the distribution network redundant," Maxtla said.

"Yes."

"You need more than one source for the things the city can't produce itself. If all your northern goods come through one route, one bad year on that route is a problem."

"Yes."

"Our route is one source. Are there others?"

"The coastal traders. The eastern mountain people. Several smaller routes." Ix Mam looked at the ledgers on her shelves. "The problem is that none of these routes talk to each other. They're independent. Each one is someone's relationship. When a relationship fails, the route fails."

"They need to be a network," Maxtla said. "Not individual routes but a system."

"Yes." Ix Mam looked at her steadily. "You've thought about this."

"I'm building it, from my end." Maxtla was thinking out loud now, the way she did with Gedeon or Ixchel when an idea was forming and needed air. "If each route connects to the others at the key points, if there's a way to reroute when one segment fails, the system is much more resilient. Each individual trader is still operating their own business. But the network as a whole is a public good."

"Like the road," Ix Mam said.

"Exactly like the road."

They sat with this for a moment, two women from opposite ends of the same road, sitting in the working center of a Mayan city, arriving at the same idea from different directions.

"This is a twenty-year project," Ix Mam said.

"At least. But the first step is documentation. What routes exist, where they go, what they carry, who runs them."

"I have some of that," Ix Mam said. She rose and went to the shelves and returned with three clay tablets covered in the Mayan script notation. "This is what I've compiled over twelve years. It's incomplete."

Maxtla looked at the tablets. She couldn't read them, but she could see the organizational logic, geographic, probably, or by commodity.

"Ahmik," she said.

"My husband's son? Yes." Ix Mam's expression was the careful neutrality she used for the third wife and the third wife's children. "He has been useful to you."

"He's been exceptional," Maxtla said. She looked at Ix Mam. "He's going to be important. Whatever happens in the succession, and I don't have a view on that, it's not my household, he carries knowledge that will matter. He has seen the charter and the governance structure and he's been teaching notation to anyone who wants to learn." She paused. "He's his mother's son."

Ix Mam looked at her for a moment with an expression that almost surprised.

"Yes," she said. "He is."

A small silence.

"The documentation of the routes," Maxtla said. "If I can get Ahmik to translate your tablets, and I add what I know about the northern routes, and we agree to share updates as the network develops, we're starting the map."

"Who holds the map?"

"Both of us hold copies," Maxtla said.

Ix Mam absorbed this. Then: "The credential letter I offered you. The portable reputation."

"Yes. I'm still grateful for it."

"I want to expand it," Ix Mam said. "Not just a statement that you are known here, a statement that you are a partner in the distribution network. That traders arriving from your route carry the same formal standing as traders who arrive through the road system."

Maxtla understood what she was being offered. It was not small. It was the difference between being known and being part of the system. It was formal standing without the constraints that formal standing usually required.

"What do you need in return?" she asked.

"The northern route information. Complete. And a commitment that when the network has enough nodes, you'll help me formalize it. Not just our two ends. The whole thing."

"That's a decade of work."

"I've been working on my end for twelve years already," Ix Mam said. "I'm patient."

They worked out the specifics over two more visits, with Ahmik translating and annotating and clearly barely containing his own excitement at being in the room where this conversation was happening. He wrote faster than usual and twice had to be reminded to translate before he was too far behind.

During one of those visits he showed her the city's date notation. He drew it on the edge of a clay tablet to mark when the meeting had occurred, a sequence of symbols she couldn't read but that Ahmik explained with quiet pride. The notation tracked not just the day or the season but the position of the day within a cycle that extended back thousands of years, to a specific moment so far in the past that Maxtla's mind couldn't hold it as a real time. The city knew, by this system, the exact position of today within a count that would still be running when her grandchildren's grandchildren were dust. The canyon country counted years in elder memories and seasons in harvest cycles. What she was looking at was something else entirely, a record designed to outlast not just individuals but civilizations. She was quiet for a moment looking at it. Then: "Teach me to read it." He started to explain that it required years of training. "I don't need to read it," she said. "I need to understand what kind of thing it is."

After the second visit, walking back through the inner precinct to the gate, he was quiet for a long time.

"What?" Maxtla asked.

"My mother has been trying to do this for years," he said. "The network. The documentation. The formal structure." He paused. "No one outside the city has taken it seriously before."

"They didn't have the route before," Maxtla said.

"No. But also." He stopped. Started again. "She's a wife. A second wife. In this city's structure, her authority is."

"Limited to what she can build informally," Maxtla said. "I know. That's what we have in common."

He looked at her. "Is that why it worked? Because you're both."

"Women operating in the gap between formal and actual authority?" She smiled. "Probably part of it. The other part is that she's right and the idea is good and the timing is right." She paused. "All three things need to be true. One or two isn't enough."

He wrote this down.

"Stop documenting everything I say," she said.

"I can't," he said, without apology. "You say useful things."

"It depends on whether the few can exit," Ixchel had said, in that conversation.

"What do you mean?" Ix Mam had asked.

"If the minority can leave the system when the majority takes from them, the majority has a check on how far they push," Ixchel said. "If the minority is locked in, if they have no exit, then you need a formal protection. Otherwise you just have the majority deciding what the minority owes."

Ix Mam had looked at her for a moment. "That is one of the most useful things anyone has said in this room," she said.

"My mother taught me to think about exit," Ixchel said. "She exited."

"And the thing she left?"

"Was impoverished for it," Ixchel said. "Which is the argument for making the thing good enough that people don't want to exit." She paused. "But they should always be able to."

CHAPTER THIRTEEN

The ball court

The ball court was the center of the city's social life in the way that the trading plaza was the center of its commercial life, and they were equally real centers, equally important, and occasionally the same thing.

The court itself was long, longer than Maxtla had expected, a narrow alley of packed earth between two long stone walls that sloped inward at forty-five degrees, with carved stone rings set high in the walls at the midpoint. The rings were vertical, not horizontal, which meant the players had to drive a heavy rubber ball through them from the side, an achievement, Ixchel explained, that was so rare it essentially ended the game when it happened.

She had spent thirty minutes simply looking at the rings before the first game. They were carved from single stones, each one sized just wider than the ball that was supposed to pass through it, the interior surfaces worn smooth by decades of near-misses. They were set at a height that required either a specific physical positioning or a shot of such calculated precision that anyone who made it had earned the result. She understood, looking at them, why the ring shot ended a segment.

They watched from the high wall on the south end, where a tier of stone seating gave a view of the full length of the court. Ix Tunich had arranged the viewing, partly to show them the city's culture and partly, Maxtla suspected, as a way to gauge their reactions to something the Maya took seriously.

The court filled fast. Not just the upper seating but every accessible ledge and position. The crowd was not the same crowd as the market. The market crowd was dispersed, individuated, each person with their own transaction and their own agenda. This crowd was unified, the density of people who are about to participate in something together, even as spectators. The atmosphere had weight to it.

The heat in the court was different from the heat in the plaza. The court was a canyon of stone, the two long sloped walls trapping air between them the way canyon walls trap it, and by midday that air had nowhere to go. It sat on you. The stone itself held heat from the morning and radiated it back from both sides simultaneously. Maxtla had grown up in a stone canyon; she knew what trapped heat felt like. This was the same physics applied to a crowd of several hundred people pressed together in formal dress, the combined warmth of all of them rising in layers. She was sweating before the players entered. Everyone was. The city sat in this as a matter of course, the way you sit in weather.

The players were extraordinary. There were four to a side, wearing thick leather padding on their hips, knees, and forearms, the ball could not be touched with hands or feet, only the hips, thighs, and upper arms. They were fast and agile and read each other's movements with an efficiency that spoke of deep practice, and the ball they were driving was nearly as large as a human head, solid rubber, heavy enough that being struck by it in the wrong place was a medical event.

Maxtla watched the ball hit a player's hip and understood that immediately. The impact was solid, dense, a sound like a fist hitting wet clay, and the player who received it moved through it rather than away from it, using the energy rather than absorbing it. You couldn't absorb it. It would break you if you tried. You had to meet it and direct it, which was a fundamentally different relationship with incoming force than anything the canyon country's physical training had produced.

"They train their whole lives," Ixchel said, not quite approvingly.

"The game is beautiful," Lofn said, watching with uncomplicated admiration. The movement of it was genuinely beautiful, these men were athletes at the edge of what human bodies could do, and they moved through the court with the grace of people whose bodies had been taught a vocabulary that was completely their own.

"Watch the score," Maxtla said.

They watched the score. It was complex, a system of points for wall contacts, rebounds, specific zones, and the crowd tracked it with the intensity of people for whom the outcome was not purely recreational. When the score shifted, the sound shifted. Not a shout, something more granular. The crowd had opinions about individual plays, individual moments.

"What does the winning team get?" Eijá asked.

Ixchel's expression shifted. "Honor. Prestige. Sometimes goods."

"And the losing team?"

A silence.

"I need to know," Maxtla said.

"Sometimes," Ixchel said carefully, "the losing team's captain is sacrificed."

The word landed in the middle of the group's attention and sat there.

"Sometimes," Maria said.

"Not always. It depends on the nature of the game. Certain ritual games have different stakes than others. Tournament games, prestige games between cities, games played to resolve specific conflicts, those are the ones where the sacrifice is possible. An ordinary game like this one, no."

"But we can't tell the difference," Lofn said.

"I can tell the difference," Ixchel said. "I'm watching for it."

She watched the crowd as much as the game. She watched the priests in the upper section, the specific posture of the court officials at the game's edges, the presence or absence of the ceremonial dress that accompanied the high-stakes games. Today was ordinary, she said. Today was athletes and spectators and a score that would matter tomorrow the way sports scores matter, as conversation, as pride, as the small currency of communal identity.

They watched the game. The crowd was engaged, partly sporting, partly something else, an investment of belief, as though the outcome of the game carried meaning beyond the physical result. Two teams driving a ball between stone walls was also, here, a reenactment of the cosmic struggle between forces that had no names in Maxtla's language. She could feel the depth of it without understanding the content.

She leaned toward Ixchel. "What is it re-enacting?"

Ixchel was quiet for a moment, watching the court below. "The court is the underworld. The ball is the sun. Every game is the journey of the sun through the world below the world, which has to happen every night or the sun doesn't rise. The players are the hero-brothers who went into the underworld and defeated the death gods with cleverness instead of strength." She paused. "Or depending on who you ask, the players are the death gods trying to stop them." Another pause. "Both are true at once. That's the part my mother said she never got used to."

She said it to Danijel later, when they were alone at the edge of camp.

"You noticed," he said.

"It wasn't hard to notice."

"Most visitors don't. They see the game, they see the pageantry, they focus on whether the losing captain walks out of the court or not."

"The losing captain is one man," Maxtla said. "The crowd that watches and understands what it means to lose, that's the whole city."

He looked at her sideways. "Do you know what you're describing?"

"It's just more elaborate here."

He was quiet for a moment. "What will you do with that understanding?"

"Nothing while we're here. We need their cooperation and their market access and the route. When we leave, I'll take the technique without the content." She paused. "The technique is: shared spectacle creates shared investment. Shared investment creates community solidarity."

"What would you have them watch in your settlement?"

She had been thinking about this for three weeks. "The building of something. The making of something. A shared project everyone can see growing." She looked at the pyramid behind them, dark against the night sky. "Not that. Something useful. A water system. A granary. Something that says: we built this together, and together we won't let it fail."

"That's how you counter the men who are taking things back to the old ways," he said.

"You give people something they built themselves and they'll defend it. The old ways don't have anything they built."

He said neither thing. She was going to try it regardless.

The game ended while they were talking, a clean conclusion, the winning team taking their score to the court's formal boundary and the crowd releasing its held energy in a long wave of sound. Both teams walked off the court with the dignity of men who have competed seriously and know it, the losing captain with his chin up and the careful carriage of a man who is feeling something large and has decided how to hold it in public.

"The games," Danijel said. "They're going to ask you to play."

She had been expecting this. "The women or the mixed group?"

"Women. They've been watching your team train since the second morning."

Every morning since they arrived, Maxtla's group had done their two hours of practice in an open space at the edge of the trading camp. Weapons, movement, hand-to-hand. They had been doing it for two months straight on the road and it was simply what mornings were. The city people had watched with the attention that specialists pay to other specialists, not impressed exactly, but assessing. Filing information.

"When they ask," she said, "what do we say?"

"Yes," he said.

She looked at him.

"You're going to have to say yes," he said. "Refusing is an insult here. Saying yes and performing well is the best possible thing. Saying yes and performing badly is instructive but recoverable. The problem is if you say yes and they change the stakes on you afterward."

"What do we do if they change the stakes?"

"Perform well enough that changing the stakes is inconvenient for them."

She nodded. This was what she had already been thinking. "We need two more weeks in the market."

"At least."

"Then we stay two more weeks. We train in the mornings, we trade in the days, we learn the court."

"I'll make sure someone teaches you the ring shot," Danijel said.

"That sounds like an instruction from experience."

"I've seen the ring shot decide games on short notice before," he said.

She decided not to pursue it.

The court was dark now, the game long finished. The crowd had dispersed into the city's evening, leaving behind the settling-down sound of a large gathering that has concluded, voices fading, the last argument about a point that didn't go the way someone thought it should, children being collected. In the plaza, the last food vendors were packing their goods and the priests were doing something with torches at the base of the pyramid that involved a slow measured rhythm and a low chanting.

The chanting was different from the crowd noise. Where the crowd had been various and unpredictable, the chanting was controlled, deliberate, the sound of something that had been the same for longer than anyone in the crowd had been alive. It moved through the plaza like water finding its level.

Somewhere in the city, a drum was starting. It was a slow beat, too slow for music but too deliberate for random sound. It felt like the city talking to itself.

Maxtla listened to it until she couldn't keep her eyes open, and then she slept. Maxtla attended three more ball games before the tournament.

She was watching the wrong thing at first. After the first game she understood the technical requirements. After the second, the social ones. The third game she spent watching the crowd.

The third game ended badly for the visiting team. Afterward the city had a particular stillness to it, the stillness of something resolved. Whatever had been building in the crowd over the preceding days had somewhere to go now, and had gone.

She described this to Danijel.

"Catharsis," he said. They were sitting on the low wall at the court's edge, the plaza emptying around them in the long bronze light of late afternoon. A vendor was packing his clay pots into a reed basket nearby. Priests moved in a slow procession toward the pyramid base. Ordinary life resuming.

"Can you have the mechanism without the sacrifice?" .

"Eventually," he said. "Most cultures get there. The theater develops. The games become less lethal. The ritual violence becomes symbolic violence." He paused. "It requires pressure from below.

From people who find the sacrifice intolerable and can offer something that does the same work."

She watched the vendor tie off his basket and hoist it to his shoulder. A practiced motion, done ten thousand times. He didn't look at the pyramid.

"You're doing it in the canyon country right now," Danijel said. "The charter and the granary. Shared investment instead of shared trauma. Slower. Less visceral." He paused. "The people who benefited from the old system resist it. You've seen that."

"You bridge from old to new by giving them stake in the new one," she said. It wasn't a question. She had already worked this out with Kael.

"For those who can be brought in," he said. "For the others, you wait. The next generation takes it for granted."

"Three generations."

"If the structure holds."

"That's the whole question," she said.

"Always," he agreed.

The vendor disappeared around the corner of the market wall. The priests reached the pyramid base and the slow chanting began again, the sound moving through the plaza the way it did at dusk, below the level of music, more like a change in the air.

"The specialization is sophisticated," Ixchel said one morning, watching the priests of the corn harvest argue with the priests of the rain god over the placement of an offering at the base of the main staircase. Both groups had legitimate claim to the space by different ceremonial calendars, and neither was giving ground.

"It's harder to control than one god," Maxtla said. "Multiple gods distribute power."

"Unless one family accumulates them." Ixchel watched the dispute resolve, barely, in the corn priests' favor, the rain priests withdrawing with the specific dignity of people who have not conceded but have chosen to defer. "The temple complex on the north side now holds seven of the major rituals. Ix Tunich thinks it's a problem."

Maxtla watched the rain priests go. Ohad had tried the same maneuver in the canyon country, positioning himself as Sun's interpreter. Once Danijel was gone and the mountain-top was just a mountain-top, the religious structure had become unfixed and available. She had offered the charter instead. Not a religion. Something that told people what they owed each other without requiring a priest to translate it.

"You don't believe in Sun," Lofn said to her that evening. Direct, as Lofn asked things.

"I believe in the canyon," Maxtla said. "The water. The stone that holds heat. The people who built the granary."

"The people here believe in many gods."

"Any belief works if it tells people the truth about their responsibilities to each other. When it doesn't, it's a policy."

Lofn was quiet for a moment.

"Do you think Danijel believes in anything?"

Maxtla looked up at the southern sky, more stars than the canyon showed, the air bending the light differently here, the great river of it running horizon to horizon. She had stopped trying to put a number to what Danijel was. Old in ways that didn't have a word in her language, not elder-old, not ancestor-old, but something past the edge of the categories she had. He had watched civilizations build and fail and build again; she had understood this the way you understand things through the sum of a thousand small observations, without anyone saying it plainly. And he had still been unable, when it came to it, not to care.

"The trying," she said. "I think he believes specifically in the trying."

"That's enough," Lofn said.

"Yes," Maxtla agreed. "I think it is."

The night before they departed Yaxal Nah, the real departure, the loaded-horses, no-coming-back-soon departure, Ix Tunich came to the camp for the second time.

The camp was quiet in the way of camps the night before a departure, everything already packed or sorted, the horses fed and settled, no work left to do that hadn't been done. The city's sounds came over the wall in the distant register that had become, over the weeks, simply the texture of the air here: the drum's slow beat, the occasional torch-lighted movement at the pyramid's base, the sound of a settlement of tens of thousands of people existing in the dark. Different from the canyon country's silence. Fuller. She had stopped noticing it three weeks ago. Tonight she was noticing it again, because tomorrow she wouldn't hear it.

She came, this time, with three other women from the inner precincts: her personal aide and two women whom she introduced as her daughters-by-bond, which Ixchel explained was not blood daughters but women who had been formally affiliated with her household in the manner that created reciprocal obligations.

They brought food, a farewell meal, which was a deliberate gesture of the kind this city made deliberately. The dark maize preparation from the feast. The fermented pepper sauce that Eijá had eaten three portions of. The flat corn cakes that had been their market lunch every morning for two weeks, so ordinary they had stopped tasting them, and now, the last time, suddenly specific again. The food was things they had eaten during the stay, already familiar, already associated with the city's flavors, and eating it this last time had the quality of all last times, where the thing you've taken for granted reasserts itself as exactly what it was. The message was clear: you know this place now. This place knows you.

Maxtla ate and said thank you properly and meant it.

At the end of the evening, Ix Tunich handed her a small object: a carved jade disc, smaller than the credential disc Ah Kinich had first processed but more finely made, with a symbol on it that Ixchel translated as something like: known here, or recognized here, or a person with standing here.

"She says it's hers personally," Ixchel said. "Not the household's. Hers."

The distinction was significant in this city's language, where personal and institutional were usually merged in the third wife's position. A personal seal meant: Ix Tunich herself vouches for you. Not the third wife of Ix Pakab's household. Ix Tunich, woman.

Maxtla held it. The jade was cool, which stone that size shouldn't be in this heat, it had been kept somewhere interior, somewhere away from sun. It was lighter than she expected and smoother on the carved face than on the back, the symbol worn slightly at its edges from handling. Someone had held this before. More than once.

"Tell her," she said to Ixchel, "that I'll carry it and I'll come back."

Ixchel translated. Ix Tunich smiled, a real smile, the kind this woman showed rarely, and said something.

"She says: she knows. She saw you pack. You pack like someone who is coming back."

Maxtla looked at her bags, sealed and organized for five days of southward travel before turning north onto the road. They were, she realized, packed exactly like the bags she had left the Lowland with: not the packing of someone closing out, but the packing of someone between trips.

"Yes," she said. "That's exactly how I pack."

They embraced in the city's way, hand to hand, forehead to forehead, close enough that she could smell the copal in the other woman's hair and feel the warmth of her skin and the small pressure of a forehead against her own that was, in this city's language, the gesture that meant: I see you as a person. Not a visitor. Not a useful contact. A person. It was brief because the city's way was brief. It was enough because it was real.

Then Maxtla went back to the camp.

Behind her, Ix Tunich stood in the firelight and watched the northern traders prepare to go, and something in her face was the expression of a woman watching something she has invested in move out into the world.

Pride was part of it.

Hope was part of it.

The longing of a person whose own constraints prevent them from doing what they are watching someone else do: that was the largest part.

She held it without showing it, because that was the skill she had spent thirty years developing.

Then she turned and walked back through the gate to the inner precincts, to her household, to the work that was hers.

She did not know if she would see Maxtla again.

She hoped.

GEDEON: THREE

What Merya decided

The woman's name was Jenet. She had come to the settlement six weeks ago from the group that moved the eastern plateau, arriving with a child on her back and nothing else. The circumstances that had brought her were not complicated and she had not been asked to explain them. She had been given work and a sleeping space and integrated the way the settlement integrated people who needed integrating, which was efficiently and without ceremony.

What Brak had been doing, Gedeon learned later, had been happening for two weeks before Merya acted. The specifics were not complicated either: the corner of the storage area where Jenet worked alone in the afternoon, the pattern of his appearing there, the escalation of it. Two other women had seen it on separate occasions and had said nothing because the formal structure for saying something did not exist.

Gedeon had not seen it. He had seen Brak and filed what he saw without yet having the specific information. He had been waiting for it to resolve or become visible enough to address, which was the kind of decision he would spend a long time deciding whether it had been right.

On a Thursday, Merya saw it herself.

She told Gedeon about it afterward with the flat precision of someone filing a report rather than seeking comfort. She had seen it. She had gone to find three of the founding women. She had come back with them and given Brak until dark to be gone from the settlement.

"He argued," Merya said.

"I know. I heard."

"He had standing with Kael. Kael came to me afterward."

"I know that too."

She looked at him. "Are you going to tell me I should have waited?"

"No," Gedeon said.

"He was going to hurt her."

"I know he was."

"Then what?"

Gedeon was quiet for a moment. The plaza was settling into evening, the cook fires lighted, the low sounds of the settlement at rest. A normal evening. The kind that happened because someone had built the conditions for it.

"You were right about what you decided," he said. "Maxtla will question how you decided it."

Merya looked at the fire.

"Because there was no process," she said. It was not a question. She had already worked this out.

"Because there was no process. Because no one could challenge it. Because the next person who does what you did may not be right."

"I was right."

"Yes. That doesn't settle the question of authority. It only settles this one case."

She said nothing for a while. In the north section, Jenet was moving between the storage buildings with the specific quality of someone learning that a place might be safe after all. Still watchful. But something eased in the way she held her shoulders.

"I would do it again," Merya said.

"I know," Gedeon said. "So would I."

He got up to check the north gate. The night was clear and cold and the canyon walls above held the last of the light in the high sandstone, the red deepening toward something between red and black before the dark took it.

He thought about what Maxtla would say when she heard. He could see her face. The first expression would be the right one: relief that Jenet was safe, that Brak was gone. The second expression would come a few seconds later, when she thought past the immediate case to what it meant.

The second expression would be the one that mattered. And she would be right about what it meant.

Two months. Less, if the road was good.

He closed the north gate and went to find Aki.

CHAPTER FOURTEEN

Scheduled violence

The sacrifices happened on a day when the sky was the color of hammered copper and the heat was heavy enough to taste.

Maxtla had been prepared, more or less. Ixchel had explained it. The priests required blood, the blood of captured warriors from opposing settlements, men taken in a particular kind of ritualized conflict that was less battle than harvest, designed to produce captives rather than casualties. The sacrifice was, within its own logic, an act of maintenance: the gods who held the world together required feeding, and what fed them was the most precious possible thing, which was life.

Ixchel had explained this in the neutral tone of someone reporting facts rather than endorsing them. Maxtla had heard the explanation and set it beside what she knew of the Breeding in the canyon country, and the two things sat side by side in her mind as examples of the same fundamental technique, the consecration of violence through the claim that a higher power demanded it.

What she had not fully prepared for was the sound.

They were at the market when it started, and the market went quiet with a speed that told her this was not ordinary ceremony. The buyers and sellers stopped their transactions and turned to face the pyramid with the unified attention of people for whom the event was not performance but genuine. The vendors who had been calling out prices and adjusting displays went still. A woman near the water vendor set down the clay jugs she had been carrying without looking at them.

On the pyramid's summit, figures in elaborate dress were visible. At this distance they were small, smaller than her hand at arm's length, and she could not make out their faces or the specific motions of what they were doing. What she could see was color: the headdresses catching the light, and the blue of the ceremonial dress, a blue so saturated it read as wrong at this distance, too vivid, the color of something that was not supposed to exist in ordinary daylight. Smoke rose in a column from somewhere near the summit and the wind slowly tore it apart. The figures moved in patterns that were clearly choreographed. Then one figure was horizontal and the others were not, and then the smoke thickened. She understood, watching from down here, the specific economy of distance: you saw enough to know what was happening. Not enough to be certain of the detail. The city had decided, long ago, exactly how much to show and from how far.

The chanting was the thing she had not prepared for. It was not melodic in the way she understood melody, not the rise and fall of a song. It was a sound that operated below song, a sustained controlled tone from many voices that created a physical pressure in the chest when you stood in the plaza. You didn't hear it so much as receive it.

The drum's beat was slower than a heartbeat, which was wrong, which was, she understood, intentional. Too slow for comfort. Slow enough to make you breathe to its rhythm rather than your own.

"We should look away," Lofn said, very quietly.

"Don't look away," Maxtla said. "Watch."

"Maxtla."

"You need to know what this place is. All of it."

Lofn watched. Her face went very still, which was different from the blank face she sometimes wore, this was the stillness of controlled horror, of a person deciding to stay in a place they very much wanted to leave.

Maria watched without comment. Her expression was flat and unreadable and only her jaw gave her away, the slight forward set of it that Maxtla had come to recognize as how Maria looked when she was putting something into the account she was keeping, the long tally of what the world had done and what the world owed.

Eijá watched with the expression of someone taking notes. Maxtla had seen this expression on Eijá when she was studying a joint technique or examining a tool she didn't recognize. The same focused neutrality that preceded analysis. As if even this could be understood as a mechanism, if you looked at it correctly.

When it was over, the market resumed. Not all at once, but smoothly, like water that had been briefly interrupted and now found its level again. The buyers and sellers returned to their transactions. The prices did not change. The goods were the same. The day continued exactly as it had been.

She understood the ceremony. She had grown up inside a system that sanctified violence and had recognized the sanctification for what it was. What she had not seen before was a system so old and so thoroughly integrated that the violence and the commerce and the daily life could exist simultaneously, in the same physical space, without any apparent friction.

In the canyon country, the violence was everywhere, always bleeding into everything. Here, it was scheduled. Contained to specific days, specific forms, specific locations. The market knew when the ceremony was happening and paused for it and resumed after it the way you paused for rain and resumed when it stopped. The ceremony was part of the weather.

The completeness of it, the total integration of the violent and the mundane, was what made it so efficient. You could not oppose it because it was not separable from the other things you needed. The road was built by the same system that built the pyramid. The market was regulated by the same authority that required the sacrifice. You could not take the road and refuse the pyramid.

She was sitting that evening with Ixchel when she put it into words.

"It's not evil in the sense of individual malice," she said. "It's what happens when a system of power is old enough and organized enough to justify itself completely."

"My mother said the same thing," Ixchel replied. "She said: the problem with very old power is that it has had so much time to explain why it's right."

"How did she leave?"

"Someone offered her something better." Ixchel smiled. "My father."

Maxtla was quiet. Then: "What we're building in the canyon, does it look like this from the outside?"

"Not yet," Ixchel said. "Maybe never. Maybe something different."

"What's the difference?"

Ixchel thought about it. "Whether the people at the bottom built it or are held in it." She paused. "You built it from the bottom up. The pyramid was built from the top down. Literally, the labor was directed from above and the benefit returned to above." She paused again. "Your baskets are made by women who own their own skills. The lord's road was built by people who were required to build it."

"Ownership," Maxtla said.

"Ownership," Ixchel agreed.

The next morning, a young man came to the trader camp from the inner precincts with a formal message: the lord's court invited the northern trading group to a feast at the palace in three days. The invitation was phrased as request rather than command, but the social weight behind it made the distinction technical.

"We say yes," Maxtla said.

She spent those three days trading harder than she had traded since arriving, converting more of the remaining inventory, and reinvesting some of the jade currency into things the canyon country needed that she had identified in the market, high-quality fiber rope, a small quantity of seed corn for a variety that grew better in heat, ceramic fired at higher temperature than her own craftspeople had mastered, and three tools from the ironworkers' section that had joints she intended Eijá to reverse-engineer.

She also spent part of each afternoon at the ball court.

A young man named Hunal had been assigned, apparently informally, to teach them the game's technical requirements. He was perhaps eighteen and had the bearing of someone who had been on the court since he could walk, which was likely. He watched them train in the morning without being asked, determined they were serious, and offered his help through Ixchel as translator.

The rubber ball was heavier than it looked. It moved differently than any projectile or thrown weapon Maxtla had trained with, with a bounce that defied prediction on the first encounter and became manageable only through specific practice. The physics of it were unlike anything from the canyon country, the ball had a responsiveness to surface angle and striking force that rewarded calculation over reaction. You did not chase the ball. You anticipated where it would be.

The hip shot, the primary method, driving the ball with the padded side of the hip, took three days to develop from pure accident to something like intention. The leather padding helped, but the hip was not a limb she had ever thought of as an instrument of precision. Teaching it precision required, first, the humiliation of repeated failure, and humiliation was a useful teacher.

The ring shot took longer. You had to understand the ball's arc, track where it would arrive at the ring's height, position precisely, and drive with enough force and angle to send it through a vertical hole barely wider than the ball itself. Hunal demonstrated it on the second afternoon, making it look effortless. It was the farthest thing from effortless.

Eijá got close on the fourth day, came within a finger's width.

"The angle," Danijel said, from the side of the court.

"I know the angle," Eijá said tightly.

"The angle coming into the release, not the release itself. You're correcting too late."

She tried it the way he described. It went through.

She stood looking at the ring for a moment. Her expression was the expression she had when a structural problem revealed its solution, something private and precise that she did not share in words because words were not the right instrument for it.

"Again," she said. And worked at it until the light failed.

Maria had taken to the game with the same focused intensity she brought to knife work, there was something in the problem-solving of it, the way the body had to learn a logic it didn't naturally know, that suited the way her mind worked. She was not the best of them, Eijá's precision made her the best, but she was the most adaptable, the one who noticed in mid-game when something was shifting and adjusted fastest. In scrimmage, she had a quality that Hunal had pointed out on the third day: she always knew where everyone was. Not the ball. Everyone.

"You will have no problem with the city's team," Hunal told Maxtla, through Ixchel.

"Their women's team?"

A small hesitation. "There is not a designated women's team in the city. It would be mixed."

Maxtla looked at him steadily.

"I see," she said.

"It's not an insult. Mixed games are sometimes played. They are not common. You would be the first from outside the city."

"When they ask us to play, what team will they put against us?"

Another hesitation. "I don't know."

He knew. Maxtla decided to let him keep the knowledge for now. Whatever they put against her group, she was going to prepare for better than whatever was coming.

That evening she told the group.

"Whatever they're planning," Eijá said, "we play our game, not theirs."

"Yes," Maxtla agreed. "But first we go to the feast and we smile."

CHAPTER FIFTEEN

The third tier

The palace was at the top of the pyramid.

Not the small temple at the very summit, which was the priests' domain. The living quarters for the lord and his court were on the third tier, accessed by a staircase wide enough to carry a procession and steep enough to require attention. The steps were exactly the right height for a person of average height to climb with dignity but not comfort, a deliberate design choice, Danijel said quietly, intended to make the climber feel the height while maintaining the form of a calm approach.

Maxtla climbed it without comment.

She counted fifty-four steps, each one worn smooth in the center from generations of foot traffic. The stone held the afternoon's heat and gave it back through her feet. The formal dress bound at the stride. At the twentieth step the city opened below her and she could see for the first time the geometry of it, the orderly spacing of the market stalls, the lines of the plaza that were invisible from inside them. At the fortieth step she could see the ball court's full length and beyond it the residential quarters spreading to the jungle edge. At fifty-four she was breathing hard and a wind moved across the tier that didn't exist at ground level, and the city was below her, complete, the whole of it visible at once.

The third tier was a platform perhaps forty feet wide, enclosed on three sides by structures of stone and plastered wood, the fourth side open to the drop. The city looked smaller from above. Also, paradoxically, more complete, the way things you've been inside reveal their shape only once you're out.

The lord's household received them in the largest of the platform structures.

Inside, the room had the quality of spaces that had accumulated objects over a long time without ever being cleared. Not disordered, everything in its place, maintained, but layered, the way a life of power layered itself in things. Jade pieces. Clay vessels with painted figures. Fabric hangings in the colors of this city's hierarchy, the deep blue and red that indicated rank. A carved wooden screen at the far end whose figures Maxtla didn't have enough context to read but which carried the density of meaning that symbolic language develops over generations.

The ceiling was lower than she expected after the openness of the platform. Stone and plastered timber, close enough to feel. The torches gave a moving light that made the fabric hangings shift without shifting and turned the painted vessels into things with shadows. After the wind of the climb, the room's stillness was its own pressure.

The smells were layered too. Copal incense, which had been burning in this building long enough that it lived in the walls. The clean oil of the torches. The food being prepared somewhere below them, something with the dark fermented depth of the corn preparations she had been eating here, and something sharper, a pepper or a spice she hadn't encountered yet.

Ix Pakab was older than Maxtla had expected based on the third wife's youth. He was perhaps fifty, thin in a way that spoke of illness despite his careful presentation, with deep-set eyes that were clearly still intelligent. He sat in a chair elevated slightly above the other seating, which was a deliberate spatial claim to authority, and his clothing was the most elaborate thing Maxtla had seen since entering the city, jade at his neck and wrists, headdress with the specific featherwork that Ixchel had identified as reserved for the lord's rank, fabric in patterns that were not decorative but functional, in the sense that every element communicated status with the precision of a formal record.

He did not look at her the way powerful men in her experience usually looked at women who arrived in their presence. He looked at her the way an experienced trader looks at a competitor's goods, with the attention of someone trying to determine value. Not dismissive. Not predatory. Assessing.

She met the look without performing either deference or aggression. The middle register, the register of equals engaging each other.

The first wife, Ix Akbal, sat on a lower chair to the lord's right, which was still elevated above the guests. She was a handsome woman in her mid-forties who wore her status like a second skin, naturally and deliberately. She looked at Maxtla and then at Ixchel and then at the group. She missed nothing. She was the kind of woman who had been the most capable person in every room for thirty years, with the patience of someone who had long since stopped needing to prove it.

The second wife, Ix Mam, sat on the other side, lower than Ix Akbal but in a position that gave her equal sight lines across the room. She was younger than Ix Akbal and had a face that had been beautiful and was now more interesting. She caught Maxtla's eye once during the initial placement and looked away. She had already decided something about Maxtla. The decision was not available yet.

Ix Tunich sat slightly apart from the other two wives, which was probably the correct social choice for the third wife in a room with both predecessors present. She held her position with the deliberate ease of someone who had practiced holding this position. She looked at Maxtla briefly and her expression said: I brought you here. The rest of this is yours to navigate.

The food was extraordinary. Maxtla had not been badly fed since arriving at Yaxal Nah, but this was a different order of preparation, dishes she had no names for, using ingredients she couldn't fully identify, presented with a care for visual arrangement that was as deliberate as the architecture. The first dish was a preparation of the maize in a dark sauce that had layers she could not fully trace, something dried and ground as its base, something roasted, something fermented, something fresh. The whole was more specific than the sum of what she could identify. It tasted like the city, she thought. Complex and organized and old.

A sauce of such complex depth that Eijá ate three portions of it, which was unusual for someone who approached food primarily as nutrition. When Maxtla raised an eyebrow, Eijá shrugged with the unembarrassed shrug of someone who has found an exception to their own rule and sees no reason to pretend otherwise.

Maxtla ate carefully, noted what she tasted, and kept most of her attention on the room.

The conversation through Ixchel's translation was skilled and pleasant and accomplished little. This was also a form of information, the lord's household was assessing them exactly as she was assessing the household. What they were doing with the food and the show was the same thing she did with the market display. The product was a setting in which real decisions could eventually be made, but tonight was not for real decisions.

She asked, through Ixchel, about the road system, how far it extended, who maintained it, whether new sections were being planned. The lord's face showed genuine interest at this, and he talked for several minutes about the engineering challenges of the southern extension and the politics of getting three separate settlements to cooperate on maintenance costs. It was a topic he clearly knew well and cared about, and Maxtla stored every detail.

She asked about the rubber trade, where the trees grew, how the material was processed, how far it traveled. Ix Mam answered before her husband could, with specific numbers that suggested she either managed this trade herself or was closely involved in it. She answered without apology for speaking before her husband, and the lord showed no sign of displeasure, which told Maxtla that the formal hierarchy in this household and the actual hierarchy were probably not identical. The first wife noted the exchange without commenting on it. She had been noting exchanges without commenting on them for a long time.

Danijel said almost nothing during the meal. He ate, he observed, he occasionally smiled at something in the room that wasn't visible to anyone else. The household's attention kept returning to him with the attention that a room gives to the person they can't quite categorize. He was not the oldest man they had seen, Maxtla was certain of that, this was an old city with old people, but he was the oldest differently. Not decay. Accumulation. The household could feel it without naming it.

She caught his eye once, during the second course. He was watching the lord's youngest son, a boy of perhaps eight, seated at the far end of the table, who was asking careful questions of the servant beside him about the dishes being served and listening to the answers with the concentrated attention of someone who intended to remember. Danijel was watching this the way he watched things that mattered to him. When Maxtla looked at him, he turned to her and said nothing. But the expression was one she had learned to read: he had seen something here that he had not expected. Something that made the long view look better than it had when they arrived.

Late in the evening, when the food was finished and the drink had been circulating long enough to soften some edges, the lord raised the topic of the ball game.

"I have heard your people practice daily," he said, through the translation chain.

"We maintain our physical training always," Maxtla said. "Travel is easier if the body is kept ready."

"Your training on the court was observed."

"Hunal was kind enough to show us the rules. We are learning."

The lord smiled. It was an honest smile, she thought, the kind that came from genuine pleasure rather than political calculation. "I would like to see your group play."

"We would be honored," Maxtla said.

"In five days. A friendly game. For entertainment."

"We look forward to it."

"Our teams play for points and prestige only," he added, which was also information. He was telling her, in this careful way, that the stakes for this game would not be the high ones.

"Of course," she said.

Ix Akbal had been watching this exchange with the attention of a woman who had spent decades monitoring the implications of everything said in this room. She spoke.

"She says," Ixchel translated, with a slight carefulness in her voice, "that she, too, heard of your trading goods. She says she would have liked to have been informed of your arrival before the third wife."

The sentence sat in the air.

Maxtla had not been told of Ix Akbal directly until the gate meeting with Ix Tunich. The first wife had not sought the meeting. This, Maxtla now understood, had been exactly what Ix Tunich had intended, to be first, to appear as the wife who recognized an opportunity before the household's formal authority did.

She answered the first wife directly. "We arrived at the gate, we were processed at the gate, and the invitation came to us from there. We did not choose the order of the introductions. We simply accepted what was offered." She paused. "I would have been very glad to meet you first."

The translation. Ix Akbal looked at her steadily. The assessment continued, Maxtla could feel it as a physical thing, the attention of someone trying to determine whether they had been deliberately maneuvered or whether the maneuvering had happened around them. The distinction mattered.

"She says: she will see your goods tomorrow morning, before the market opens."

"We would be honored," Maxtla said.

She met Ix Tunich's eyes briefly across the room. The third wife's expression was perfectly neutral. But she had heard every word.

The game within the game.

They descended the steep pyramid stairs in the dark, torches held by servants illuminating the way, the city spread below them like the reflection of the star river in still water. The market plaza was empty now, the daytime commerce gone. Without the crowd, the space became what it actually was: enormous. A plaza that could hold thousands, built to hold thousands, currently holding no one but the night watch and the slow orange light of the perimeter fires.

"The second wife," Maxtla said quietly to Ixchel as they descended.

"Said almost nothing," Ixchel agreed.

"Watched everything."

"Yes."

"She's the one I want to talk to alone."

"I know," Ixchel said. "Give it a few days."

They descended in silence after that, fifty-four steps down, the city rearranging itself around them as they left the height and rejoined the level where ordinary people moved.

Below them, in the plaza, the drum started its slow measured beat.

It felt, Maxtla thought, like a clock she was running against without knowing the time.

CHAPTER SIXTEEN

The knowledge keeper

The woman's name was Ix Chab, and she did not look like someone who held power.

She was perhaps fifty-five, small and round in the way of women who have eaten well and worked hard across a long life, with deep-set eyes that had the quality of someone who had been observing people professionally for decades. She sat in a low building behind the market's western wall, in a room that smelled of dried herbs and something sharper, a resin of some kind, medicinal, and she looked at them with the patience of someone deciding how much to say and to whom.

Ix Tunich had arranged the meeting. This was itself significant: the third wife had the relationship with Ix Chab, which meant Ix Chab was either formally attached to the third wife's household or was someone whose knowledge base the third wife had chosen to cultivate independently of the first wife's domain. In either case, Maxtla understood she was being offered something through a specific channel, and the channel was part of the gift.

"She keeps the women's knowledge," Ixchel had explained. "Not the temple knowledge, that belongs to the priests. Not the healing knowledge, that belongs to the healers. The knowledge of." She had paused, finding the right framing. "The knowledge of how women manage their own lives. How women make decisions about their bodies and their households and their relationships that are not covered by the formal structures."

"That sounds like the most important knowledge in the city," Maxtla had said.

"Yes," Ixchel had said. "Which is why it's kept by a woman who appears to have no formal standing."

Ix Chab looked at them now, in the herb-smelling room, and spoke.

"You want to know about the prevention of children," Ixchel translated. "She asks: is this for yourselves or for your people?"

"Both," Maxtla said. "And for the women who come to us from old ways, who have not had the choice before."

Ix Chab looked at her for a long moment. Then she nodded, once, and began.

The first session began with Ix Chab setting three plants on the low table between them, dried, still in their stalks, different enough in structure that Lofn could see they had come from different sources and different seasons. She placed each one with space between them. Not a display. A lesson structure.

She spoke. Ixchel translated in the careful low register she used when the content required precision.

The first plant: a preparation of the root taken during the specific window of days before the possibility, not after. Timing was the whole of it. The plant's action was narrow and required understanding what narrow meant. She described it without hedging. The failure modes, the edge cases, the conditions under which it did not work. The conditions under which it worked reliably.

Lofn was writing before the first plant was finished. Her notation moved fast and she did not look up except to ask, through Ixchel, two questions, the first about the preparation method, the second about the timing window. Both were specific. Both indicated she had understood the mechanism before the full description was complete.

Ix Chab looked at her when the second question arrived. She said something to Ixchel without waiting for the question to be fully translated.

"She says: you are a healer," Ixchel said.

"Yes," Lofn said.

A pause while Ixchel translated.

"She says: a specific kind. She says: you are the kind who is angry," Ixchel finished. "About what you cannot cure."

Lofn looked up from the tablet.

A silence in the herb-smelling room in which something between them became a different thing.

"Yes," Lofn said again.

Ix Chab picked up the second plant. The session continued.

"Why doesn't everyone know this?" Lofn asked. Through Ixchel.

Ix Chab answered at some length. Ixchel translated carefully. "She says: everyone who needs to know, knows. The women of the households that have this knowledge share it with their daughters and with women they trust. The knowledge does not go to the temple, which would use it to control it. It does not go to the lord's administration, which would regulate it. It lives in the relationships between women."

"But the women who don't have access to those relationships?" Lofn pressed.

"She says: that is the problem she has spent thirty years working on."

Lofn looked at Ix Chab with a recognition that crossed the language barrier entirely.

"She's doing what you're doing," Maxtla said quietly. "For the women here."

"Yes," Lofn said. She looked at Ix Chab. "Tell her we'll carry it north. Tell her every woman who comes to us will have access to it."

Ix Chab listened to the translation. She said something short.

"She says: she knows. That's why she agreed to the meeting."

The third session included the plants themselves, dried samples packed in sealed clay pots with the same notational system Tinga used, which had been adapted from something older than anyone

Maxtla knew could trace. Ix Chab also sent a small bundle of seeds for two of the plants that grew in the hot lowlands: they would not survive the canyon's cold, but might grow with careful cultivation and the right slope exposure.

She sent one other thing: a rolled strip of pressed reed on which she had drawn, in the fine notation of her city's writing system, a complete record of what she had taught. Ahmik had agreed to translate it into the simplified notation system before they left, so the information would survive intact.

When they left the herb-smelling room on the fourth day, Maxtla felt the weight of what she was carrying. Not the physical weight, the pots and the seeds and the rolled reed were light. The other weight. The weight of knowledge that had been kept in women's hands through deliberate invisibility, now moving north to a place where it could be distributed without the need for invisibility.

"She's remarkable," Ixchel said, when they were clear of the building.

"Yes," Maxtla said.

"She could have had formal standing. She's chosen not to. The formal structures constrain what she can do."

"She made the same calculation I made," Maxtla said. "Formal standing costs you scope. Informal standing costs you protection but gains you room."

"Where do you want to end up?" Ixchel asked.

Maxtla thought about it honestly. "Both. The charter is the formal standing. The informal scope is what I do inside it."

Lofn had been quiet during this. Now she said: "I'm going to name her Chab."

They both looked at her.

"If I ever have a daughter," she said. "I'm going to name her Chab." She looked at the sealed pots in her pack. "For the woman who kept the knowledge safe until it could go somewhere better."

Neither of them pointed out that Chab was not a northern name, or that naming a child after a Mayan woman they had met for three days was unusual. Some decisions didn't require justification.

"Good name," Maxtla said.

The birth control knowledge was not the only thing Ix Chab taught them, but it was the one that Maxtla found herself thinking about most in the weeks after, as the city's rhythms folded around them and the market stall became familiar territory.

"The death problem," Lofn said.

"Yes," Maxtla said.

"Which is why the priests control the writing system," Ixchel said.

"Which is why we teach it to everyone," Maxtla said.

They were sitting in the shade behind the market stall on a slow afternoon, the rain had come suddenly and reduced the market traffic to the hardiest buyers and the most dedicated sellers, which was a smaller and more focused group. The rain here was not the hesitant occasional rain of the canyon country. It fell as if it meant it. Everything got wet.

Lofn liked the rain. She had liked it since the first tropical downpour three days into their time in the city, which had driven the market to shelter and given her forty minutes to sit in it and feel it and think.

"You were not like this at home," Eijá observed, when she found Lofn in the rain for the third time.

"Like what?" Lofn said.

"Content to sit and not do anything."

Lofn thought about this. "I don't think I was ever not content to sit. I just felt like I wasn't allowed to."

Eijá absorbed this. "Who didn't allow it?"

"No one specifically," Lofn said. "Just, the general pressure of things that needed worrying about."

"Things that needed worrying about still exist," Eijá pointed out.

"Yes," Lofn agreed. "But from here they look smaller. Or differently sized." She tilted her face up at the rain. "I think I needed to get very far away from them to see what size they actually were."

Eijá sat down beside her in the rain. This was unusual behavior for Eijá, who generally treated water as a practical material rather than an experience. But she sat in it and they were both wet and the market went on being traded around them and nothing was required.

"Do you miss him?" Eijá asked, after a while.

"Dewii?" Lofn didn't hesitate. "Always. Less completely than before."

"What does that mean?"

"It means he was the whole thing for a while. And then he wasn't the whole thing anymore, because other things were also things." She paused. "That's not the same as forgetting. He's still there. He's just not, all the way across the horizon."

Eijá thought about this. "I don't think I've ever felt that way about a person," she said. Not sad about it. Observational.

"I know," Lofn said. "I've wondered what that's like."

"Not empty," Eijá said, after considering. "Just, specific. The things I feel strongly about are problems. And things that are made. And sometimes people who are making things, but mostly the things." She paused. "I don't know if that's a loss."

"I don't think it's a loss," Lofn said. "I think you got a different thing instead."

They sat in the rain.

"The water channel," Eijá said. "The one at the settlement. If we extend it from the creek to the south storage area, it would serve the new buildings going up on that side. The gradient is right. We'd need to."

"Eijá," Lofn said.

"Yes?"

"You're doing it right now," Lofn said. Not accusatory. Fond.

"Am I?"

"Thinking about the things." Lofn smiled at her sideways, rain-soaked. "You're sitting in the rain in a Mayan city thinking about a water channel in a canyon you're several months away from."

"The gradient is quite good," Eijá said after a moment.

Lofn laughed.

What Lofn took home was the sitting. The understanding that stillness was not the absence of useful activity.

CHAPTER SEVENTEEN

What Lofn built

The charity operation started because Lofn couldn't help herself.

On their sixth day in the market, she saw a child. The child was thin in a way that had nothing to do with today's hunger, which was ordinary and correctable, but in the specific hollow way of a child who had been insufficiently fed long enough that the body had begun accommodating to it. She was perhaps five, sitting near the wall of the market with a blank patience that children develop when they have stopped expecting much from the world.

Lofn bought food from the nearest vendor. She fed the child.

By afternoon, three other children had found the position near the wall, and Lofn was feeding them too.

By the following day, there were seven children and two adults, the adults being women who had the same hollow quality as the children in the eyes rather than the body, the hollowness of people who expected to remain invisible.

Maxtla found Lofn that morning already redistributing a portion of the previous day's earnings to this unofficial welfare operation.

"You know I can't have you spending the trading inventory on," she began.

"I'm spending my share," Lofn said, with a firmness Maxtla hadn't heard from her before.

"Your share is part of the collective."

"It's also mine. You said it was mine."

Maxtla stopped. That was true. She had established, clearly, that each woman in the group held an individual stake in the operation's returns.

"The market people are watching," she said instead.

"I know."

"They don't know what to make of it."

"Good," Lofn said. "Maybe thinking about it will be useful for them."

Maxtla thought about this for half a day and then came back to it.

"Spend conservatively," she said. "And keep a record. Every transaction."

Lofn blinked. "Why the record?"

"Because when I tell the story of this trip to people back home, I'm going to talk about what you're doing here. And the numbers will make the story real."

The operation grew on its own, which was what happened when you addressed a need in a place where the need existed and no one had yet thought to address it. By the second week, Lofn had organized a small feeding operation in the space behind their market stall that ran for two hours at midday and provided a meal to anyone who came without the means to trade.

The market people watched this with the attention of a professional community encountering an alien business model.

On the ninth day, a man from the inner precincts, junior staff, not household, came to the market and stood near the feeding operation for most of an hour. Then he left.

"That's the second wife's household," Ixchel said.

"How do you know?"

"His arm wrap. I've been tracking the household markings since the feast." She paused. "The second wife runs what amounts to a welfare function for the city herself. She has for twenty years. She maintains it through a system of clan obligations that I haven't fully mapped yet."

"And now she's seeing Lofn do it in the market."

"Yes."

"Is that good or bad?"

Ixchel considered. "Interesting is what it is. Lofn is doing it differently than she does, Lofn does it publicly, in the market, at the cost of her own funds. Ix Mam does it through the obligation network, which is less visible but more systemic." She paused. "From Ix Mam's perspective, Lofn is either a competitor, or proof of concept, or both."

"Get me the meeting," Maxtla said.

"The second wife doesn't meet casually."

"I know. Find the mechanism."

Ixchel found the mechanism the next morning. The second wife, she had determined, managed the distribution of charity through a series of what were, essentially, market transactions, clans with surplus contributed to clans in deficit, with her household keeping the ledger and taking a small administrative fee. It was, when you looked at it correctly, a welfare system structured as a trading operation.

Maxtla sent Ix Mam a message through the appropriate intermediary: she would like to discuss the operational principles of her distribution system. She was interested, she said, in establishing something similar in her settlement in the north, and believed they might have things to learn from each other.

The meeting was arranged for the following day.

Ix Mam met her in a courtyard in the inner precincts that was smaller and more functional than the official meeting spaces, a working space, not a ceremonial one. She was accompanied by a single aide and brought no guards. She looked at Maxtla with an intelligence that had been sharpened by twenty years of moving in the gaps of the formal power structure, which was a specific kind of intelligence that Maxtla recognized because she was developing it herself.

"Your woman with the food," Ix Mam said through Ixchel. "The blonde one."

"Lofn."

"She doesn't charge anything for what she gives."

"No."

"How does she fund it?"

"Her share of our trading profits."

Ix Mam absorbed this. "Why?"

Maxtla thought of Lofn's face when she'd found her feeding the first child. She thought of how to translate that impulse into something this woman, who operated through systems rather than impulse, would respect.

"Because someone in our group who has experienced need recognizes it faster than someone who hasn't," Maxtla said. "And because in the settlement we're building, the people who are helped remember who helped them, and that memory becomes a kind of investment."

"That is a colder way of putting it than your woman intends," Ix Mam said.

"She intends to help people who need it," Maxtla said. "I see the system even when I approve of the impulse."

Something shifted in Ix Mam's face.

They talked for two hours. About clan obligation systems and how they could be made equitable rather than coercive. About what the north had that the south didn't, and vice versa. About the problem of bad harvests and how a system of stored surplus and coordinated distribution could prevent the catastrophic failures that killed settlements.

About women and power, which Ix Mam raised herself, directly and without preamble: "Your group has only one man."

"Yes."

"By choice?"

"Yes."

"This is unusual here," she said. "I understand it is unusual where you come from as well."

"It's becoming less unusual," Maxtla said. "Slowly."

"How do you maintain the authority?"

"I earn it daily," Maxtla said. "That's the only way it works."

Ix Mam took that in.

"I have maintained my position in this household for twenty years by earning it," she said. "Not daily. More like hour by hour." She paused. "It is exhausting."

"Yes," Maxtla agreed. "It is."

A small silence between them, not uncomfortable.

"I would like to send a message with you when you return north," Ix Mam said. "Written, in our script. I understand you have no equivalent. I will explain what the script says to your translator before you go, and she can teach it to whoever you choose."

"What will the message say?"

"That you are known here. That you are reliable. That merchants arriving at Yaxal Nah who mention your name will receive good faith treatment." She paused. "A credit note, essentially. Portable reputation."

Maxtla looked at her. "That's worth more than anything in my pack."

"I know," Ix Mam said. And smiled, for the first time, entirely real.

She walked Maxtla to the courtyard gate.

"Your Lofn," she said at the gate. "Tell her: it is not charity. It is investment."

Maxtla delivered the message.

"Both," Lofn said. "It's both."

"Yes," Maxtla said.

The feeding operation had a second effect that Maxtla had not anticipated and Lofn had not planned for: it became a source of intelligence.

The children who came knew the market in the way that children who spend their days in a place know it, not the formal structure but the underside. Who argued with whom. Which stalls were fronts for other arrangements. The locations of water, of shade, of the specific positions where you could hear two conversations at once. They did not volunteer this information. It surfaced in the interactions, in what they noticed and pointed at and reacted to.

Lofn was not, by nature, an intelligence-gatherer. She was a healer and a record-keeper and she had the record-keeper's eye for what was precise and verifiable. But she was also, Maxtla had known for years, someone who paid attention to people, genuinely, without agenda, and people responded to that quality. The children talked to her more than they talked to anyone else in the group, partly because of the food and partly because she looked at them in a way that said: you are a specific person and I am noticing which one.

By the end of the second week, Lofn had mapped the market's underside.

"There's a second market," she told Maxtla. "East of the ball court, near the residential neighborhood. It runs at night. Goods without legal standing, some stolen, some in-between categories. Medicines. Agreements. Information."

"Stolen?"

"Some. The formal medicine system costs more than everyone can meet. The second market's medicines are cheaper and less regulated and sometimes dangerous. But sometimes they're the only option."

"I want to go," Lofn said. "To see what they have."

"For documentation."

"And because Ix Chab talked about preserving the knowledge the official systems don't preserve. That knowledge lives in the second market."

"Ixchel and Maria," she said. "Not alone."

"I wasn't going to go alone," Lofn said, with a slight expression that suggested this should have been obvious.

They went the following night. Maxtla did not go herself, someone needed to hold the camp, and three was the right number for the purpose, and she was recognizable enough by now that adding her to a group moving through unofficial spaces was more conspicuous than useful.

They came back two hours later.

Lofn was carrying three small sealed packages and had the expression of someone who had seen things that required processing before they could be reported.

"Tomorrow," Maxtla said, looking at her.

"Tomorrow," Lofn agreed.

What she reported the following morning, systematically and with the documentation she had already begun: six plant preparations not available in the formal market, two of which were for conditions that the canyon country had no treatment for. A preparation for the specific kind of fever that took children in the canyon's cold seasons. A preparation for the infection that followed deep wound injuries, the kind that killed people who had survived the initial damage.

She had paid for the preparations with her own funds, as she had paid for the feeding operation. She had also paid for the knowledge of how they were made, which had cost more than the preparations and which she had in her records as a sequence of written instructions that Ixchel had translated and which would need translation back on arrival. She had also, without complaint, been working the entire time in the city from a kit that was half what it should have been, rationing the fever treatment and the wound-closure preparation with the specific care of someone who knows they cannot replace what they spend.

"The fever preparation," Maxtla said.

"Yes," Lofn said. "I thought of Bren."

Bren had been seven years old. Three winters ago. The fever had taken her in two days. Her mother had not left the settlement for a month afterward.

"How reliable?" Maxtla asked.

"The woman I bought it from said: reliable when caught early. Not reliable when the fever has been running three days." Lofn paused. "Which means the knowledge we also need is how to identify the fever earlier, before the third day."

"Can you get that knowledge?"

"I already did," Lofn said. "It cost me the last of my share."

She spread the documentation on the ground between them, the clay tablets with their careful notation, the sealed packages with their identifying marks, the sequence of instructions.

"This is why we came," she said.

Maxtla looked at what was in front of her. The trading goods in the stall were worth more in jade currency and would weigh more on the horses going north. What Lofn had spent her share on would weigh almost nothing and was worth more than anything else in the inventory.

"Your share," she said. "For the next trip, I'm doubling it."

Lofn looked at her. "You don't have to."

"I know I don't have to," Maxtla said. "I'm doing it because the return on what you spent is the highest return in this expedition." She paused. "And because Bren's mother deserves to know we tried."

CHAPTER EIGHTEEN

The exchange

The technology transfer happened in two parts: one intended and one not.

The intended part was Eijá.

She had been patient for two weeks, which for Eijá was the equivalent of a longer person's lifetime of patience. She had watched, catalogued, and mapped the technical landscape of the Yaxal Nah market with the systematic attention of a woman who had been thinking about structural problems all her life. The rope fiber. The ceramic firing. The fitted stone joint system used in the road and the buildings. The rubber processing.

She approached each exchange the same way: she came to a craftsperson's stall, watched without buying, asked through whatever translation was available for a demonstration, and paid fair value for the lesson. Not the product, the lesson. The craftspeople were, most of them, initially uncertain how to price this, which meant Maxtla had to negotiate, which she did by suggesting a price and then suggesting that the craftsperson tell anyone who asked that they had been fairly treated by the northern traders.

Reputation as currency.

In exchange for these lessons, Eijá demonstrated her own techniques, the obsidian beveling, the self-tightening rope weave, the basket pictography method. These were given freely, as Maxtla had promised at the toll gate.

The unintended transfer happened with the weapons.

She hadn't planned to share the weapons. The outline in Maxtla's mind had included them as a trade good, show them, get interest, negotiate for considerable value, deliver on the next trip. They were the highest-leverage items in the pack.

What she hadn't planned for was Parruk.

Teya's second-in-command had found, in the ball court, something that agreed with his temperament. He trained with the ferocious focus of someone who had discovered a physical problem worth solving, and he trained alongside the city people without the friction that Maxtla had feared, because the ball court had its own language and in that language he was fluent.

He had also, in his time at the market, developed a friendship with a young man from the craftworkers' district who made arrows and spear tips. The friendship was conducted mostly in gesture and demonstration, the common language of people who work with their hands, and in its third day had arrived at the obvious question of whose arrow-making technique was better.

Eijá found them at the back of the market on the tenth day, both demonstrating to each other, both genuinely interested, both entirely forgetting they were supposed to be from different cultures with proprietary knowledge.

She stood and watched for a while. Then she sat down beside them and got involved.

By the end of the afternoon, Teya's people, the city craftspeople, and Eijá had produced a composite arrowhead design that combined three separate techniques in a way none of them had seen before. It was significantly better than any of the source techniques.

Maxtla found Eijá after the market closed.

"The arrowheads," she said.

"I know," Eijá said. "I didn't plan it."

"I know you didn't. What happened?"

"We were each trying to show the other that our way was better, and we were both right, and we ended up with something that used both, and it was better than either." She paused. "I couldn't stop it and I wasn't sure I should."

Maxtla thought about this. "What did it cost us?"

"They can make the composite now. But they can't make it consistently without our source materials, which don't exist here. And they can make the component techniques but not the junction technique, which is the part that makes it work." She spread her hands. "We gave away two things and kept the key."

"That was deliberate?"

"No. But it turned out that way."

"Next time," Maxtla said, "make sure you don't share the key even by accident."

"I didn't share the key."

"Deliberately. I know."

Eijá nodded. This was a fair correction and she received it as one.

The composite arrowhead was discussed across the market by the following morning. They had become more interesting.

"The spear thrower," she said to Eijá.

"Atlatl. Yes."

"How long to teach the basic operation?"

"An hour. Accuracy is days of practice."

"Do you have one with you?"

"I brought three. I thought they'd be worth showing."

"Show them today. Don't explain the construction yet. Just show the range and the power."

Eijá demonstrated the atlatl, a throwing board that functioned as an extension of the arm, effectively doubling the leverage and tripling the range of a standard spear throw, in the open area behind the market, with a target made of stacked reed bundles thirty yards out. Her first throw punched through three bundles and buried the point in a fourth.

By the time the market closed that day, six separate buyers had approached about acquiring an atlatl, and two craftspeople had approached about learning the construction.

"We teach the construction on the next trip," Maxtla told the craftspeople. "We sell the finished goods now."

She sold two atlatls that evening for more jade currency than she had made in the previous three days combined.

In the evening, sitting with the group after the trading closed, she took stock.

The trading was substantially complete. She had the goods. She had the currency. She had the relationship with Ix Mam and the credential letter, the connection with Ix Tunich, the demonstrated trust with Ah Kinich at the gate.

What she had not had, what had appeared without being planned, was the beginning of a relationship between Teya's people and the craftspeople of Yaxal Nah. Not a trading relationship yet, but the groundwork.

She looked at Teya across the camp, who was watching Parruk and the arrow craftsman argue cheerfully about something she couldn't hear.

"Your people," she said to Teya. "Do they want to come back here next trip?"

Teya didn't answer immediately. "Some."

"Parruk?"

Teya glanced at him. "He has found his thing, I think."

"We'll make room," Maxtla said. "The route needs reliable protection both ways. People who know it and have reason to care about it."

Teya looked at her. "You're building a system."

"I'm trying to."

"The road," Teya said. "The Maya built the road so trade could move. Trade moves, more people prosper, the city grows."

"Yes."

"You want a road between here and the canyon country."

"Not stone," Maxtla said. "But yes. Something that functions like a road. Safe passage, known route, reliable relationships at intervals."

"And we are one of the relationships."

"If you want to be."

Teya was quiet for a moment. Then she said: "Parruk will be your worst problem and your best asset."

"I know," Maxtla said. "I'm counting on both."

The night settled around them, warm and wet and loud with insects in the way of the deep south.

Five more days before the ball game.

Five more days before the alliance with the lord's court was tested in the most public possible way.

She was ready. More or less. More or less was what you had, usually.

The evening after the atlatl demonstration, Danijel sat with Eijá at the edge of camp for a long time.

Maxtla could see them from where she was doing inventory, Danijel's characteristic stillness, Eijá's characteristic restless hands, the clay tablet and the writing instrument between them, and the specific quality of two people who think in similar ways discovering this about each other.

Gedeon sat down beside Maxtla.

"What are they talking about?" he asked.

"Engineering," Maxtla said. "What else?"

"He knows things she doesn't know."

"He knows things none of us know," Maxtla said. "He's been deciding, since before we left, what's appropriate to give us and what isn't."

"How do you know?"

"Because he's been choosing carefully for as long as I've known him." She did not say: because he told me so, because that conversation was not hers to share. "He doesn't give knowledge carelessly. He gives it in specific amounts at specific times."

"For what reason?"

"Because he's seen what happens when he gives it carelessly," she said. "I think. He's never said it directly. But the care has a reason behind it."

Gedeon watched Danijel for a moment. In the city's firelight, the old man looked, as he always looked, like someone from a different country who had been living in this one long enough to know all the customs and still get them slightly wrong in small ways that no one could identify specifically. Not wrong, different. The kind of different that was only visible if you were paying attention.

"He's going to leave," Gedeon said. "When we get home."

"Yes."

"He told you?"

"He told me on the way south," Maxtla said. "Not when or how. Just that the journey was the last one. He has a place he goes when a place is finished."

"How does he know when a place is finished?"

She thought about this honestly. "I think he means when the thing he came to see has happened. When the experiment has run far enough to know the direction." She looked at the fire. "He came here to see whether people could build something different from the Breeding. We built it. The experiment has a direction."

"It might still fail," Gedeon said.

"Yes. He knows that. But it's not going to fail for lack of trying, and that's what he was watching for." She paused. "I think he's seen a lot of things fail for lack of trying. He stays for the trying. When the trying is going, he goes."

Gedeon was quiet for a while.

"What will you do?" he said. "When he's gone."

"The same thing I'm doing now," she said. "Minus one person who sees around corners I can't see around." She paused. "I've been watching how he sees around them for years. I've learned some of it. Not all. But some."

"He's been teaching you."

"He's been living near me," she said. "I've been learning. Those aren't the same thing, but the result is similar."

Across the camp, Eijá had stopped writing and was drawing. The drawing was a structural diagram of something Maxtla couldn't see clearly from this distance, the specific organized lines of an engineer working through a problem. Danijel was watching the drawing the way he watched most things: with the attentiveness of someone for whom watching was never passive.

"I'll miss him," Gedeon said.

"Yes," Maxtla said. "So will I."

She went back to the inventory. The count was right, as it always was when Ixchel had checked it before her. The goods were organized, the currency was accounted for, the knowledge was sealed in Lofn's clay pots and recorded in Eijá's documentation.

She was, she thought, ready to go home.

Two more days in the market. One day of packing. Then north.

She had what she came for. She also had things she hadn't come for, which were always the more interesting category.

CHAPTER NINETEEN

The stakes

The ball game changed things.

The day before the game, the young man Hunal came to the camp looking uncomfortable.

"What is it?" Maxtla asked.

He spoke to Ixchel. She translated, carefully: "He says the game tomorrow is not a small prestige game between friends. He says the court officials have arranged it as a formal tournament game. Two teams from the city's best players against your group."

A silence.

"The stakes," Maxtla said.

"He says: the stakes are the stated friendly ones. No sacrifice. No formal consequence for the losing team." He spoke again. Ixchel's face shifted. "He says: the crowd will expect a demonstration game. The city's best players are known. If your group performs badly, the market standing will not be formally affected but informally."

"The market will see us differently," Maxtla said.

"Yes."

"Who arranged this?" Ixchel asked him.

He answered. She went still for a moment.

"The first wife's household," she told Maxtla.

Ix Akbal. Who had been patient since the feast and had now found the lever. If the northern traders were shown up on the city's court by its best players, the balance of household politics that Ix Tunich had temporarily disrupted would restore itself. The third wife who had gotten there first would look like she had backed an entertaining but ultimately minor novelty.

And there was nothing Maxtla could do about it directly. Refusing the game was worse.

"Thank him," Maxtla said to Ixchel. And then, to Hunal directly: "We will play well. Thank you for telling us."

He left, looking somewhat relieved.

"Options," Eijá said.

"We play the game," Maxtla said.

"We play it perfectly," Eijá said.

"We play it our way," Maria said.

Both of them looked at her.

"Their best players are their best players in their game," Maria said. "It's their court, their rules, their ball. They're going to be better than us technically. But it's a seven-player game and we have five."

"Six," Danijel said. He had been sitting outside the circle of this conversation, apparently thinking about something else.

They all looked at him.

"Six," he said again. "I'll play."

"Can you play?" Eijá asked.

He looked at her.

"That was a stupid question," Eijá said.

"Yes," he said, without heat.

"They said their best players," Maxtla said. "Seven of them."

"Against six of us." He settled back. "I've seen worse odds than six to seven. The key is what you said: play our game, not theirs." He was quiet for a moment. "I've watched their best players for two weeks. They have three technical virtuosos and four competent supporters. The virtuosos drive the score and the supporters protect them. The virtuosos' weakness is tunnel vision, when they have the ball moving well, they focus on the score and lose track of the support map."

"We disrupt the support map," Maxtla said.

"We make the virtuosos feel unsupported," Eijá said, catching it.

"We don't need to outscore them," Danijel said. "We need to make them look as if they're fighting for it." He paused. "And Eijá needs to make the ring shot."

"Once?"

"Once. At a high-pressure moment. In this city, the ring shot ends a game segment and resets the crowd. One ring shot at the right moment remakes what the crowd thinks they're watching."

"I can make the ring shot," Eijá said.

"I know. I've been watching you practice for five days."

The game took place the following morning, court opening before the full heat of the day.

The crowd was larger than any casual game crowd, word had traveled and the seats on the high walls were filled, with more people standing in the accessible areas around the court's edge. Maxtla recognized faces from the market, from the inner precincts, from the craftspeople's district. The second wife's staff was in the upper seating on the west wall. The lord was present, an unexpected appearance that sent a ripple through the crowd, in a shaded platform on the east wall.

The city's team came onto the court to noise. They were well-known. The crowd knew their names and shouted them.

Maxtla's group came on to a different sound, not hostility, but the specific uncertainty of a crowd that doesn't know what it's looking at yet. Northern women and one old man, in their northern clothing, which was different from the court dress.

They had discussed whether to wear the court padding. They had decided against it. The padding was for players who expected to be hit by the ball at full speed. Not wearing it was a statement of confidence that might turn out to be painful.

The first segment of the game went to the city team by one score. Which was, Maxtla had decided in the pre-game discussion, exactly what should happen. Let them have the first segment. Let the crowd relax into what it expected. Let the city team begin to feel the slight loosening of concentration that came with an early lead.

The second segment started differently.

Maxtla had told her team one thing: watch each other, not the ball. The ball would be where it needed to be. What mattered was the shape of the whole court, who was where, what was open, what opportunity existed before anyone else saw it.

This was how she traded. Not watching the individual transaction but watching the room. Not negotiating this piece but negotiating the whole arrangement.

It turned out to apply to ball courts.

The city team's virtuosos were confused by players who seemed not to be reacting to the ball and were instead reacting to them. They were used to opponents who chased the ball. Opponents who anticipated their movement instead of the ball's movement were a different problem.

In the middle of the second segment, with the score even, Eijá got the ring shot.

The ball came off the south wall at an angle that was genuinely difficult, most of the crowd could see why it was difficult, which was why the court went quiet in the beat before Eijá moved. She moved early, before the ball arrived, positioned by calculation rather than reaction, and drove the hip shot through the ring.

The ball went through.

The court exploded.

In the reset that followed, the ring shot earned a significant score and a formal pause, Maxtla's team stood in the center of the court while the crowd did something she had not expected. They cheered, yes, but more than that: they argued. The crowd was arguing with itself, the way a crowd argues when the thing they're watching has suddenly become more interesting than they came prepared for.

The third segment, the city team played harder. This was also what she wanted. A team that was fighting was a team that had stopped showing off, and a team that had stopped showing off had made a small admission.

The game ended with the city team winning by two scores.

The lord's platform was empty. He had left before the end, she had noticed, which was an unexpected development. The second wife's staff were talking among themselves with animation.

Coming off the court, the city team's best player, a young man named Xaman who had clearly spent fifteen years perfecting the hip drive and moved with a physical intelligence that was genuinely beautiful, came to Maxtla.

"The old man," he said, through gestures mostly and the few words they shared. "How old is he?"

"Old," Maxtla said.

"He never." Xaman paused. "He never needed to look at the ball."

"No," Maxtla agreed.

Xaman looked at Danijel, who was standing apart from the post-game crowd talking to no one. Then at Maxtla.

"Who are you people?" he asked.

"Traders," she said. "Going south."

"Going home now?" he asked.

"Soon," she said. "Soon."

Hunal came back the following morning with a piece of equipment.

It was a hip pad, heavy, worn leather, the surface scuffed from years of ball contact. He offered it to Maxtla without explanation and she understood immediately: it was his personal practice pad, the one he had trained with since he was a child, shaped to his use in a way that new equipment wasn't. He was lending her the accumulated form of his own years of practice.

She took it with a nod.

Eijá had reached the ring shot seven consecutive times in the previous afternoon's session. Her percentage from set positions was high, consistent, deliberate: find the geometry, trust the geometry, repeat the geometry. Her weakness was the moving shot, the ring shot from unexpected position, the ring shot when the sequence leading to it had not been planned.

Danijel had identified this on the fourth day: "The planned shot you have. The unplanned shot you're still developing."

"How do I develop it faster?"

"You stop planning," he said.

She had looked at him with the specific expression she used for imprecise advice.

"Not entirely," he said. "You already plan too far ahead. You're calculating three steps in advance and trying to position for the shot you've already decided will come. The ball doesn't care what you've decided." He paused. "The ring shot finds you. You don't find it. Your job is to be in the right condition to receive it."

The sessions after that had a different quality. Eijá moved differently, less calculated, more continuous, the specific flow of a body that has stopped interrupting itself.

The ring shot count climbed.

Maria worked on the court the way she worked on fighting: not against her own limits but through them. The hip drive had not come naturally, her fighting training was all hands, arms, feet, the specific physical vocabulary of someone who had learned to protect herself with the tools available to a person who had spent years not being allowed to be large or visible. Reconfiguring to use the hip required deliberate unlearning, slower and more uncomfortable than learning something new.

She did not complain about the discomfort. Complaining about discomfort was not part of Maria's repertoire.

By the end of the second week she had the hip drive. Not Eijá's precision, different, something else. Maria on the court had the quality she had in a fight: the capacity to be somewhere nobody had anticipated before anyone else had processed that she needed to move. Not speed exactly. Anticipation translated to action before the action was visible to anyone watching.

Hunal had named it on the ninth day: "She's already there," he told Ixchel, pointing at Maria in the court. "Everyone else arrives. She's already there."

The five days before the tournament game they practiced three times a day, morning, midday, evening. Maxtla's ribs took three impacts she could not protect against and she arrived at the morning of the tournament game with a bruise along the left side that she had wrapped tightly, not enough time to be good, enough time to be adequate, and adequate was what they needed.

Lofn found her at it.

She had come for the morning check, the weekly thing she did without ceremony, the two minutes that confirmed what they both already knew. She stood in the doorway of the small enclosure and looked at Maxtla wrapping the left side and did not speak for long enough that Maxtla felt it.

"Say what you're going to say," Maxtla said.

"You're six months along and you're getting hit in the ribs." Lofn's voice was flat in the way it went flat when she had already decided what she thought. "Three times yesterday."

"I know how many times."

"The child is fine. I checked." She set her kit down. "I'm telling you that you are taking risks with someone who cannot consent to them."

Maxtla finished tying the wrap. She pressed it with the heel of her hand. The bruise ran from the bottom rib to the hip and had gone from purple to the yellow-green of something working through. She had been walking carefully for three days without saying so. She turned to face Lofn.

"If we don't play, we can't come back. No route, no settlement in twenty years. The child grows up in something smaller than what this journey was trying to build." She held Lofn's eyes. "I ran the numbers. This is the number I got."

Lofn was quiet. She had the expression she wore when she was arriving at the same answer against her will.

"It's not a good number," she said.

"No. It's the best one available."

Lofn looked at the wrapped ribs. She looked at Maxtla's face, not at the bruise, at her face. She had known her long enough to understand that the decision had not been made this morning. It had been made weeks ago, alone, before anyone could argue.

"Stay low on the hip drive," Lofn said finally. "Keep the left side turned away. And if you take another impact in the same place, you come off the court."

"If I come off the court we lose a player."

"If you don't come off the court when I tell you to, I will tell Gedeon exactly what these five days looked like. In detail."

A silence.

"That's not fair," Maxtla said.

"No." Lofn picked up her kit. At the door she stopped without turning. "He would understand the calculation too. That's what makes it work as a threat."

She left.

Maxtla stood alone in the small space. She looked down at the wrapped ribs, adequate, not good, and at her hands, and at the morning light coming through the gap in the reed wall. She thought about what she was carrying and what she was doing to protect it and whether those two things were in conflict or the same thing, and she could not entirely separate them, and she had to go to the court anyway.

She picked up her spear and went.

She had thought about this honestly in the mornings, alone in the hour before the camp woke: what they needed was not to be the best team. What they needed was to be a team that couldn't be easily defeated. A team that required real effort to beat. A team that showed, in its performance, that the people in it were worth knowing and worth hosting and worth the complexity of the political arrangement that the game was embedded inside.

The rest would follow from that.

Or it wouldn't.

GEDEON: FOUR

The formal filing

The challenge was formally filed on a Tuesday, forty days after Brak's expulsion.

Kael had waited longer than Gedeon expected. He had been patient about it, which was either discipline or calculation, and with Kael it was usually both. He came to Gedeon the day before the filing, not to ask permission and not to announce it, but to say what he was doing and why, which was more courtesy than he was required to give.

"The land assignments," Kael said. "Without a formal basis, they are individual decisions made by a single authority. Individual decisions made by a single authority can be unmade by the same authority or challenged by the council under the old customs."

"I know," Gedeon said.

"I am not saying they are wrong. I am saying they are not settled."

"I know that too."

Kael looked at him. He was not a bad man. Gedeon had been clear about this in his own mind since before Maxtla left. Kael was a man with a framework that had worked for his entire life, and the settlement had grown up around a different framework, and the two frameworks were now in the same space and one of them was going to have to change. Kael understood that if he did not formalize his framework now, it would be formalized out of existence when Maxtla returned. So he was doing what anyone with standing and a sense of timing would do.

"She's coming back," Gedeon said.

"I know."

"With what she's bringing, the challenge will be harder to sustain."

Kael met his eyes. "I am not trying to win the challenge. I am trying to ensure the outcome is settled by a legitimate process rather than by individual authority."

Gedeon looked at him for a long moment.

"Then you and Maxtla want the same thing," he said.

Kael's expression did not change. But something in it shifted.

He filed the challenge the next morning.

The settlement took three days to adjust to it. Not crisis, the work continued, the water system ran, the trade stalls opened and closed. But the shape of the air changed. People made decisions more carefully. The women who had been running operations looked at each other in the morning with the look of people comparing notes without speaking.

Merya came to Gedeon twice and said nothing both times, which was how Merya handled things she was still deciding.

He gave her the space and waited.

Aki had begun talking in sentences that made partial sense, which was a development Gedeon found genuinely interesting and occasionally exhausting. The child had his mother's habit of observation and his father's habit of taking time before speaking, which in an adult was precision and in a twenty-month-old produced long silences followed by pronouncements that required investigation.

"Man sad," Aki said one morning, watching Kael cross the plaza.

Gedeon looked at Kael. He was not, visibly, sad.

"What makes you say that?"

Aki considered. "Face."

He looked again. There was something in Kael's walk, not defeat, nothing that direct. The set of a man doing what he believed was right and not being fully certain it was enough.

"You might be right," Gedeon said.

He did not count the days until Maxtla returned. He had decided not to and had kept to it, mostly. What he counted instead was the work: the fence posts repaired, the water channel extended to the new north section, the storage inventory completed before the rains, the three new families integrated and working. The settlement Maxtla had built. He was maintaining it.

What the settlement was going to require when she came back was not more maintenance. It was the document. The thing that settled what individual authority could and could not do, and made the charter real.

He had started drafting it. Not formally, he did not have Ahmik's skills, and the formal version would need to come from people who knew what they were doing. But he had written, on a piece of prepared hide that he kept folded behind the medicine stores, the things he thought it needed to contain. He had been adding to it for six weeks.

He would give it to her when she arrived. Not as the document. As the beginning of it. The places where the settlement had tested the boundaries and found them insufficient.

She was going to arrive with sixty people or more, if the reports from the southern traders were right. She was going to arrive with goods and alliances and the formal structure of a trading network that didn't exist six months ago. She was going to walk through the canyon gate and see what the settlement had become in her absence and she was going to know, immediately, what needed doing.

He was going to let her see it. Then he was going to hand her the hide.

The canyon held its patience the way it always held its patience. The walls did not change. The creek ran. The light moved across the red stone at the angle it had moved for longer than anyone's memory, indifferent to the small urgent lives below.

He sat at the place in the canyon wall that caught the last light and waited for the sound of the column coming up the southern approach.

It would come.

CHAPTER TWENTY

The workroom

The lord sent for Maxtla alone.

Not through the usual channels. Not through a household staff member with a formal token. A message through Ah Kinich at the gate, informal, suggesting she come to the inner precincts not at the palace but at a smaller building on the north side of the complex that she had noticed but not entered, a building with no ceremonial function that she could identify. Low, plain, practical in the way of working buildings everywhere.

She told Ixchel where she was going. She did not bring anyone else.

The building was a workroom.

It was a working room. Maps on the walls, not pictures but genuine functional maps, scratched onto plaster with careful notation, covering territory that she could, with effort, orient to the world she knew. The coast to the east. The mountains to the west. Trade route lines running in both directions with symbols she couldn't read but whose organizational logic she could follow, clustering around the city, thinning as they moved toward the map's edges, a few lines extending to points that had no names she could recognize.

The routes she knew were not on this map. The canyon country's location was a blank. She was standing at the edge of the world these maps described.

A table with clay tablets, organized by a system she could see was systematic without being able to read the categories. A writing instrument. Two small oil lamps whose clean-burning flames told her the oil was good quality, the kind of detail a person who managed resources paid attention to. A second table against the far wall with measuring tools she recognized as for distance calculation, and one she didn't recognize at all, a device of wood and string that she filed for later.

Ix Pakab was already there, seated behind the first table, and he had brought one aide, a young man with the look of a person whose function was to be trusted. Not a guard. Someone who processed information and kept it. No guards.

The lord's illness was more visible here than at the feast. His breathing was audible, his movement deliberate in the way of someone managing energy. At the feast he had been performing. Here he was not.

He spoke without preamble. The aide translated.

"He asks: where is the road you're building?"

She had not told anyone about the road she was building. She had told Ix Mam about the trading network, the informal route with relationships at intervals. That was not the same language as "the road."

"I don't know what he means," she said carefully.

The aide spoke to the lord. The lord made a sound that was either dismissal or impatience and pointed to the map behind him. To the north. He touched a point on the map that was, Maxtla thought, roughly where the canyon country was, roughly, at the edge of what the map described. He pointed to a line running south from that point. Not a line that was on the map. A line he was drawing in the air.

"He says: the road you're making. Here. To here." The aide pointed again. "The relationships, the protection, the guide posts, the safety. This is a road."

She looked at the map. The route she had traveled, the alliance with Teya's people, the tolls paid, the relationships at the springs and in the mountain pass, when you put it on a map, it looked like what it was.

"It's the beginning of one," she said.

He spoke again.

"He says: how many trips before it is reliable?"

She thought about this honestly. "Three. Maybe four. Depending on how many problems I can solve on the return."

"He says: what do you need to make it faster?"

She looked at the maps on the wall, then back at him. He had built his family's power on roads, she knew this from Ix Mam, from the palace feast conversation, from the practical intelligence of the road system she had walked. A man who understood roads understood what they required.

"Support from this end," she said. "A formal introduction to the merchants who use your road system. A message from your household that the northern route has your acknowledgment." She paused. "A small station at the road's northern junction with your road, a way marker, a place travelers know to stop, would reduce the first trip's confusion for parties coming from this end."

The aide translated. The lord nodded slowly, the kind of nod that was processing rather than agreement, the movement of a mind organizing new information against its existing structures.

"He says: the road built his family's power over four generations. A new road does the same for whoever builds it."

"Yes," Maxtla said.

A silence. The small oil flames moved in some air current neither of them could feel.

"He says: his wives."

She waited.

"He says: the first wife wants you to leave because you have made the third wife's position more comfortable than it should be at this time. The second wife wants you to come back because she believes you will make the distribution system more efficient. The third wife wants you to come back because she finds you interesting and trusts you." He paused. "He says: he wants you to come back because you are building something useful and he wants to be connected to it before it becomes large."

"What does he want in exchange?"

The aide translated.

The lord looked at her, and something in his expression was a little rueful, the look of a man who understood the transaction completely and was uncomfortable with it.

"He says: the thing your old man can do on the ball court. The thing with seeing. He would like to know what that is."

Maxtla went still.

She had known, from the first morning of the market, that the lord would eventually ask about Danijel. He was too anomalous. Three hundred years of living in a human body and being seen had not produced a version of him that didn't draw attention when attention was being paid.

"He says: he has not seen eyes like that. He has met the traders from the far east, the ones who come by sea. He has met people from fifteen different peoples in thirty years. He has not seen eyes like that."

She said nothing for a moment.

"I can't explain it," she said. "I have wondered about it myself."

The aide translated. The lord looked at her for a long time. His deep-set eyes were steady and assessing and also, she thought, tired, the tiredness that came with illness and with being responsible for a city that required constant management and with being a man who had been inside power long enough to know that most of the interesting things that happened to his city arrived in forms he hadn't anticipated.

Then he spoke.

"He says: he will accept your answer. He says: he did not expect you to explain it. He only wanted to see how you held the question."

The last three days of trading went well, but the market had shifted in a way she could feel more than quantify. There was a current in it now, she and her group had become something more specific than "northern traders with good goods." They had played the game. They had fed the poor. They had met the wives. They had sat in the lord's workroom. The market knew all of this, as markets know everything, through the specific distributed intelligence of people who spend their days watching other people conduct business.

The knowing had two effects.

The first was more business. More buyers came to her stall, some from the inner precincts, and prices settled at levels that reflected the shift in status. The credibility display had worked in the way she had designed it to work, the standard baskets had been the foundation and the specialized goods had been the confirmation. Now both worked in each other's favor.

The second was attention from a different direction. On the third-to-last day, Maria came to Maxtla with her flat, accounting expression.

"The men," she said.

"Which men?"

"The market vendors near the south gate. Not traders. They've been watching the stall for two days and Lofn's feeding operation with the specific look of people trying to understand what it is in order to decide whether they're threatened by it."

"Threatened by charity?" Lofn said.

"By change," Maxtla said. "The city has a way it distributes to the poor. It has people who have standing in that system. We came and did something that worked differently and got popular quickly." She thought about it. "The second wife's system and Lofn's are not in competition, they work in different spheres and Lofn's will be gone when we leave. But the people who watch the second wife's system and profit from being near it feel the threat."

"What do we do?"

"We leave on time," Maxtla said. "We don't overstay."

She had already been planning the departure date. Two more days of trading. One day of packing. Then the road north.

On the second-to-last day, the trouble arrived without warning.

The court officials, not the lord's men, the separate ceremonial officials who managed the ball court and its associated rituals, sent a message at midday. The message said: your group is invited to play a second game. The message said: this game has different stakes.

"What stakes?" Maxtla sent back.

The answer was not good.

She called the group together.

"Tournament stakes," she said. "Formal. The losing team captain is subject to the ritual consequence."

Silence.

"Can we refuse?" Eijá asked.

"We can. But the refusal will be read as fear, and fear changes our market standing and our ability to return here safely." She paused. "They have waited until we are ready to leave. They've chosen the timing deliberately."

"The first wife," Ixchel said.

"Most likely."

Maria was very quiet. Then: "What is the ritual consequence exactly?"

"Sacrifice," Danijel said. "Execution, done in a formal ceremonial way. The captain of the losing team."

"Which would be you," Maria said, looking at Maxtla.

"Yes."

"No," Maria said. Not arguing. Deciding.

"If we refuse, we can't come back," Maxtla said. "And the route needs this city."

"If you lose and die, you definitely can't come back," Maria said. "And the route doesn't have you."

Maxtla looked at her for a moment. "We won't lose," she said.

They had two days.

CHAPTER TWENTY-ONE

The night before

The night before the game, Ix Tunich came to the trader camp.

She came alone, without staff, wearing plain clothing rather than court dress, a transgression of protocol that was also, Maxtla understood, a statement of alliance. She sat in the camp the way an ally sits and not the way an official visits. She accepted water when it was offered and did not ask for anything else, and the directness of her sitting-down said: I am not here as the third wife. I am here as a person who has something to tell you.

"The game tomorrow was not authorized by my husband," she said through Ixchel. "He did not agree to it."

"Then who authorized it?"

"The court priesthood. They have authority over the court that is separate from the lord's authority. This is an old division of power." She paused. "The first wife did not order it. But she did not prevent it, and she had the standing to prevent it."

"She let it happen."

"Yes."

Maxtla thought about what this meant. "Can your husband stop it now?"

"He could. But stopping it now, the morning before, would require him to invoke his authority over the priesthood directly. This would cost him significantly." Ix Tunich's expression was careful. "He is ill. He does not spend his authority carelessly."

"He chooses his battles."

"As everyone must."

Maxtla sat with this. Around them the camp had quieted, the group had been preparing since the afternoon, and preparation of the internal kind, the preparation of the mind, required quiet. The fires were low. Someone had the watch but was holding it without movement.

"Can he influence the game?" she asked.

"Not the play. The stakes he can adjust if he moves carefully. Not elimination, that is the priesthood's domain. But the definition of the ritual consequence for the losing captain can be quite specific. There are different types of sacrifice. Some are symbolic." She paused. "Some are not."

"Would he do this?"

"If he believed the relationship was worth it." Ix Tunich looked at her. "He asked me to come and tell you this. He asked me to tell you that he would adjust the definition of the consequence if you agreed to one thing."

"What thing?"

"On your next trip north, you will send back his second son. Nineteen years old. Healthy. The second son has expressed interest in traveling the northern route and learning the trade. The lord wants him to have this experience. He wants him out of the city for a year and in the hands of someone he trusts to teach him something real."

Maxtla looked at Ixchel.

"Political," Ixchel said quietly. "The second son is the second wife's child. He's of an age to be a factor in the succession. Getting him out of the city for a year removes him from the immediate competition and demonstrates the lord's confidence in you."

"And confirms us as a reliable northern connection," Maxtla said.

"Yes. For the lord, it's multiple problems solved."

She turned back to Ix Tunich. "Tell your husband yes. We will take the second son north and teach him what we know. He will come back with skills that are useful."

"And you will play tomorrow?"

"We will play tomorrow."

Ix Tunich rose. "Then my husband will attend the game. His presence will convey what his authority cannot formally state." She paused. "Win," she said. "Win clearly."

"Yes," Maxtla said. "That is the plan."

The camp was quiet after she left.

Danijel was the one who spoke first. "The ring shot changes games. Your team can make the ring shot. Three of them. Only one of them matters."

"Eijá's the most reliable," Maxtla said.

"Eijá is reliable in calm conditions with time to prepare. Maria is reliable when everything is wrong and pressure is high."

They all looked at Maria.

Maria looked back. "I've made it eleven times in practice," she said.

"How many in chaos?" Danijel asked.

"Three times. In the last practice session when Parruk was." She stopped. "When things were complicated."

"Tomorrow will be more complicated than that," Danijel said. "The crowd, the stakes, the pressure. You'll need to make it when everything in you is screaming to just hit the ball anywhere."

"I know," Maria said. She was quiet for a moment. Then she looked at Maxtla. "I'll make it."

"Yes," Maxtla said. "You will."

She didn't say it encouragingly. She said it the way she would have said: the sun will rise.

She lay in the dark and looked at the stakes clearly, then put them down.

She slept well. The night before difficult things, she always did.

The court was full an hour before the game started.

Not just the upper seating. The walls themselves, the road entrance, the viewing platforms the city hadn't opened for the friendly game. There were people on rooftops. There were children in the trees along the court perimeter who were being neither noticed nor removed. The sound of the crowd was different from the friendly game, not louder, but denser, as if each person's attention had more weight.

The other team was different from the first one.

This was the city's formal tournament team, not the showcase players from the friendly game, who were athletes and showmen, but the players who were sent to the inter-city tournaments that determined genuine political relationships. They were older, on average. They moved with less flash and more economy, and they looked at Maxtla's group with the professional attention of people who had been in high-stakes games before and knew what they were looking at. They took note of the number: six against seven.

The lord's platform was occupied. Ix Pakab sat in the shade, attended, watching the court below with his measured intelligence. His presence was visible to the crowd in the way that formal authority is always visible when it wants to be seen. It was also visible to the first wife, who sat in the upper tier on the opposite side of the court, and whose expression on seeing it shifted by exactly the amount you would expect it to shift if you knew the private politics of this household.

The game started.

The first segment was the worst. The tournament team was calibrated for this, their transitions were faster than the friendly players, their court sense deeper, and they read Maxtla's group's positioning with an accuracy that told her they'd had observers in the practice sessions. They had known what was coming and had prepared for it specifically. The ball moved through gaps before the gaps had opened. They were not showing off. They were winning.

She had expected this. She had also scouted, which was the only reason the first segment's outcome was close rather than overwhelming. They went down by one score. One was manageable.

In the break, she said one thing to the group: "Eijá, hold the ring shot for the third segment. Everyone else: the middle player, number four in their line. Watch number four. He is the link between the virtuoso and the support structure. Take the link."

The second segment ran closer and ended at even, and by the end of it the crowd knew it was watching something other than a demonstration. The uncertainty had left the sound and something more committed had replaced it. The crowd was engaged now in the way it had been engaged at the friendly game, invested, with opinions about individual plays.

The third segment was where it happened.

The tournament team came out of the break playing harder. They had felt the second segment's evenness and understood its implication: this group was not going to be overwhelmed by the obvious advantages of experience and home court. They were adaptable. They had to be beaten directly.

Maxtla played in the third segment in the full-attention state she had been in twice before, both times when the situation was bad enough that analysis and reaction collapsed into a single thing. You stopped thinking about what to do and started knowing it. The court became very clear and very quiet inside the noise of it.

She watched number four.

He was good, not the team's best player but its most necessary one, the point through which the virtuoso's talent was made useful. Without him, the technical skill of the team's best player became an isolated phenomenon instead of a sustained system. She and Maria spent the third segment making number four feel watched, which was its own kind of pressure, different from physical challenge but no less real. A player who knows they are the key will eventually try too hard to compensate, and overcompensation opened spaces.

The space opened in the twenty-seventh minute.

Maria got the ball at a difficult angle, on the far side from the ring, with two opponents between her and any clean shot. She did not try the ring shot from there, the angle was wrong. She drove the ball off the east wall in a ricochet that Eijá had taught her in a moment of technical inspiration two days ago, and the ricochet put the ball in a position where it arrived at ring height on the west side at a moment when none of the tournament team was positioned to intercept.

Eijá was there.

She made the shot.

The ring shot sound, the sound of the heavy rubber ball passing through the stone ring rather than bouncing off, was a distinctive hollow thud, different from every other sound in the game. It was a sound that everyone on the court and in the crowd recognized immediately and completely. The crowd heard it and went into the frenzy of people watching something rare. Not the frenzy of celebration, the frenzy of witnessing, of a thing that had happened that they would describe to people who had not been here.

The reset. The score.

The tournament team, their support structure disrupted by the sustained pressure on number four, spent the final section of the third segment trying to recover their equilibrium. They were good enough to prevent the deficit from growing. They were not good enough, in those final minutes, to win back what they had lost.

Maxtla's group won by one score.

One score. The minimum possible winning margin.

The tournament team's captain stood in the center of the court and met Maxtla's eyes. He was a serious man who had just lost a high-stakes game to people from a place he had never been, and he was holding it with a dignity that cost him something. His team stood behind him, breathing hard, in the specific posture of people who had fought and lost and were not pretending otherwise.

She inclined her head. He returned the gesture.

The crowd was making a sound that wasn't quite either celebration or protest, something more complex, the sound of a people encountering an event that exceeded their categories. They had come to watch the northern women lose. The northern women had not lost. This was going to require some recategorizing. The recategorizing was audible.

In the lord's platform, Ix Pakab sat without visible expression. But he was still there. He had stayed to the end. In this city, in this context, staying to the end was its own kind of statement.

The court officials spoke, something formal about the outcome, which Ixchel translated quietly as: the game is concluded, the terms of the ritual consequence are hereby defined as symbolic tribute and not ceremonial sacrifice, as the losing captain has demonstrated honor in defeat and the winning captain has demonstrated honor in victory.

It was exactly what the lord had arranged through his wife's visit.

They walked out of the court through the crowd, which parted for them with a kind of uncertainty in it, not quite respect, not quite wariness, something that was the beginning of a longer-term relationship that hadn't decided yet what it was.

Maxtla thought: we have two days to become something specific to these people before we leave. If she left them uncertain, the next visit started from uncertainty. Clear category, clear start.

She spent those two days making sure every person who had interacted with them in any way understood exactly what category that was: reliable northern traders who would return, who kept their word, who worked hard and fought hard and valued their relationships.

She paid every debt and settled every account.

She said goodbye in person to Ah Kinich, to Ix Mam, to Ix Tunich, to Xaman the ball player and to the craftsperson who had collaborated with Eijá, and through the appropriate intermediary, to the lord himself.

The lord's second son, whose name was Ahmik, who was nineteen and had his father's intelligent eyes and, she suspected, his second wife's strategic patience, joined the group on the morning they departed.

He had one pack and a clay tablet on which he was already writing.

PART TWO: THE RETURN

———————

CHAPTER TWENTY-TWO

What she counted

The road north felt different loaded.

Going south, they had traveled with the lightness of people carrying possibility. Coming back, they had weight, physical weight on the horses, carefully balanced and secured with Lofn's tightening system. And the harder-to-describe weight of knowing what they had done and returning to it.

Maxtla counted, walking, on the first day of the return.

The trading inventory: converted entirely into jade currency and local goods assessed for the canyon country market. The final tally was approximately six times the value of what they had left with. Not all of it in her hands, Lofn had her individual stake, Maria had hers, Eijá and Ixchel had theirs, and Teya's group had been paid the first installment of the promised protection fee.

The non-material returns: the credential letter from Ix Mam, the lord's second son walking behind her with his clay tablets, the relationship with Ah Kinich that would smooth the next entry, the connection with Ix Tunich, the informal understanding with the second wife, and the specific knowledge that Eijá had acquired, techniques, materials, dimensions, processes, every detail she had observed and could reproduce.

The route itself, now known rather than guessed. Three allied relationships at intervals. Teya's group as the backbone.

She had left thinking she was building a trading route. She was returning understanding it was something larger. The route was an artery. The settlement was the heart. Four months south had clarified what the heart needed: governance, not just people. Rules, not just customs.

Seven months now. Maybe seven and a half. The body had adapted to walking, the way bodies did, and Lofn checked her weekly without ceremony. Nothing wrong. The child was still there.

She had not let herself think about it directly on the journey south. On the return, with the city behind her and the desert ahead and the child more present than it had been when she left, she had started to let it in.

Not the fear. She knew the fear's shape, understood its specific texture, the way it arrived without warning at the third month and again at the eighth. She did not give the fear more room than it needed.

This one she would give it to.

She filed it. Not dismissed. Held. Then she walked.

Ahmik walked near the back of the column for the first week, watching everything and writing on his clay tablets and asking Ixchel careful questions. By the third week, he told her he spoke four languages and was working on a fifth.

"This one?" Maxtla asked.

"The one you all use when you talk fast," he said. "I understood most conversations for ten days. I didn't correct the misunderstanding because I was learning faster that way."

She felt irritation followed by genuine appreciation. "You're your father's son," she said.

"My mother's, more," he said, and went back to his tablets.

The jungle thinned over the first week. They made good time, the road running true and the toll point coming and going without incident. Then the desert and mountain country began, and with it the harder work of the return.

Danijel had been quieter than usual since leaving the city. Not with visible difficulty, he functioned perfectly, saw everything, moved without effort, but with an inwardness she had not seen before. Or had seen once: the day after the cliff fall, when ten people died and he sat in a curl on the ledge and fought to come back to himself.

She walked beside him on the morning of the twelfth day.

"What are you thinking about?" she asked.

He didn't answer immediately. Then: "What happens next."

"We go home."

"Yes. And then what you do next matters more than everything before it." Not harshly. As one does when pointing at a fact they want to make sure lands properly. "The route is established. The goods are in hand. When you get home, the men who have been testing the boundaries will see what you've brought back. They'll understand the trade value. Some will try to attach themselves to it, trade their existing social standing for influence over the new wealth."

"That's predictable."

"What's harder to predict is whether the structure you've built, the women who work for you, the young women who have grown up watching you, is strong enough to hold when the pressure comes from inside rather than outside."

"What do you mean, inside?"

"The settlement has grown. Not everyone who has come is of your original group. New people bring new assumptions. Some of those assumptions are the old ones dressed in new circumstances."

"What do I do?" she asked.

"What you're already planning. The shared project. The granary or the water system. Something everyone builds together and everyone has a stake in. The ownership principle you described before you knew you were describing it."

"And if it isn't enough?"

He was quiet for a long moment.

"Then you build again," he said. "From whatever is left. That's what people who build things do."

She walked with that for a while.

"Danijel," she said. "Are you going to leave again?"

He didn't answer immediately.

"Eventually," he said. "Not soon."

"Where do you go?"

The longest pause.

"Home," he said. "Eventually."

"Is it better there?"

"It's older," he said. "Which is not the same thing as better. Sometimes it's worse. It has had more time to get some things right and more time to make other things calcified." He paused. "What you're doing here is not old yet. It's new enough to still be possible in any direction."

"That's the best time," she said.

"Yes."

They walked without talking, the blue mountains sharpening against the sky.

Somewhere behind them, Lofn was asking Ahmik about the climate in the southern city and whether it rained frequently, and Ahmik was explaining with his careful incomplete vocabulary, and Lofn was periodically saying "oh" in the specific tone she used when new information was being added to her worry list.

Then Maria, from the rear, called: "Dust. South ridge."

They stopped.

The dust was a small organized cloud, the kind produced by moving people, coming from the south ridge on a path that would intercept their route in perhaps half an hour.

"Teya," Maxtla called.

Teya was already looking. "Not ours," she said.

"How many?" Maxtla asked.

"Not few," Teya said.

The column tightened without being told to, the horses moving to the center, the fighters spreading to the periphery. Ahmik stopped writing and looked at the dust and then at Maxtla with the expression of someone encountering the real version of something he had read about.

"Stay with the horses," Maxtla told him. "Your value is your knowledge, not your fighting. Protect the knowledge."

He stayed with the horses. He kept writing, which she found unexpectedly admirable.

The dust resolved, over the next half hour, into approximately thirty people. Armed. Organized in the loose but experienced formation of a working raider group. Moving to cut the trail.

And from the north ridge, she heard the sound of Targat's people moving.

They were being approached from two directions simultaneously.

She stopped the column. Both groups slowed as they saw her stop.

She raised her right hand, open palm forward.

She waited. Both groups stopped.

In the space between them, she stood with forty people behind her and two raider groups in front of and above her, loaded horses and six months of work in her custody, the sun still high, the day still long.

She took a breath.

"I'd like to talk," she said loudly, in two languages, one after the other.

And she waited to see who answered.

The southern group sent a man forward. He was young, mid-twenties, with the bearing of someone who had been given authority for this moment and was being careful not to waste it.

From the north ridge, after a longer pause: a single figure descended. Older than she had expected. A man of perhaps fifty-five, compact and deliberate, with a face weathered by decades outside.

He stopped on her left, the southern man on her right, both at equal distance from her.

Targat. She had been aware of him since before the Teya negotiation, the figure on the ridge above that first camp, the pattern of movement that had shadowed them south and north with patient attention. She had known he would arrive eventually. She had not known he would arrive at the same moment as thirty armed strangers from the south.

The southern man spoke first. Ixchel did not know his language and Maxtla did not know his language and for a moment they were in the position she least wanted: three people in open ground, none of them sharing words. She held the silence without filling it and looked at Targat, who was watching the southern man with the specific attention of someone translating without showing the translation.

"He wants the horses," Targat said. Flat. Informational.

"All of them?"

"Three. And a share of the load."

She had forty people behind her with weapons and the organizational discipline of a group that had been moving together for four months. The southern group had thirty and the geography. She could probably hold and probably extract a cost high enough to make the raid unprofitable. Probably was not a word she liked when the alternative was conversation.

"Tell him: I know what he wants. Tell him what I'm offering instead." She looked at Targat steadily. "Tell him Teya's people were doing the same work six months ago and are now on the route with a fair share of every caravan that passes. Tell him the arrangement has conditions. Tell him if he wants to hear them, I'll explain them myself, through you."

Targat looked at her for a moment. Then he turned and spoke to the young man in the southern language. The young man listened without expression, then turned and walked back to his group. There was a long minute of silence with work in it.

"You know who I am," Targat said.

"I know you've been watching since before the Teya negotiation. Which means you know what the Teya negotiation produced. Which means you already have more information about what I'm offering than he does." She nodded toward the southern group. "So why are you still on the ridge?"

He was quiet for a moment. The quality of the quiet was not hostile. It was the quality of a man who had been waiting a long time for an opening and was being careful about whether this was one.

"The northern confederation has fifteen families," he said. "We move between the high desert and the canyon country. We have been raiding settlements that don't defend themselves because the alternative was watching our children go hungry in a bad winter. This is not what I would have chosen. But choice was not what the winter offered."

"I understand that," she said. "I'm offering a different winter."

The young man came back from the southern group. He spoke to Targat. Targat listened, then looked at Maxtla.

"He'll hear the terms," Targat said. "He says he wants to hear them from you, not from me."

"Good," she said. "That's the right answer."

She spent the next two hours in the open desert with the sun declining, Targat translating, the southern group's leader, a short, serious woman named Olli, listening to the same argument Teya had heard six months ago with the attention of someone who has been offered things before and knows how to check for the catch. There was no catch and Maxtla did not perform the absence of one. She stated the terms. She produced the trade record from the expedition. She had Teya speak, which was the most effective thing she did all afternoon: not Maxtla explaining what the arrangement was but Teya explaining what the arrangement had been, in the plain language of a person who had been on the other side of the offer and accepted it and was still alive and still employed and still eating.

Olli agreed to terms before dark. Targat agreed separately, in the specific formal way of a man who needed the agreement to be his own.

They made camp together that night, sixty-three people from six different groups, speaking four languages between them, eating around a fire that was larger than anyone had built since the city. Ahmik, who had kept writing during the confrontation without being told to stop, had documentation of all three agreements by the time the food was gone.

Maxtla sat at the edge of the fire and felt the specific quality of exhaustion that was different from the physical exhaustion of the road. The negotiation had required something that walking did not require: the sustained performance of certainty she did not fully have, maintained long enough that certainty arrived to fill the space she had held for it.

Targat sat beside her at the fire's edge. He did not speak for a while. Then: "You were pregnant the whole time."

"The whole time," she agreed.

He looked at her. His expression was something between assessment and something older, the look of a man revising a story he had been telling himself for a long time.

"The northern confederation will hold its section of the route," he said.

"I know. You've been holding it for six months. You just weren't getting paid."

Something moved in his face. Not quite a smile. Close enough.

Three days north of the city, the road ended.

She had known it would end somewhere. The Mayan road extended north for a considerable distance, but it had an edge, the point where the city's maintenance territory ended and the unmaintained began. She had expected the edge to be more dramatic. The road simply became less precise over the course of half a mile, the fitted stones giving way to larger rougher placement, the edges losing their definition, and then the stones stopped and the path continued in packed earth.

She stood at the transition point and looked back south, then north.

"The maintenance is the work," she said to Ixchel. "The trading is the reason. But the maintenance is what makes the difference between a route and a road."

"Who decides for our section?"

"The people who use it. Their income depends on the route being used. Their standing depends on it being in good condition. Pride and self-interest combined, same as the Mayan road."

"Talk to Teya," she said to Ixchel.

"She already understands it," Ixchel said.

"I know. I want her to hear me say it."

Ixchel smiled. "You want her to feel consulted."

"I want her to be consulted," Maxtla said. "There's a difference."

Eight days south of the Mayan city on the return, Danijel sat with Maxtla by the fire and said: I want to tell you something before I go.

It was not a surprise. She had known, in the way she had come to know his moods, that he had been building toward something. The way he had been watching the group over the past weeks had a different quality, not the professional observation of a man cataloguing information, but the watching of someone trying to hold onto a picture before it changes.

"You're going north," she said.

"Yes. When you are settled. When the settlement is past the critical moment."

"Which is when?"

"The charter signed and functioning. The granary through its first full cycle. Maria's training established. When the structure exists independently of you. When it would continue without you, not because you are replaceable but because the systems are real."

"You've been monitoring for the critical moment for years," she said.

"Yes. I was wrong about when it would arrive, several times. I expected it earlier. You kept having more problems." The corner of his mouth moved. "You are very good at finding problems."

"The problems find me," she said.

"That is usually how it works with people who are doing things." He was quiet for a moment. "I want to tell you what I am, as precisely as I can, because you deserve to know and because I have been imprecise, for a long time, about what I am and what I am doing here."

She waited.

"I am from a place very far from here," he said. "Not a different valley or a different continent. A different world. A different star."

She had suspected something. Not this specifically, not a different star, but something past the edge of the world she had names for. She had known the technology was not from here and that he was not from here more fundamentally than place of birth. But the direct statement landed differently than the suspicion. Suspicion was a question you carried. This was the answer, and it had weight.

"How far?"

He looked up at the stars. "Do you see that bright one, low in the west?"

"Yes."

"From where I come from, your sun looks like that. Small and distant and unremarkable unless you know what it is."

She looked at the star.

She sat with it for a while. She had built a settlement. She had walked to the southern sea and back. She had negotiated with a lord in a pyramid and made three wives into allies. She had done all of this, and now she was sitting in a desert camp with a fire going low and the man she had trusted since she was young was telling her he had watched her the way she watched birds, from a different order of existence, from a different sky.

He waited. He knew how to wait.

"Three hundred years," she said finally. "On this world."

"Yes."

"How many worlds?"

"Twelve."

She looked back at the star. It didn't look different. It looked exactly like what it was: a point of light in the dark, unremarkable unless you knew.

"All right," she said. "Tell me the rest."

"Why are you here?"

"To observe. My people study civilizations the way your healers study the body, to understand what they need, what makes them fail, what makes them persist." He paused. "I have been here three hundred of your years. In that time I have watched more civilizations build and fail than I can count. It becomes difficult, after a while, not to say something."

"Ohad," she said.

"Ohad was watching the same things I was watching and made the opposite choice. Where I tried to give people the tools to build for themselves, he used what he knew to take." He was quiet. "We are the same kind of person. The difference is only what we wanted."

"What do you want?"

"This," he said.

She understood it was complete.

"I've had three hundred years of the long view," he said. "I am very tired of watching. I want, before I go, to have been in something. Fully. Not observing it."

"You've been in it," she said. "Since you helped me leave the canyon that first time."

"Yes." He paused. "It has been the best thing I have done here."

They sat for a while.

"The device," she said. "The one in my neck."

"Yes?"

"What is it doing?"

"Monitoring your health, primarily. Providing small corrections when something is wrong, not healing, exactly, but giving your body better information about what it needs to fix." He paused. "The regenerative capacity you have. The wound that closed faster than it should have, when Tokh's people attacked. That is the device."

"How long will it work?"

"Your lifetime," he said. "It draws energy from your body's own processes. It will not run out before you do." He looked at her steadily. "Your children will not have it unless I give it to them."

"Aki," she said.

"I will give him one before I leave, if you want."

"What are the consequences?"

"The same ones you have had. Better wound closure. Somewhat better disease resistance. A longer life than the average, though not dramatically." He paused. "No consequences beyond those."

She thought about Aki, the child she was carrying, seven months along, who would grow up in the first generation to be born inside the charter's protections.

"Yes," she said. "Give him one."

Danijel nodded.

"And the others?" she said. "The people in the settlement?"

"I don't have enough for everyone," he said. "I have enough for Aki. Enough for Ixchel's children, if she has them. Perhaps one or two more." He looked at the fire. "I have been giving them where I could, carefully. Eijá has one. Lofn has one, though she doesn't know it, I gave it to her after Dewii died, because the grief was doing something to her body that concerned me."

Maxtla absorbed this. "She doesn't know."

"No. I will tell her before I leave."

"She'll be angry," Maxtla said.

"Probably. But she'll also understand. Lofn understands most things eventually. She just needs to be angry about them first."

Danijel looked at her with the specific expression of someone who has watched someone else for a long time and is pleased by what they see.

"I will miss this," he said.

"Watching?"

"Talking. Specifically talking with you. You think like someone who was trained to think, which you were not. It's partly natural and partly what you taught yourself, and partly what the problems gave you."

"The problems made me," she said.

"The problems gave you the material. You made yourself." He was precise about this. "That is the distinction. Many people have problems. Not all of them become what you became."

She did not deflect this or discount it, because it was not flattery and he did not flatter. She took it as the information it was.

"What does it look like, from the long view?" she asked. "What you are building?"

He was quiet for long enough that she thought he might not answer.

"In most of the civilizations I have observed, the moment that corresponds to yours is fragile," he said finally. "The systems are new enough that they have not yet been tested against everything that will eventually test them. The people who built them are still alive, which means the systems still depend on them more than the systems' designers realize. The generation that grew up inside the systems is not yet old enough to carry the systems forward."

"But?" she said. Because there was a but.

"But this one feels different," he said. "I have learned to distrust my own optimism, I have been wrong before, optimistically, about civilizations that looked like yours and failed. So I distrust what I am about to say. But this one feels different. The writing is more distributed. The ownership of the charter is more distributed. The knowledge is in more heads and more hands than I have seen at a comparable stage. That is harder to lose."

"Harder," she said.

"Not impossible. Nothing is impossible to lose. But harder."

She took this in. The reassurance was the kind that came from someone who had earned the right to offer it.

"When you leave," she said, "is there any way to see what happens? After?"

"Not easily," he said. "I will be very far away. The monitoring capability I have here will not be available." He paused. "I will not know how it turns out."

The honesty of this was more than she had expected, and hit harder.

"That's terrible," she said.

"Yes," he agreed. "It is."

A long silence.

"It is also what makes it real. The direction is up. Slowly, with terrible moments when it seems to go down. But the direction is up."

"Yes." He looked at her. "I will not see it. But I have seen enough of the pattern to know you are part of it. What you are building is part of why the floor is higher in the next century than in the last one. That is not nothing."

"No," she said. "It's not nothing."

The fire burned low. Around them the camp slept, the sixty people of the return journey, wrapped and easy in the safety of the desert night.

"Thank you," she said, finally. "For the three hundred years of it. For deciding to get into it instead of just watching."

He made a sound that was not quite a laugh but was in the same register.

"Thank you," he said, "for making it worth getting into."

They sat together until the fire went out.

CHAPTER TWENTY-THREE

Targat

Targat came down from the north ridge, older-looking than the three days she had spent watching him prepare her for, a man in his forties, lean and weathered, with the specific watchful stillness of someone who had survived by being exactly as still as necessary for exactly as long as required. He descended the slope without hurrying and stopped ten feet away and looked at her.

She looked back.

"You've been following us," she said.

"Since the canyon country," he agreed. His language was close enough to hers to work, with effort. "You saw us on the ridge."

"Yes."

"Why didn't you address us then?"

"You weren't ready. You were scouting. I waited until you'd finished."

He regarded her. "You knew we'd come."

"You waited for the return. That's always the plan. Wait until the goods are loaded and the group is tired and then intercept." She kept her voice even. "It's a reasonable plan."

"Yes," he said.

"Who is the southern group?"

He looked past her to the approaching dust. "The mountain bands. They want what your allies have."

Teya had also turned to look at the southern approach. Her face had gone flat and watchful.

"Teya," Maxtla said.

"I know them," Teya said. "The Xom bands. We have history."

"Bad history?"

"There is no other kind with the Xom."

The Xom bands had stopped perhaps seventy yards south, assessing. Their leader had clearly calculated the same thing Targat had: that the two groups of raiders had arrived simultaneously at the same target, which complicated matters considerably.

Maxtla turned back to Targat.

"Here is the situation," she said. "You want what we're carrying. The Xom want what Teya's people are carrying, which includes a piece of what we're carrying, since they were paid. We are better armed and better organized than you're expecting. If either group attacks us, you will get some of what you want and lose a significant number of people in the getting. If both groups attack us simultaneously, neither group will get enough to justify the losses."

She paused.

"So the question is not whether you take what we have. The question is whether you take it the expensive way or the cheap way."

Targat looked at the Xom leader, and then back at her.

"What's the cheap way?" he said.

"The same offer I made Teya's people. You join the system. You get a piece of the returns in exchange for protecting the route, which is permanent and its value grows." She let that settle. "One raid on a loaded caravan is a one-time event. One piece of a permanent trading network is something different."

He was quiet.

"You already figured this out," she said. "That's why you didn't raid us going south."

"I thought about the bigger prize," he said.

"The long-term prize is bigger."

He was quiet for a moment. Then: "My people don't eat percentages."

"No. They eat the food and tools and medicine that the percentage buys."

"The first payment is when?"

"When the second expedition passes through your territory. A year from now. Maybe a year and a half."

"That's a long time to trust a stranger's promise."

She had not planned the next part. She was doing the math in real time and saw that it required something concrete now or the whole proposition collapsed into the abstract.

She looked at the loaded horses. She thought about what she was carrying and what it was worth and what she could afford to separate from it.

"I'll leave one pack with you today. Not a percentage. Goods. Weight you can carry and use before my next expedition arrives to confirm the arrangement." She watched his face. "In exchange you protect the route from here to the canyon edge until the second expedition. If the second expedition doesn't arrive, the pack was fair payment for this season's safe passage and we're done. No further obligation either side."

He looked at the horses again. Then back at her.

"One pack," he said.

"One pack. You choose which."

He had not expected that either. Giving him the choice was either stupidity or confidence, and she was clearly not stupid.

She was watching his face. He was doing the math. She could see it, the change in his expression as the calculation arrived at an unexpected place.

"What about them?" He tilted his head toward the Xom.

"That's the other problem. The Xom are here because they're opportunistic and they identified a target. They haven't been watching the way you have. They don't have the context."

"They're going to attack," Targat said.

"Probably. Unless you help me convince them not to."

He stared at her.

"You have standing with them," she said. "Northern confederation is known to the mountain bands. A word from you means something. And your cooperation on this problem is part of the demonstration of what cooperation with me looks like."

A long silence.

Then Targat turned and said something to two of his people, who moved to flank his right side, and he walked forward toward the middle space between the column and the Xom.

He called out to the Xom leader in a language that bridged theirs and Teya's, and the Xom leader stiffened and then after a moment walked forward to meet him.

They talked for perhaps ten minutes. The Xom leader looked at Maxtla twice during this, and once at Teya, and once at the loaded horses. The calculations were visible on his face in a different way than they had been on Targat's, this man was faster to anger and slower to revision.

At the end, Targat came back to her.

"He wants to meet you directly," Targat said.

"Of course he does," she said.

She walked forward into the middle space.

What happened next was the part she had not planned for. The Xom leader, his name, through Teya's translation, was something close to Hrakt, looked at Maxtla and decided, without much deliberation, that the problem was that she was a woman and therefore could be moved. He reached out and grabbed her arm.

Maria moved faster than Hrakt could track. She was past Maxtla and had his arm in a joint lock that had him down on one knee before the arm that had reached for Maxtla had completed its grab. She had her knife at his throat.

She did not use it.

She held it there and looked at Maxtla.

The entire scene stopped.

Maxtla looked at Hrakt, on his knee with Maria's knife at his throat, and at the Xom fighters who had half-moved and then half-stopped.

"This is what cooperation looks like," she said to him, evenly. "My people defend my position, as yours would defend yours. That is not disrespect. That is competence."

She waited.

He was humiliated, which was dangerous. She needed to give him a way out that preserved enough dignity to work with.

"Maria," she said.

Maria held for one more second, a specific second, intentional, saying: I could finish this, and then released him and stepped back, sheathing the knife in one motion.

Hrakt stood. He was breathing hard, which was the only sign. His face had settled into the careful neutral of a man rebuilding control.

"Your woman is fast," he said, through Teya.

"My women are all fast," Maxtla said. "This one is the fastest."

A beat.

He looked at Maria. Something in his assessment of the situation was rearranging itself.

"You come back this way?" he said.

"On every trip south. Twice a year, if the route holds."

"Every trip, you bring goods."

"Every trip, I bring goods. And every trip, I need the route between here and the canyon country to be safe. People who make the route safe get a share of what the route produces."

He was a different kind of person than Targat. Targat had done the math and arrived at a reasoned conclusion. Hrakt was doing something more visceral, a recalibration of who this woman was and what that meant for him.

"You fight yourself?" he asked.

"When I have to."

He looked at her for a long time. Then he made a gesture that Teya told her, quietly, meant something like: you have surprised me.

"We talk tonight," he said.

"We talk tonight," Maxtla agreed.

They made camp in the desert with three separate groups, which was uncomfortable and required constant awareness and a carefully managed seating arrangement at the fire. But they made camp together, which was the essential thing.

Maria sat beside Maxtla at the fire that night and didn't speak for a long time.

Then she said: "I could have killed him."

"I know."

"I didn't."

"I know." Maxtla looked at her. "That was the harder thing."

Maria was quiet again. "Is it always like this? Knowing when to stop?"

"No. Sometimes it's knowing when not to stop. The harder skill is knowing which situation you're in."

"How do you know?"

"Practice," Maxtla said. "And a lot of mistakes." She paused. "You made no mistakes today."

That, apparently, was enough. Maria looked into the fire, and after a while her breathing settled, and she slept.

The negotiation with Targat took the rest of that day and the evening and the following morning.

Not because it was contentious, Targat was not a difficult negotiator, being the kind of person who said what he meant and expected the same in return. It took long because there was a great deal to work out, and the working-out required the patience of people operating across a partial language barrier.

The terms they reached were clean. Targat's confederation patrolled the northern section. They received a percentage of passage fees. They committed to leaving any party traveling under the settlement's sanction unmolested. Any raider group outside the confederation that interfered with the route was the confederation's problem.

"That last part," Ixchel said to Maxtla, in the evening.

"I know."

"You're giving him the enforcement responsibility."

"I'm giving him the incentive. He protects the route because protecting the route protects his income. I don't need to enforce it. The income enforces it."

"What if the income isn't enough? What if one of the groups in his confederation decides a loaded return expedition is worth more than the percentage?"

"Then he has a problem with that group, which is a problem he'd have anyway, except now he also has the motivation to solve it." She paused. "I can't police the whole route. I have to build systems that police themselves."

"You've been thinking about this since before we left," Ixchel said.

"Since the first time one of the raider groups hit us going south. Replace the raiding with something that pays reliably and the raiding is less attractive."

"And the ones who like raiding?"

"Targat handles them. That's what I just paid for."

She slept that night with the weight of the loaded packs visible from where she lay, the goods from Yaxal Nah, the currency, the knowledge in Lofn's sealed clay pots and in Eijá's documentation and in Ahmik's clay tablets.

In the morning, Targat's confederation fell into position around the column, not as adversaries but as perimeter.

North. Home.

By the third evening the camp had found its rhythm. Three different peoples, three different customs, one mutual interest in reaching the canyon safely. Maxtla managed it the way she managed the market: held the structure, let the content move within it.

The conflicts that came to her were mostly small. A dispute about water access at a spring. A question about whose fighters walked the outer perimeter. A moment of genuine tension on the fifth night when one of Targat's men and one of Teya's reached the same conclusion about each other that men from rival groups often reached, and Maxtla had to be between them before the conclusion became physical.

She had done it without drama. She had stood between them and waited, which was the technique that worked for this: not assertion, not argument, just the presence of a person who had decided this was not going to happen. Both men had more intelligence than anger. The anger drained away and they had avoided each other after that.

"How do you do that?" Lofn asked her, the night after the near-fight.

"Stand in the middle of something like that without flinching."

Maxtla thought about it honestly. "I've been the thing in the middle before. The thing that was going to be damaged if the situation went wrong. After a while you stop flinching at situations that aren't going to damage you."

"But you didn't know it wasn't going to damage you."

"No. But I knew the alternative was worse."

Lofn was quiet.

"The canyon," she said after a while. "What do you think it looks like?"

"The same."

"But different."

"Different because we're different. The canyon doesn't change. We do."

Lofn was quiet for a moment. "I keep thinking about what Ix Chab said. About the knowledge that doesn't die when the person dies."

"Yes."

"The canyon doesn't have that. We have what people remember and what people pass down and what doesn't get lost when the person who knew it isn't there anymore." She paused. "We're bringing more than we took."

"That's the whole point," Maxtla said.

"I know. I just wanted to say it out loud." Lofn looked at the fire. "Dewii would have wanted to do what we did. He would have wanted to come south and see the city and learn the knowledge and bring it back." Her voice stayed even. "That's the thing I think about. Not that he's gone. That he didn't get to do what he would have done."

"We'll do it for him," Maxtla said. Not sentimentally. As a plan.

"Yes," Lofn said. "We will."

The nights also felt like return nights, the nights of people who have done a hard thing and are coming home from it, who know they are going to arrive.

Eijá used the nights to document. On the return the documentation took on a different quality, more organized, more systematic. She catalogued the techniques, the observations, the specific measurements she had made. She catalogued what she had given away and what she had kept. She catalogued what she did not yet know how to do.

By the time they reached the desert crossing, she had filled three clay tablets.

"You're going to need more tablets," Maxtla told her.

"I know. I'll finish when we're home. These are the rough notes." She looked at the tablets. "I don't want to forget the order. The order matters for understanding how things connect."

"Does the order change what you do with it?"

"Sometimes. The rope fiber technique and the ceramic firing technique have a connection I didn't see until I documented them in sequence. The high-temperature firing changes the material's water resistance in a way that's relevant to rope fiber treatment." She paused. "If I'd seen them separately I wouldn't have made the connection."

Maxtla sat with this. She was doing the same thing with the political information, the sequence of the three wives, the sequence of the market to the feast to the lord's workroom, the sequence of the friendly game to the tournament. The sequence was the meaning.

"Tell me the most important thing you learned," she said.

Eijá thought about it seriously. "The road joints. The zero-gap fitting technique. I have it documented but I need the right chisel to implement it, and the chisel design is what I gave away my best obsidian blade for." She touched the tool at her belt. "This is the most important thing I'm carrying. Not the tablets. This."

"You traded for it."

"He wanted the knowledge preserved. He knew what he was doing. He was old enough to know that the tool and the technique would outlast him, and he wanted them together." She looked at the chisel. "I'll preserve them together."

On the eleventh night of the return, rain came.

Not the tropical rain of the south, which arrived with weight and intention. This was the high desert's grudging rain, thin and cold and barely committed. The camp adapted without complaint, which Maxtla noted as evidence of the group's integration. Forty days ago, rain would have produced three different responses from three different contingents. Now it produced one: the organized efficiency of sixty-three people who had been traveling together long enough to have learned each other's competencies.

Targat's people had the waterproofing. Teya's people had the fire maintenance in wet conditions. Maxtla's group had the medical coverage, because Lofn had positioned it that way early in the return.

The rain stopped by midnight and the cold that followed was significant.

In the morning, Hrakt came to Maxtla before the camp broke.

He said something to Ixchel.

She translated. "He says: we talked last night. His people and Targat's people and some of mine. He says: the route is good. He says: the route is good for us."

"Yes," Maxtla said.

"He says: we want to be part of it. Formally. Not just the protection arrangement, he says that works. He means they want to be stakeholders. They want their families to benefit from the trade in a direct way."

Maxtla looked at Hrakt. He was watching her with the calm attention of a man who has decided something and is waiting to see if the decision was correct.

"The waystation," she said.

Ixchel translated the question.

Hrakt answered.

"He says: they know the desert crossing. They know where the water is that isn't on the obvious route. They know the seasonal changes. They could run a waystation at the desert crossing."

"Run it how?" Maxtla asked.

The conversation took thirty minutes, with Ixchel translating back and forth, and produced a rough agreement that Kael would formalize when they got home: Hrakt's people would build and maintain a waystation at the desert crossing, supply it with their local knowledge, and take a percentage of the passage fees in exchange for the service and for the security guarantee that their presence implied.

It was, Maxtla realized, the route building itself. She had not organized this. She had set up the conditions that made it possible and the people who saw the value had built the next piece themselves.

"Good," she told Hrakt directly, before the translation.

He looked at her. He understood the word.

"Good," he said back.

It was the first word of her language any of them had tried.

CHAPTER TWENTY-FOUR

The cold crossing

The desert was cold now.

The season had turned while they were in the south, and the desert they crossed returning north was not the desert they had crossed going south, the heat had broken, replaced by a dry cold that came off the mountains to the west at night, dulling the scrub from summer gray-green to winter gray-brown. The ground was harder underfoot. The shadows came earlier. The sunlight, when it arrived, had the specific quality of winter light in open country, bright and clean and without warmth.

The pack animals moved better in the cold. The loads were heavier on the return, but the animals were conditioned now, and the cold replaced the heat's exhaustion with a different quality of endurance.

Lofn, who had catalogued every weather concern available at the beginning of the journey, said nothing about the cold.

She had changed on this trip. The grief was still there, Maxtla could see it in the occasional unmanaged expression, but it had redistributed, the way old injuries settle into the healed body. Present, integrated, no longer in control. What had replaced it was purpose. The look of someone who has discovered what they are for.

"She's different," Ixchel said to Maxtla on the fourth day of the desert crossing, watching Lofn run the midday medical check on two of Targat's people who had developed sores from the pack straps.

"Yes."

Ixchel watched Lofn finish the check and move on to the next person in the same efficient unhurried way. "She'll build a training."

"She'll build a training. The moment she gets home. She's probably already planning it. She's been planning it since the third day in Yaxal Nah."

The desert crossing was three days. The route was the same one they had walked going south. The rock formation that looked like a shoulder, the dry creek bed at the halfway point, the section where the ground color changed from red to brown that meant they were out of the worst sun exposure and could push the pace.

On the second day of the crossing, Targat walked beside Maxtla for an hour.

He did not speak for the first ten minutes. He seemed to think through what he was going to say before saying it, cultural habit or personal one.

"The second intercept," he said. "At the desert's edge."

"Yes."

"That will not happen again."

She looked at him.

"I spoke to the families. The six bands whose territory covers the route's northern section. I explained the route and the protection arrangement and the income. I explained that a group of my fighters attempted an intercept and failed." He paused. "I explained the consequences for the route if this happened again."

"What consequences did you describe?"

"That the route would avoid our territory. Find a path around us. We would receive nothing and the route would go elsewhere."

She absorbed this. He had done the work she had been planning to do, the consolidation of the protection arrangement from a personal agreement with him into something his people understood and supported. Without her asking.

"Why?" she said.

He was quiet for a moment. "Because the income is real," he said. "My people have not had reliable income from the northern passage in twenty years. The old routes stopped being used. A reliable income changes what is possible. I want my people to understand that the income requires protecting the thing that produces it."

"That's the argument for the granary," she said.

"Yes. Your man told me about it. Gedeon. He said: you protect the system that feeds you, not just the food. I thought about it for four days."

Gedeon. Who had been on the first short expedition before the southern trip, making exactly the relationships she had sent him to make.

"He's a good person to think with," she said.

"Yes. He thinks without showing it, which is the useful kind of thinking."

They walked in silence for a while, the desert opening around them in its winter stillness.

"The second son," he said. "The lord's son."

"Ahmik."

"He asks me questions about the route every morning. Where we are, what the terrain means, who controls what territory. He writes down what I say. He's going to know it better than I do, eventually. He's young and he's systematic and he has the writing." Targat said this without resentment. As information. "Is that a problem for the arrangement?"

"No. The more people who know the route, the stronger the route. One person knowing it is fragile. If that person dies or leaves, the knowledge goes." She paused. "The route needs to be in many heads. Including yours. Including Ahmik's."

"And yours."

"And mine. Though mine is less important every year as more people know it."

He looked at her. "That doesn't worry you?"

"No. The route is the point. Not being the only person who knows it."

He walked with this for a while. She could see him thinking it through, the specific contemplative forward gaze of a person working through an unfamiliar idea against their own experience.

"In my world, knowledge is power because knowing what others don't know gives you advantage."

"A route that only I know can be stopped by stopping me. A route that a hundred people know requires stopping a hundred people."

"Different game," he said.

"Different game."

The desert stretched ahead of them, winter-brown and cold and known now in the way that places you have spent time in become known. Known terrain was a form of safety.

The canyon was two weeks north.

She walked toward it without hurrying. The canyon would still be there when she arrived. What she was bringing home was more important than the speed of arriving.

On the last night before the desert ended and the plateau country began, Maxtla sat with Ahmik.

He had been on the edge of the conversations throughout the return, present, attentive, writing, translating when useful, observing when not. He was the ideal person to travel with: he required nothing and produced much. His questions were always the right questions.

He had asked her, on the third day of the return, if he could keep a route log. She had said yes and he had been keeping it since, a running record of the route's conditions, the contact points, the approximate travel times between waypoints. It was already more organized than anything she had produced herself.

"The log," she said.

He looked up from the clay tablet he was working on. "It's a copy for you. I'll keep one as well."

"Two copies," she said.

"Two copies is how important things survive. When you go back to Yaxal Nah, you'll take a copy south. We'll keep one in the canyon. On the next trip, we update both. The route log accumulates. It becomes more useful every trip."

"You've thought about this," she said.

"It's what I would do. The documentation is the most valuable thing I can contribute. The route is yours and Targat's and Teya's."

"Then make it better than anyone," she said.

He went back to the tablet.

The night settled around them, cold and clear, the stars of the high desert spread in their winter density. Sixty-three people breathed and slept and kept their watch and moved toward morning.

Somewhere in the clay tablet Ahmik was writing, the route was becoming permanent. Not permanent in stone, the stone road to the south had taken generations. Permanent in the written word, which was faster and more portable.

Both said: something passed here, and it mattered, and here is where it went.

CHAPTER TWENTY-FIVE

The western ridge

They were four days from the canyon when the Raiders hit them.

Not Targat. Not the Xom. Not any of the groups she had already accounted for. This was a different group, a large one, twelve or perhaps fifteen fighters, working from the western ridgeline, and they had not come to negotiate.

The first warning was the sound. A crack and whistle of a thrown spear in flight, and then Eijá made a noise and went down.

Maxtla was moving before the next spear landed. The battle formation they had practiced came together fast, fighters to the periphery, horses to the center, the column compressing and turning to present the smallest possible target. Teya's people were already returning fire, moving uphill with the focused efficiency of people who had been waiting for someone to try this.

"Eijá," Maxtla called.

"I'm up. Shoulder. It's in the shoulder. Keep moving."

Maria had already moved to her, had her, was assessing the wound. Not an artery. Not the killing location.

Targat's people came off the north slope fast and hit the western ridge from the rear. This was the advantage of sixty-three people arranged correctly, the western ridge attackers had planned for a trading column, not a mobile force with flanking capability.

The engagement lasted perhaps twenty minutes.

When it was finished, three of the western ridge fighters were dead, seven were taken, and the rest had run. Targat's people had two wounded, neither life-threatening. Teya's group had one wounded.

Eijá had a spear wound through the left shoulder, a long gash that had passed between the bone and the muscle, which was exactly as painful as it sounded and considerably less lethal than where it would have been if she had not moved fractionally in the wrong direction at the right moment.

Ixchel, who had learned basic wound treatment from Tinga before they left, cleaned and packed and bound it. Eijá endured this with the focused patience of someone counting seconds until it was over.

"You'll have a scar," Ixchel said.

"Good. Fast scars are good ones."

"That's a stupid saying," Ixchel said.

"Tell her, not me."

Maxtla was looking at the seven captured fighters. They were young, most of them not yet twenty, poorly equipped by the standards of the experienced raider groups.

"Where are you from?" she asked.

The eldest one, eighteen, maybe, met her eyes. He had the look of someone who had expected to die and hadn't yet.

He named a place. Teya knew it, a small encampment two days east, a group that had been a trading family until three years ago when a drought had decimated their stores and a rival group had taken the rest.

"Survival," Teya said quietly.

Maxtla looked at the seven of them. Young. Frightened. Hungry enough that she could see it in how they looked at the trail rations being distributed to the group.

She made a decision in one breath.

"Feed them," she said. "And then tell them what the route offers."

"They just attacked us," Targat said.

"They failed. Which is the only reason we're having this conversation instead of a different one." She looked at him steadily. "A failed attack by desperate people is an indictment of their circumstances, not their character."

He stared at her.

"Or we can leave them here," she said. "In the desert. With nothing. And they'll try again on the next caravan, and they'll get better at it. Or we absorb the cost of feeding seven people for four days and gain seven people who have personal evidence that the route system is better than raiding."

"You can't trust everyone who tries to rob you," Hrakt said.

"No. But I can trust that people with a better option usually take it."

They fed the seven. Maxtla sat with the eldest one and talked for an hour through available translation and gesture.

His name was Tok. He had a sister in the encampment to the east who had two small children and had been sick for three months. He had been raiding because there was nothing left to eat.

"Your sister needs medicine," Maxtla said.

She reached into the pack beside her and found the sealed clay pot with the herb preparation that Tinga had identified for fever, and one of the smaller pots that addressed infections of the gut. She held them out.

"These are for her. Instructions are scratched into the seals." She waited while Ixchel explained the scratched notations. "Come to the canyon settlement in the spring. Bring your family. There is work and there is food and what you produce is yours to keep."

He looked at the pots. He looked at her. He looked at the column around them, the organized movement of sixty people who had just defeated his group without losing anyone.

"Why?" he said.

"Because a settlement that turns away desperate people is eventually a settlement that runs out of people. And because your sister's children are worth more than a grudge."

She stood and walked back to the head of the column.

Danijel was waiting for her.

"You know he may not come," he said.

"I know."

"Or he'll come and it won't work out."

"I know that too."

"Then why?"

"Because the other option is leaving him in the desert. And I've done that and I know how it feels." She walked. "Someone could have offered me something different earlier than they did. Someone could have looked at what was happening and said: this is fixable, here is the beginning of the fix." She walked. "I do what I can. Not because it works every time. Because it's right even when it doesn't."

He walked beside her.

"You know," he said finally, "that is very close to what my protocols were supposed to be and very far from what they were in practice."

"Your protocols?"

He said nothing for a moment. "Observe without interfering. Let the culture develop naturally."

"You've interfered quite a lot," she said.

"Yes. I have."

"Do you regret it?"

He thought about this honestly. "Not one action," he said. "Not the cliff, not the protection against Ohad, not this." He paused. "I may face consequences for it. But no. Not one action."

She looked at him sideways. "You keep saying things like that. Consequences. Like there are rules you've been breaking."

"Yes," he said simply.

"Tell me," she said.

Another long pause.

"There are people who sent me here to watch. Not to participate. Not to lead, or protect, or advise, or interfere. They believe, correctly, that when observers participate, they change the outcome. And changing the outcome is not their purpose."

"But it was yours," she said.

"It became mine. Over three hundred years, it became impossible not to care. And caring meant acting." He stopped.

She walked with that for a while.

"The people who sent you," she said. "What do they look like?"

"Like me," he said. "But less tired."

She laughed at that, a real laugh, sudden, and he looked at her with the expression of someone who had not expected to cause that and found it welcome.

"When you go back," she said, "what will you tell them?"

"The truth. I'll tell them what happened."

"And what happened?"

He was quiet for the last time.

"Something better than they planned," he said.

Above them the sky was the specific blue of the high desert in autumn, saturated, enormous, honest in the way that large open spaces are honest. The canyon country was four days ahead.

Aki was four days away.

She increased the pace again.

They lost two horses in the attack. Not dead, the animals scattered when the first volley came in and two went north without stopping. Targat's people found one by evening. The second was not found.

The load redistribution took the remainder of the afternoon and required a specific accounting of what went where, because the loads were not equivalent. The medicines and the documentation that Lofn and Eijá carried could not go on an animal driven by someone else, they went on their own backs.

"The second horse," Lofn said.

"Gone," Maxtla said.

"The pack on the second horse."

"Maria got it off before the animal ran. She moved fast."

Lofn let out a breath.

Maria had moved fast, Maxtla had seen it from the other side of the fight, the specific economy of Maria's movement in crisis situations, the absence of hesitation that came from someone who had learned to decide quickly because slow decisions had cost her too much. She had cut the pack free and moved it to ground before the horse bolted, and had done it while maintaining her position in the defensive line.

"I owe her something," Lofn said.

"She knows that. You can tell her later."

"I want to tell her now."

"Tell her now. And then help with the redistribution."

The new group, the fifteen fighters from the western ridgeline who had attacked and failed, had separated themselves to the perimeter of the camp. Not fleeing. Not integrating. Existing in the specific position of people who have lost and are waiting to find out what that means.

Their leader was a woman about Maxtla's age who had fought with competence and had not broken when the fight went wrong, which was information. She sat apart from the group with the contained posture of someone managing both the external situation and an internal one.

Maxtla walked to her.

She sat down without announcement or request, not asking permission. The woman watched her with alertness but not aggression.

Maxtla had been in this conversation three times now. The structure was always the same.

She waited. She let the silence sit long enough to become something specific rather than the absence of words.

Then she said to Ixchel: "Ask her what she expected to find."

The translation. The woman's expression shifted, not the answer she had been braced for.

She answered.

"She says they expected a smaller group with more goods and less defense. She heard north from the mountain families that a trading expedition had come through with six people. She heard wrong about the six."

"We were six when we came south. We are not six now."

Translation. A pause.

"She says: she sees that."

"Tomorrow we talk," she said. "Tonight you rest."

"She says: yes. Tomorrow."

The camp absorbed the aftermath of the attack in the specific organized way that sixty-three experienced people absorbed an aftermath: medical check, load accounting, perimeter reset, fire rebuilt.

By dark, the camp looked like what it was: a large traveling group that had experienced a disruption and had managed it.

Maxtla sat the first watch herself. The night after a fight had its own texture, and she needed to be outside rather than inside it.

The stars were clear. The cold was significant. Across the camp, in the place where the wounded were sleeping, she could hear Eija's breathing, changed since the afternoon, carrying the particular quality of someone managing pain in sleep. Not in danger. Managing.

She had been managing things for six months.

She sat with that for a while and let herself feel the full weight of it, the way you felt the weight of something when there was no work left to do and the night was too cold for anything except the truth.

Sixty-three people. Four days. A child she hadn't held in six months, who had been learning to walk while she was south of the desert. A man who would be gone before the canyon, whose leaving she had been preparing for since somewhere on the road and still had not fully prepared for. A settlement she had built that was being unmade while she was away, she was certain of it, in the specific quiet way that things unmade themselves when the person who held them together was gone.

She did not know the details. She didn't need them. She had left something fragile and it would be in whatever state it was in and she was four days away and could not change any of it from here.

The fire had burned down to coals. The camp breathed around her, sixty-three people, three cultures, a dozen languages between them, sleeping close enough that the warmth was shared. She had built this in six months out of threats and negotiations and the repeated demonstration that the route was worth more than what it cost.

It was real. She had built something real.

And yet.

She put her hand on her stomach. The child moved, not urgently, the way the child moved when she was walking, but the slow shift of something getting comfortable. She was going to arrive home seven and a half months along, and there was going to be a council, and the council was going to be the kind of problem you could not outrun by moving faster.

She had never been good at the kind of problem you could not outrun.

She sat in the dark a long time.

What she arrived at, finally, was not a plan. She had made every plan available to her. What she arrived at was simpler: she was going to walk through it. She had walked through the desert and through the jungle and through three hundred miles of difficult terrain and through every kind of person who had wanted what she was carrying, and in four days she was going to walk through a canyon gate, and whatever was on the other side of it she was going to walk through that too.

Not because she was certain. Because there was nothing left to do except finish.

She watched the night until the second watch came. She handed off and went to sleep with the completeness of someone who had decided something.

CHAPTER TWENTY-SIX

The approach

The last day before the canyon, they made camp at the foot of the southern approach. The air smelled different here, sharp with juniper and the mineral smell of red stone.

The canyon was an hour's walk above them.

She did not push the pace to arrive at dark. She made the deliberate decision to arrive in daylight, properly, with the column organized and the horses sorted and the group looking like what it was.

What they looked like mattered. They were arriving home with sixty-three people where they had left with six. The settlement had been watching, and by now most of them knew the expedition was on its way back and had some version of what it was bringing with it. What they would see when the expedition arrived would fill in the gaps. She wanted what they saw to be the right thing.

She spent the afternoon organizing. Not the goods, those were already organized. She organized the people. Teya's group in the outer positions, visible. Targat's people in the middle, in sight without prominence. The Xom bands at the rear, which was the position of least prominence and also the position Hrakt had requested.

Her group in front. We went, we came back, we brought what we said we would bring.

Lofn was checking the medical packs for the last time. She had been doing this daily for the last week, not because the packs needed checking but because the proximity of home had produced a specific anxiety about the condition of the things she was carrying.

"They're fine," Maria told her.

"I know they're fine."

"Then why."

"Because knowing they're fine is different from knowing they're fine," Lofn said, and went back to checking.

Maria looked at Maxtla.

"Let her check," Maxtla said.

Eijá was sharpening the chisel from the old mason, an unnecessary activity, but Eijá's hands needed to be doing something. She worked with the specific focused quietness of someone who is both present and somewhere else simultaneously.

Ahmik was writing. He had been writing continuously for the last two days, filling the final clay tablets with the route log, the inventory of what they carried, the names and positions of the groups they were traveling with. He wrote with the speed of someone who had many things to say and understood that the tablet couldn't hold them all but was going to try anyway.

"The writing," Maxtla said to him.

He looked up.

"When we arrive, the settlement will want to understand what we brought. Not the goods. The knowledge." She paused. "Can you produce a document for them? Not the log. Something explanatory. What the city is, what we found there, what we established."

"How long?"

"As long as it needs to be."

He looked at the remaining blank space on his current tablet. "I'll need materials from your archive."

"You'll have them."

He nodded and went back to writing, switching from the log to something else, the beginning of the document she had described, visible in the change of pace and the way his hand moved differently across the clay.

She walked the perimeter of the camp twice before dark, not for security but for the specific quality of attention that walking produced in her. The perimeter of any camp she had been responsible for contained the whole of what she was responsible for, and walking it was a way of understanding the whole.

Sixty-three people. One thousand two hundred pounds of goods and currency. Three contingents from three different cultures that had spent five days trying to kill each other before becoming reluctant partners and were now, six months later, sleeping near each other's fires with the settled ease of people who had spent enough time in each other's company to have moved past the initial assessments.

She noticed it late in the afternoon. One of Targat's younger women, she did not yet know her name, had been marking her by the blue cord she wore in her hair, was standing at the northern edge of camp doing nothing. Just standing. Looking north.

Maxtla followed her line of sight. Canyon country from here was only a suggestion, the light changing quality at the northern horizon, the desert floor darkening where the plateau began, a faint line of red that could have been rock or could have been the last of the afternoon.

She went and stood beside her. Neither spoke for a while.

"That is your home," the woman said finally. Not a question.

"Yes."

"What is it like?"

Maxtla thought about how to answer. The canyon walls and the way light moved through them at different hours. The sound of the creek in the morning. The smell of juniper after rain. The feeling of walking a canyon path and knowing every turn of it.

"Vertical," she said. "And red. And the kind of place that takes a long time to leave."

The woman looked north for another moment. "I have not lived in a place that was worth staying in," she said. Not self-pity. Information.

The canyon country had been organized around the opposite principle for as long as anyone could remember: groups competed, and the losses in the competition were the cost of the system, and the cost was borne by the people at the bottom of each group's hierarchy. Mostly women. Mostly the young. Mostly people who had not been given the choice about the system they were born into.

The canyon was an hour above her.

She stood at the foot of the approach in the last of the afternoon light, and she thought about what she had left with and what she was returning with, and she let herself feel the weight of it completely, because there were not many moments when you could let yourself feel the full weight of something without it interfering with the work.

Then she turned back to the camp and the work of organizing the morning's departure.

Behind her, the canyon walls rose into the coming dark, red fading to purple fading to the first black of night.

They had been waiting. They did not mind the wait. The canyon was patient in the way of stone.

The four of them were at the fire late, her, Ixchel, Lofn, Eijá. Maria had taken the first watch. The camp was mostly sleeping around them, the low sound of sixty-some people breathing.

They did not talk much. They had been talking for six months, across every kind of situation that produced talk. What was left was the specific silence of people who know each other well enough that silence is not an absence but a form of company.

Lofn had her hands around a clay cup of the herbal preparation she drank at night, the one she had started making three weeks into the journey and had been refining since. She looked at the fire with the expression she wore when she was not working, a softer quality than her working face.

"What is the first thing you're going to do?" Ixchel asked. No one in particular.

"Sleep in a real bed," Eijá said, without hesitation.

"You've slept on harder ground than this."

"I've slept on harder ground than this for six months. That's different from choosing to."

Lofn smiled without looking up.

"You?" Ixchel asked her.

"Find the children who were sick when I left. See which ones made it. Then start the training."

"The training will take years," Maxtla said.

"I know." She did not say it as a complaint. She said it with the specific satisfaction of someone who has identified a problem large enough to be worth their lifetime and is glad to have found it.

Ixchel looked at Maxtla.

"I don't know," Maxtla said. Because she didn't. The settlement had governance problems she had been thinking about for three months. The route needed formalization that only Kael could provide. Gedeon needed to hear everything that had happened. Aki needed his mother to stop being somewhere south of the desert.

All of it was the first thing.

"You'll find out when you get there," Ixchel said.

"Yes. That's how it always works."

Maria appeared at the edge of the firelight, second watch finished, handing off to the next. She looked at the four of them and then sat down without asking, because she had stopped needing to ask a long time ago, and took the cup of preparation that Lofn passed her without looking.

They sat in the last of the night.

The canyon was an hour above them.

The fire held.

She was at the edge of the firelight when she heard him.

Not footsteps. The specific quality of the air near a person who moves without announcing himself. She had learned it over four months. She did not turn.

He sat beside her. His pack was behind him, set with the particular neatness of someone who had packed for the last time. She looked at the pack once and looked away.

"When?" she asked.

"Before the settlement. I'll come in with the column as far as the southern approach and then not come in. It's better that way."

"Better for who?"

"For the settlement. New people arriving, existing relationships to manage. A man walking out instead of in is a distraction." Another pause. "And for me."

She understood the second reason without needing it explained. He had been inside the settlement once, briefly, years ago. That was enough of inside for a man whose entire function was outside.

The fire shifted. Something in the wood gave way and the flames settled lower and the darkness beyond the camp moved a step closer.

"Where?" she asked.

"Home." He said it without inflection. She had no way to know what the word cost him.

She had spent four months not asking questions about what he was. She did not ask one now.

"The interference," she said. "What it costs you."

"I don't know yet."

"But you're going to find out."

"Yes."

She looked at the fire. He looked at whatever Danijel looked at when he was looking at something no one else could see. They sat in the quiet of two people who have said the important things and are now sitting in what's left.

"The child," he said. "Give him a name that means something. Not something decorative. Something that carries weight."

"I already have one."

"I know. I'm saying it anyway."

She looked at him. He was three hundred years old and he was looking at her the way a person looks at something they are committing to memory because they are leaving and they do not know what the leaving will cost. The eyes she had never learned to read.

She did not say: come back. It was not a thing that could be said to him.

She said: "The interesting part is what happens next."

He almost smiled. "Always."

He rose, picked up his pack, and walked out of the firelight. Gone in the way he had always been able to be gone, completely, without sound, as if the dark had been waiting.

She sat at the fire alone.

She had known this was coming for months. She sat with it anyway, the knowing and the fact of it arriving being two different things. Three hundred years on twelve worlds, and he had ended up here, in a desert camp, talking with her until the fire went low. She did not know what waited for him on the other end. She knew only what it cost to watch him go, that the cost was real, that he had known it would be, and that he had stayed until the fire went out anyway.

She went to sleep. The night before grief was like the night before difficult things. You rested well because the body understood what the next day would require.

In the morning, they went home.

The canyon received them in the early afternoon.

The light was still in the upper walls, the red stone at the angle that turned it the color of something older than fire. They came through the southern approach with the column organized and the goods visible on the horses and the sixty-three new arrivals spread across the trail in a length that communicated what words couldn't.

The settlement came out.

Not in a rush, not the panicked gathering of people waiting for bad news. The deliberate gathering of people who had been told something good was coming. They stood in the plaza and along the creek path and on the flat rock above the trading stalls, and they were quiet the way crowds were quiet when they were taking in more than they could process.

Sixty-three strangers behind her. Horses loaded past what the settlement had seen a horse carry. Ahmik with his clay tablets. Teya's fighters in their northern dress. Targat's people reading the settlement with the guarded assessment of those who had learned that the difference between a welcome and a trap was a question of who was asking.

She walked through the crowd to where Gedeon was standing.

He looked at her. He looked at the column behind her. He looked at her again.

She was seven and a half months along and she had been walking for four months and she was standing in the canyon she had built and her husband was looking at her the way he looked at things that cost him something to hold.

She did not say anything. Neither did he. He put his hand on her face, briefly, the gesture of a man making sure something is real, and then she stepped into him and let herself be held.

Around them, the settlement was beginning to move. People talking. Children running toward the horses. Someone had started a fire larger than the cooking fires.

She stepped back and looked at him.

"The council," she said.

"Three days. I bought you three days."

"Good," she said.

PART THREE: THE SETTLEMENT

CHAPTER TWENTY-SEVEN

The council

The elder council met three days after their return.

They had been waiting, Gedeon told her, for five weeks. The challenge to the land assignments had been formally filed and formally pending, and the settlement's informal governance structure had been straining under the weight of the question it couldn't answer.

She spent the two days before the council meeting doing several things.

First: she met with every woman who had run the settlement's operations during her absence. One by one, in the trading stall that served as an informal office, she listened to what they had managed and how. She asked questions. She showed respect. She made notes.

The settlement had functioned. Some decisions had been made differently than she would have made them, and one had been made badly enough that the cost was still in the settlement's air.

A man named Brak had been expelled by Merya, one of the founding women, who had decided on a Thursday that his behavior toward a new-arrival woman warranted his removal and had organized his escort to the canyon's edge on a Friday.

The behavior had warranted removal. The problem was process. No formal accusation, no response from Brak, no decision by any body that could be held accountable. Merya had decided, Merya had acted, and the settlement had watched a man expelled without understanding on what authority.

"He deserved it," Lofn had said, when Maxtla raised it.

"Yes. And if Merya had expelled him for the wrong reason, or the wrong person, or been wrong about what she thought she saw, there is no record and no process and no way to know."

Lofn was quiet.

"The next person expelled might not deserve it. And the authority Merya used will still exist, because we used it and didn't question it and it worked."

This was the thing that had kept her awake on her first night back. Not Brak, Brak was gone and the settlement was safer for it. The thing that kept her awake was the template. The informal, undocumented exercise of individual authority, correct in this instance, waiting to be used incorrectly in the next one.

She could not undo it. Brak was gone. She could make sure it never happened that way again.

This was the actual argument for the charter. A specific Thursday when someone good had made a decision alone that should have required a process, and the decision had been right.

Second: she met with the men who had filed the challenge. Not to argue. To listen.

Four of them. None stupid. They had identified a real vulnerability in the settlement's structure. The land assignments were legitimate by the logic of the system she had built, but the system had not been written down, had not been made formal, had not been made into something that existed beyond her individual authority.

"You are right that it isn't formal," she told them. "I'm going to make it formal."

They had expected an argument.

"The council decides under the old customs," Kael said, a man named Kael, not malicious but traditional.

"The old customs don't include trading networks to Mayan cities. The old customs don't include women who make the ring shot in tournament games. The new customs are developing. The council needs to develop with them."

"A woman cannot govern the council."

"No woman has asked to govern the council. I'm asking the council to recognize the governance structure that has been operating for the past two years and that produced the returns you counted two nights ago."

He said nothing for a moment.

"You want a formal vote," he said.

"I want a formal structure. Not a vote, a document. A statement of principles and rules that everyone in the settlement has agreed to and can be held to."

"Where does this document come from?"

"We write it. Together. The council participates. So do the women who have been running the operations. So does Ahmik, who comes from a city that has been doing this for four generations and has things to teach us about how it works." She paused. "And after we write it, everyone signs it. Or marks it. And then it exists outside any individual person's authority."

Kael looked at her for a long moment.

"This is not the old way," he said.

"No. It's better."

Third thing she did: she asked Ahmik to describe how the governance structure of Yaxal Nah worked.

He spent an entire evening on it, drawing in the dirt, explaining the layers, the lord's formal authority, the priestly authority, the market authority, the clan authority, the distribution authority, the way these layers interacted and counterbalanced and the role of written records in making each layer accountable to the others.

The settlement people who had gathered to listen became quiet in that specific way when people are hearing something that reorganizes their understanding of what is possible.

"The writing," a young woman named Peli said. "You can hold someone accountable through writing?"

"Through writing that multiple parties have witnessed and signed," Ahmik said. "Not just through it. Writing is the record. The accountability comes from the witnesses."

"We don't write," another man said.

"You can learn. I can teach anyone who wants to learn."

By the next morning, six people had asked Ahmik to begin teaching.

The council met in the plaza under the open sky. She did not want it in a closed space where things could happen without witness.

There were eleven elders. Four of them were women. Three of the four women had been in the settlement since the beginning; the fourth was a new arrival who had been given elder standing because of her particular skill with medicinal plants.

Kael led the challenge, as she had expected. He laid it out formally and correctly: the land assignments were not made by established custom, they were made by individual authority, that individual authority was not sanctioned by the elder council, and therefore the assignments were provisional pending review.

Maxtla stood and waited for him to finish.

Then she said: "May I speak?"

Formal. She was operating in the council's language.

"Speak," Kael said.

She spoke for twenty minutes. She did not argue against the challenge directly. She did not defend the land assignments as they were. She argued for the document, for the settlement charter. She laid out what it would contain: the land assignment principles, the governance principles, the rights and responsibilities of all residents, the dispute resolution process.

When she finished, the plaza was quiet for a moment. Then a woman stood.

She was younger than Maxtla had expected. Thirty, perhaps. Her name was Brea and her family had been in the canyon since before the settlement had a name for itself. She had survived two bad winters and a raid and the kind of loss that left marks you carried rather than moved past.

"You built something good," Brea said. Her voice was steady. "What this settlement is now, compared to what it was five years ago, my family knows the difference. We lived the difference."

Maxtla nodded. She did not speak.

"My objection is not to the document. My objection is to what the document erases. We were here when there was nothing. When the water system broke, my father fixed it in the dark with his hands because no one else was available. When the raiders came the second time, my mother stood at the north gap with four other women and held it for three hours while the children were moved." She paused. "Those people are dead now. Most of them. What they bought with that work is in every house in this settlement. I am asking that the document remember them."

The plaza was quiet in a different way now.

Maxtla stood with it. The full weight of what Brea had said. The founding families had paid a price that the later arrivals hadn't. That was true.

The question was what that truth entitled them to.

"The charter will remember them," Maxtla said. "Their names. What they built and when. That is a record, and records outlast the people who hold the memory in their heads. Your mother at the north gap will be in the document. Not because I require it. Because it happened and happened here and belongs to the settlement's history."

Brea was quiet.

"Memory is not land," Brea said.

"No. Land given by origin becomes a claim that never ends. Every generation extends the claim. Every new family that comes to build something here finds that the ground was already claimed by someone who isn't using it, on the basis of something that happened before they were born." She paused. "Your father fixed the water in the dark. That built this settlement. What it built was a place where the next person could also build something, and the one after. That is the inheritance. Not the first right to land. The right to a settlement that keeps building."

Brea sat down. Something closer to a person who had needed to say the thing and had said it and was now deciding what it meant.

She would be in the room when they wrote it.

Maxtla made clear that the document would protect the men in the room as much as the women. That it would define the council's authority, not abolish it. That it would give Kael's position formal grounding.

"Who decides what the document says?" Kael asked.

"We do. Everyone in this plaza right now. We debate and we agree and when we agree, we write it down. Ahmik knows how to make it permanent, on prepared hide, which lasts."

"And when we disagree?"

"We keep talking until we agree. Or until the group decides to put it to a vote. One person, one mark."

"Women as well," he said. Not a question. Testing.

"Women as well. Women have been running this settlement for five months. Women bring goods from the south. Women maintain the water system. Women make the baskets that feed the children. Yes. Women as well."

He looked at the eight other male elders. He looked at the women elders. He looked at the gathered settlement people behind Maxtla, two hundred of them, including Teya's group and Targat's people's representative and Ahmik and Tok, who had come already and was standing at the back of the crowd.

"I will participate in writing this document," Kael said. "I make no commitment to what it will contain."

"That is all I'm asking. Come and say what you think should be in it. Listen to what others say should be in it. And let us make something together that outlasts all of us."

He sat.

The council did not dissolve. But it shifted, the challenge that had been pending became the document that was beginning, and those are fundamentally different things.

After the meeting, in the evening, Gedeon sat beside her with Aki sleeping between them.

"You're tired," he said.

"Deeply."

"You didn't show it."

"No."

She looked at the sleeping child. Six months she had been gone. He looked like Gedeon when he slept, the same forward tilt of the head, the same absolute surrender of it. She had been afraid, at seven months along, that she wouldn't know him when she saw him. She had known him before she reached Gedeon. She had known him from across the plaza, running toward her with a sound like everything she had missed.

"He looks like you when he sleeps," she said.

"He looks like his mother when he's awake. Watching everything. Not deciding yet what it means."

She put her hand on the child's back and felt the small breathing, steady, indifferent to her relief, simply continuing as it had continued the whole time she was away. He had not needed her to breathe. That was the thing she had known intellectually and had to feel to believe.

She did not speak for a while. The canyon held the last of the day's light in the upper walls. The settlement moved around them in its evening rhythms. Six months of getting here, and here was this: warm stone, the smell of the canyon after summer rain, the weight of a child's breathing under her hand.

"We need the granary," she said finally. "The shared project."

"I know. I started the planning."

"Of course you did."

She leaned against him and rested in the way that was the closest thing available, not fully down, not fully up, just paused, in the canyon that was home, with the work still ahead and the weight of it no longer feeling like burden.

Just weight. Just real. Just hers.

She spent the days after her return walking the territory, the canyon walls and the upper ridge and the farming sections and the places where the new arrivals had been absorbing into the settlement. She walked it the way you walk a thing you are responsible for and have been away from: slowly, with attention.

The granary was finished. She stood in front of it for ten minutes. Four months of work, and the construction showed it, the foundation was level, the walls were plumb, the roof sealed tight. Eijá had designed it and the settlement had built it and the building itself had the specific quality of work that people had put care into, not because they were required to but because they had decided the thing was worth caring about.

Sixty-three new people had joined while she was gone, plus Aki's arrival and the natural growth of the existing families. The settlement was large enough now that she did not know everyone's name.

She spent part of the first day correcting this. Kael walked with her and made introductions, and she spent each introduction with full attention, not the greeting, the person. Where they were from, why they had come, what they did.

"The council composition," Kael said, when they reached the upper ridge at the end of the day.

"Tell me."

"Seven elders. Three are from the original settlement, Merya, Shan, and Pollo. Four are from the groups that have joined in the last two years. The challenge to the land assignments came formally from Brea, who is from Shan's group. But it has support from two of the four newer elders."

"What's the core of the challenge?"

"That the founding families should receive priority in the land allocation because they took the greater risk." He paused. "Brea's argument is not unreasonable on its own terms. Her family did take real risk in the early period."

"Her family took real risk in the early period. So did families who came later and found less certainty, not more. Later arrivals joined a settlement that was not yet proven. They took a different kind of risk." She looked at the canyon below them. "The question isn't who risked more. The question is what the settlement's principle is."

"The charter says contribution, not origin."

"Yes. And the charter was made by people who were here when it was made, which includes Brea's family. If we change the principle for founding families, we change what the settlement is. Not just this decision. Everything that comes from this decision."

Kael nodded slowly.

"The meeting," she said. "Open it."

"To everyone?"

"To everyone who wants to come. The charter is everyone's document. The challenge to it should be heard by everyone."

He processed this.

"Brea will not expect that," he said.

"No. She won't."

The canyon held the light in its specific late-afternoon way. She had built something here. She had been away from it for five months. It was larger than when she left, more complicated than when she left, and more worth defending.

She would defend the principle. That was what Brea's challenge was testing, and the defense would be its proof.

"Three days from now," she told Kael. "Set the meeting for three days from now. Open notice to the settlement. Anyone who wants to come, comes."

He walked back down into the canyon. She stayed on the ridge until the last light went.

The canyon was patient. She had always loved that about it.

CHAPTER TWENTY-EIGHT

The granary

The granary took four months.

Not because four months was the minimum time required. It could have been built faster, if Maxtla had simply organized the labor and directed it. But she had not built the granary to store grain. She had built it to build something. The grain was the useful result. The building was the point.

She gave Eijá the design specifications, stone foundation, thick walls, sealed roof, sized to hold the surplus of a two-hundred-person settlement through a full winter and the possibility of one additional bad season.

Eijá spent a week on the design, incorporating three techniques she had brought back from the south and one she had adapted from the cliff dwellers' methods.

Then Maxtla called the settlement together.

"We need a granary. Everyone in this settlement benefits from a granary. Everyone in this settlement will help build it. Anyone who works on the granary earns a proportional share of the credit they can draw against in shortage years." She let that settle. "No one is required to work on it. But everyone who doesn't work on it doesn't earn the credit."

Voluntary participation in a system that was broadly beneficial, with the incentive calibrated to the benefit.

Three people did not participate. Two of them were injured and their non-participation was recognized as circumstantial. The third was a man named Brak, one of Kael's informal allies who declined on what he called principle.

Kael himself worked on the granary. He mixed clay for the mortar on the first day and was surprised to find himself doing it, and more surprised to find that working alongside people from Teya's group and from Tok's family, who had arrived two weeks after the return, made the work faster and more interesting than working in the old patterns.

This was not accidental. Eijá had designed the work teams.

On the third day, a man from Tok's family who had been in the settlement for six weeks and had been polite but cautious in all his interactions brought his two oldest children to the work site without being asked. The children mixed clay. By the end of the day the man had stopped being cautious.

On the seventh day, one of Teya's women, Sura, who had been on the return journey and who had the reserve of someone who has decided to try a new place before deciding whether to trust it, sat down at the mid-morning break beside one of the canyon's founding women and they had a conversation that ran through the whole break and was still running when the work resumed.

By the end of the second week, the walls at shoulder height, the work site had developed the specific social texture of a shared project, jokes that only made sense if you had been there, the vocabulary of a particular kind of labor, the small private history of this work and not any other work. People who had arrived separately were now in the same story.

She had seen this in the Mayan road's construction, the physical residue of shared effort, the way work done together left a different mark than work done alongside. The granary would store grain. It would also store this.

On the fourteenth day of construction, the walls had risen to shoulder height, and Kael brought his draft of the land assignment section of the charter to the evening fire.

It was not what Maxtla would have written. But it was real, a genuine document that had been worked on by a man who had initially opposed the idea.

She read it carefully. She made two annotations in the margin, both of which strengthened Kael's original position in ways that also strengthened her position. She returned it to him the next morning.

He read her annotations.

"You improved it," he said.

"We improved it."

He thought about this. "You always do this."

"Do what?"

"Turn the thing I resist into something I helped make." He was not angry. He was assessing. "Because the thing you helped make is stronger than the thing I made alone, and is something I'll actually defend when it needs defending."

He was quiet for a moment.

"I would have been a better man younger," he said.

The granary was finished in the fourth month, before the worst of the winter. Eijá supervised the final seal of the roof with the material she had adapted from the southern technique, a mixed clay and fiber preparation that, when dried, was nearly waterproof.

The day it was finished, the whole settlement contributed the season's surplus to its storage. The contribution ceremony was Lofn's idea, not elaborate, just present. Each family carrying their surplus to the granary, the surplus being counted and recorded, the record becoming the basis of the credit system.

Ahmik wrote it all down.

He had also, over the four months, taught seventeen people the basic system of notation. Not the full Mayan script, but a simplified version he had developed specifically for record-keeping: numbers, names, weights, dates, transactions. Enough to make the credit system real. Enough to make agreements binding. Enough to give the charter permanence.

The charter itself was finished six weeks after the council meeting. It covered: land assignment principles, governance structure, trading rights, contribution requirements, dispute resolution process, the terms under which new members could join, and the terms under which members could leave.

It was twelve paragraphs. It was the most important thing written in the canyon country in living memory.

Kael signed it first. Maxtla had asked him to.

Then the four women elders. Then the other men. Then the broader settlement, everyone who could make a mark.

Three hundred and fourteen marks.

Maxtla held the finished document and felt the weight of it, which was not the weight of the hide it was written on.

"How long will this last?" she asked Danijel, who was standing nearby.

"The hide? Years. The principles?" He thought about it. "That depends on the people who defend it."

"Will they?"

"The granary will help. People defend what they built."

She set the document in the storage case that Eijá had made for it, sealed against moisture, set on a high shelf in the trader's building.

Then she went back to work.

The settlement was now larger than she could hold in her mind at once. The charter's informal implementation was showing strain at the edges, people invoking its principles in ways it hadn't anticipated, the governance structure making decisions she would have made differently. This was correct and also uncomfortable. The structure was real now.

The second trading expedition was being planned. The route was established. Targat's representative had been in the settlement for two weeks and was now part of the spring departure plan. Hrakt had sent a message indicating his group would hold the middle segment through the mountain country.

The route was two seasons old. It was beginning to be reliable.

Danijel left on a morning when the sky was clear and the first breath of spring was in the air, not warmth yet, but the potential of warmth.

The night before, he had found Lofn at the herb table in the medical room, doing inventory by lamplight.

She had known he was leaving.

"I have something to tell you," he said.

"I know. Sit down."

He sat. He told her about the device. What it was, what it did, how it worked. He told her he had given it to her after Dewii died, without asking, because the grief had been doing something specific to her body that concerned him.

She stopped writing.

She was quiet for a long time.

"You gave it to me," she said, "without telling me. Without asking."

"Yes."

"That is not something you should have done without consent."

"No. It isn't."

She looked at the inventory in front of her. The lamp made the room warm and small.

"After Dewii," she said. "What specifically were you seeing?"

He told her. The technical specifics, the physiological markers, what the device had detected and what it had done. He said it plainly, because she would want the plain version.

She listened the way she listened to medical information: without expression, taking it in, placing it against what she had known and not known about herself in that period.

"I'm angry," she said. "You should know that clearly."

"I do know that."

"And I understand why you did it. Which makes me angrier, because it would be simpler to stay angry." She picked up her stylus and set it down again. "My body. My decision. Those are not provisional principles that suspend under emergency."

"No. They are not. I made the wrong choice by the principle, for the right reason. I'm not going to argue that the reason makes the choice correct. It doesn't."

She was quiet again.

"I'm still angry," she said. "But not only angry. That's enough."

He rose to go. At the door he stopped.

"The device will continue to work. You don't have to do anything. You don't have to think about it. It's just there."

She looked at him for a long moment. "Dewii would have wanted to know. Everything about it. He would have asked you every question he could think of for a week."

"Yes. He would have."

She turned back to her inventory. "Good night," she said.

"Good night," he said.

He came to Maxtla before the settlement woke.

She had known he was leaving.

"Is it safe?" she asked.

"The mesa?" He glanced at the high ground above the canyon. "Yes. The way I go is safe."

"That's not what I meant."

He looked at her.

"The things you said about consequences. What you'll face when you go back."

"Ah." He was quiet for a moment. "I'm not certain. I was honest about what happened here. There will be discussion. But I also have the record. Three hundred years of observation. Full documentation of what these people are capable of, demonstrating the kind of progress that the protocols are supposed to be protecting." He paused. "When you know someone has advanced beyond what you feared for them, that they've moved from survival to governance in one generation, the case for continued non-interference becomes harder to make."

She understood. "You're going to argue that we don't need observation anymore. That we're past the point where it helps."

"I'm going to argue that we were past that point before I got here, and that the best thing that happened on my entire posting was the interference."

She was quiet.

"Will you come back?" she said.

"Probably not, in my professional capacity. Personally." He looked at the canyon walls, the red stone in the early light. "I'll come back when I can."

She walked with him to the base of the mesa. They did not say much.

At the base of the climb, he turned.

"Tell Aki. When he's old enough. Tell him there were people who came from far away and watched you build something real."

"I'll tell him," she said.

He began to climb.

She watched him until the mesa rim swallowed him.

She knew he was going. That was enough.

There was always more work.

CHAPTER TWENTY-NINE

The second expedition

Spring came to the canyon the way it always came, too fast on some days and too slow on others, the warm patches alternating with cold returns until the cold finally ran out of ambition and the warmth settled in.

The second expedition departed on the first reliable warm day of the season, loaded heavier than the first and moving faster because the route was known and the stops were already arranged and Teya's people were waiting at the mountain junction.

Maxtla was not on it.

This was the hardest decision she had made about the business. She had planned the route, trained the team, selected the lead, Ixchel, who was ready and knew it, and then she had stepped back.

If the system required her presence on every operation, it was not a system. It was a personal practice. She stood at the canyon mouth and watched the departure and felt both the loss of the road and the rightness of the ground under her feet.

Lofn was not on the trip either. Her feeding operation in Yaxal Nah had stayed with her. She had expanded it in the settlement, not as charity. As a distribution system. A way for the settlement's surplus, which was now real and documented and stored in the granary, to reach the people in the settlement who ran short: families with illness, families with new children, families in the specific limbo of being new arrivals.

She had been running it for three months and it was working, which meant she was needed here.

Maria was on the trip. She had asked to be, which was different from the first trip, where she had simply showed up at the gate.

"Why?" Maxtla had asked.

"I want to see it again. Now that I know what it is." She paused. "The first time I was running toward something without knowing what. Now I know. I want to go back and see it clearly."

"You're not running from anything this time?"

Maria thought about it. "I'll let you know when I get back."

She had said goodbye to Maxtla in the morning before the departure, in the trader's building while the expedition was loading.

"The charter," Maria said. "Will it hold while we're gone?"

"Kael will hold it. He helped build it. And Peli has the notation now. She keeps the records."

"Peli is seventeen."

"Peli is precisely as old as she needs to be. She's been keeping records for four months without an error."

Maria looked at her. "You've been building this the whole time. Since the trip south."

"Since before the trip. The trip was the route. This is the thing the route serves."

"A city," Maria said.

"The beginning of one." Maxtla looked around the trader's building, the record shelves, the communication system, the growing collection of Ahmik's notations and Eijá's technical documentation and the expedition reports that Ixchel had been writing since the return.

Maria looked at it all without speaking.

"You'll send word from the southern junction," Maxtla said.

"I'll send word. I'll remember."

Maxtla smiled. "I know you will."

The expedition left. The canyon was quieter for it.

Eijá had gone with them, her shoulder mostly healed, the scar already a settled part of her landscape. She had brought the complete documentation of everything she had learned in the south, organized in a system she had taught to two apprentices before leaving. The documentation would stay here, in the trader's building, accessible to anyone who needed it.

Ahmik was still in the settlement. He had decided to stay until the second expedition returned, he wanted to document the governance system in operation, he said, which was true, and also he was seventeen months from home and in no particular hurry to return to the political dynamics of his father's household.

Maxtla found him in the archive building one evening, sitting with a clay tablet he wasn't writing on.

She sat down across from him. She didn't ask.

"My father died. Six months ago. The news came in a trade dispatch three days back."

"I'm sorry," she said.

He set the blank tablet down. "What I keep thinking is: if the route had been formalized two years ago, if we had the dispatch system we're building now, the news would have come in three months. Maybe two."

She didn't say anything.

"I don't know if that would have helped. I couldn't have gone home in time regardless. The distance is what it is." He paused. "But I keep thinking about it anyway. The faster record. Whether knowing sooner would have made it different."

"Would it have?" she asked.

He thought about it for a long time. "No. He still would have died. I still would have been here." He looked at the tablet. "But there's something about receiving a record of a person's death. You find out they died on a specific day, in specific circumstances, documented and dispatched. And the record is precise and the record is accurate and you were not there, and the precision of the record makes that more true rather than less."

She held that a moment.

"The dispatch that told me my father was dead arrived the same way the route condition reports arrive. Same notation. Same format. Same seal."

Maxtla did not say that the system wasn't built for this. It was obvious and would not help.

They sat in the archive together, surrounded by the clay tablets and the sealed cases and the organized shelves of everything the settlement had committed to record, and neither of them spoke for a while, and eventually Ahmik picked up the stylus and went back to writing.

She stayed until the lamp needed oil, and then she added oil, and then she left him there.

He was teaching notation three mornings a week and had thirty-four students.

CHAPTER THIRTY

What she stayed for

Maria had been running from a man named Sael.

She had not said this on the morning she appeared at the settlement gate with a pack and no explanation, and she had not said it during the first month of training, or during the journey south, or in the city, or on the return. She had said: a man who thought I was his to decide about. She had said: an elder. She had said: I'm going somewhere.

She said the name to Lofn on the twenty-second night of the return journey, sitting far enough from the camp fire that they had privacy.

Sael was not unusual. He was ordinary in the way that made ordinary men dangerous: moderately respected, moderately powerful, certain of his own rightness in the way of someone who had never once been asked to justify it. He had decided, two years before Maria left, that she was appropriate for him, and he had begun the process of making this claim formal in the ways the old customs provided.

She had refused. The settlement was new enough, and Maxtla's influence was strong enough, that refusal was available. She had refused clearly and without apology and had believed, for a while, that this was sufficient.

It was not sufficient.

The second thing that happened was that Sael began the slower process: the accumulation of social pressure, the quiet conversations with her family, the positioning of her refusal as something eccentric that reflected poorly on her judgment, the gradual narrowing of her standing in the settlement until continuing to refuse him became a daily project that required all of her energy.

She had watched Maxtla leave for the first shorter trading expeditions. She had watched the settlement grow. She had watched Maxtla return and watched the women of the settlement move differently, with more confidence, with less of the specific apologetic quality of women whose standing was contingent on men's approval.

She had wanted that. She had been trying to get there by staying, by holding her position, by refusing to be moved.

And then, while Maxtla was on the last short expedition before the southern trip, Sael had come to her house.

He had not hurt her. She made this clear to Lofn, not because it absolved him but because the distinction mattered for her own accounting. He had come to her house and he had stood in it and he had told her what was going to happen with a certainty that required no threat to carry, because the certainty was its own threat. The old customs would support him. The elder council, without Maxtla present, was tilting back toward the old customs. He had the patient righteousness of a man who had decided to wait out the disruption and return to what he believed was the natural order.

She had stood in her own house and understood, in that moment, that staying was not going to work.

She had packed that night.

She had waited until she heard the southern expedition was planning to depart and she had been at the gate the following morning with everything she owned that was worth carrying.

"You could have said this," Lofn said.

"To whom?" Maria said. Not defensively. Genuinely. "Maxtla was already planning the departure. She didn't need the complication. And I didn't want anyone to make it about him. I wanted it to be about me going somewhere."

"It's about both," Lofn said.

"I know that now. Then I needed it to be only the going."

Lofn understood this. She had needed things to be only certain things, at certain moments, to keep moving. The full truth of something could be weight you couldn't carry yet.

"What will happen when you go back?" Lofn asked.

Maria was quiet for a while. Around them the desert night moved, the wind that came off the mountains at night, the sounds of sixty people asleep, the fire's low crackle.

"I don't know. It was five months ago. Things will have shifted. He may have found someone who agreed, or lost interest, or, I don't know." She paused. "The charter is different. The charter says what I said with only my body before: I have the right to refuse. It says it in a form that Kael agreed to. That changes it."

"Does it change him?"

"No. But it changes what the settlement says about what he can do."

"Is that enough?"

Maria thought about it for a long time. A whole minute, maybe more.

"Enough to go back," she said finally. "Not enough to stop watching."

Maxtla had said: "Yes. Good. When we get home."

That was all. No elaboration, no praise, no committee to propose it to. Just: yes, this is the right thing, when we get home.

Maria had understood, in that moment, what it felt like to be seen in the way that meant: the person seeing you has assessed your capability and found it real and is now planning around it rather than around the space where it might someday be.

It felt like being handed something solid to stand on.

She had been standing on it since.

On the last morning of the return, running her circuit in the pre-dawn cool, she ran past the settlement boundary markers and she thought about where the training ground should go.

She already knew. She had known for two months.

The flat area to the south of the water channel, where the light came in the morning from the east and there was enough space and the ground was even and the canyon wall behind it created a natural backdrop.

She would build it there.

She ran back to camp in the energized lightness of someone who knows what they are going to do when they get where they are going.

Behind her, the sun came up over the eastern mesa and painted the canyon walls in the colors that the canyon reserved for the transition between dark and light.

She ran into it. He was waiting.

Not literally, he was not standing at the settlement gate when the expedition returned, had not been watching the road south, had not organized any formal reception. He was simply present in the settlement the way a man is who has spent six months calculating, and the calculation was finished, and now he was ready.

Maxtla recognized it within an hour of arrival.

She had been home for forty minutes when she first saw him. He was across the central clearing near the granary, talking with two of the elder council men, and he glanced at the returning group with the attention of someone who was not merely looking.

She had Aki in her arms six weeks later, two months old and solid in the way of babies who had been well-fed, who looked at her with the concentrated evaluation of someone who had been told about her and was now making his own assessment.

"He knows you," Gedeon said, beside her.

"He doesn't know me. He's deciding whether to know me."

Aki reached for her hair. Grabbed a handful and held it with the absolute conviction of someone who had found the thing they were looking for.

"He's decided," Gedeon said.

She spent the first two days home in the specific luxury of return, the people, the settlement's changed dimensions, the food, the light, Gedeon's company. She absorbed the reports from Kael and Peli and Tinga with one layer of attention while another layer simply felt the canyon walls around her and the quality of the canyon's air and understood: this is the place.

Sael came to see her on the third day.

She had expected him sooner. The delay was tactical, he had wanted her to settle before approaching.

She received him in the open, at the table outside the planning room, with Kael present. This was not accidental. Kael's presence said: anything said here is said to the governance structure. It also said: I am not hiding this conversation. It also said: you are welcome here but this is not your territory.

Sael sat across from her. He was perhaps fifty, a big man running toward heaviness but still carrying the physical presence of his stronger years. He had the bearing of a man who had always been listened to.

"You've been south," he said.

"Yes," she said.

"A long way."

"A long way," she agreed.

He looked at her. She looked back. The silence was not uncomfortable for her. She had been in a room with Ix Pakab and his wives and a priest. A man who wanted to claim ownership of another person was a familiar problem by comparison.

"Maria came with you," he said.

"Maria is part of the expedition team. She's a skilled fighter and a good reader of dangerous situations."

"She left without." He searched for the word. "Discussion."

"She didn't need discussion. She is a member of this settlement. She made a decision about her own life. That is what the charter protects."

He sat with this. She could see him deciding which approach to take, the reasonable-man approach, the historical-claim approach, the elder-authority approach. He was calibrating.

"The charter," he said, with the specific inflection of a man who had not quite said a dismissive thing but had gotten most of the way there.

"Yes. The charter. Which you were present for and which the elder council endorsed." She paused one beat. "Which includes you."

"Elder council endorsement of a document that Kael drafted." He glanced at Kael. "With her guidance, in a process that moved very quickly and did not allow for proper consideration."

"Sael," Maxtla said.

He stopped.

"I'm going to tell you what I know. And then you're going to decide what to do with it." She was not unkind. This was not anger. She had spent six months doing things that were more complicated than this conversation. "I know that you made a claim. I know that she refused it. I know that you pursued the claim through social pressure instead of force, which means you understood the refusal was real and legitimate and you chose a slower method instead of the faster one. The charter says the slower method is also not available. Not the pressure. Not the quiet conversations with her family. Not the positioning of her refusal as a judgment on her standing."

A silence.

"She talked to you," he said.

"She didn't have to. I watched you watch her arrive."

Another silence. Longer.

Kael had not moved or spoken. His stillness was its own statement.

Sael looked at the table. At his hands. He was not, Maxtla thought, a cruel man. He was a man who had been formed by a world that was no longer the world he was living in, and the gap between the formation and the present reality was producing behavior that the formation said was normal and the present reality said was not.

"What do you want from me?" he asked. It was not a surrender. It was a genuine question from a man who was, for possibly the first time, unsure of the answer.

"Nothing you haven't already given. Your name on the charter. Your participation in the settlement. Your contribution to the grain system. And the understanding that when a person says no, the no is real, and the settlement will stand behind it."

"And Maria?" he said.

"Maria is a member of this settlement. She is building a training program for the girls. She is good at her work and she contributes substantially. She is not a subject of discussion between you and me or between you and anyone else."

He sat with this for a long time. The table was between them, literal wood, literal distance.

"I was wrong," he said.

It was not what she expected. She absorbed it without expression.

"I know what the world I grew up in said about how this worked. And I know the charter says something different. And I know she was right to refuse me. I knew it when she refused. I kept moving anyway because the old way said the refusal was negotiable." He looked up. "It wasn't."

"No. It wasn't."

"I don't know how to." He gestured vaguely. "How to be in this structure. The new one."

"You're in it already. You have been since you signed. The way you be in it is you make your contributions and you follow the charter and you treat the other members as members. You start from where you are. Not from where you were."

He nodded. Not the nod of someone who has fully arrived somewhere new. The nod of someone who has agreed to try to arrive.

He stood. He looked at Kael, a look, man to man, that said: I know you were here.

"I'll be at the granary shift tomorrow," he said to Maxtla.

"Good," she said.

He left.

Kael was quiet for a moment after he was gone.

"He surprised me," Kael said.

"He surprised me too."

"Do you trust it?"

"Not yet. But I trust it enough to see what happens next." She looked north, where Maria was already marking out the training ground boundaries with stones. "The charter doesn't require trust. It requires behavior. Trust is what you get if the behavior is real over time."

Kael absorbed this.

"The training ground," he said.

"Yes."

"She's marking it near the water channel."

"Good placement. It'll need formal approval from the settlement."

"The elder council will want to discuss the use of that space."

"Then we'll discuss it. The charter has a process for land use decisions. We'll use the process." She stood. "Kael. How many of the elder council are with us and how many are waiting to see which way the grain falls?"

He considered this with the precision she relied on. "Four solidly with us. Two waiting. One who will never be with us but who has enough stake in the granary system that he won't actively oppose." He paused. "Sael was the sixth."

"And now?"

"Possibly with us. Probably not against us. Which is enough for most decisions."

She nodded.

"Get the four together tonight. I want to hear everything that happened in six months and I want to hear it from people who were watching, not from the official report."

"It'll take more than one evening."

"Then two evenings. Start tonight."

He moved to arrange it. She went to find Gedeon, and Aki.

Across the clearing, Maria drove the last boundary stone into the ground and stood back and looked at the space she had made.

It was exactly the right size.

CHAPTER THIRTY-ONE

The Listening Ground

The training ground took shape over three weeks.

Maria had designed it herself, with the specific practical knowledge of someone who had been learning to defend herself since she was twelve and had thought carefully about what training needed to be and what it too often wasn't. Not a weapons display. A space for people who were not yet capable to become so, with the specific safety of a place where not knowing was not punished but was the beginning.

The boundary stones marked a space large enough for twelve people to work without interfering with each other. Inside it, the ground was cleared and leveled, Eijá had helped with this before leaving. The leveling had taken four days.

The equipment was minimal and deliberately so. Maria had learned her most important things with no equipment at all, with only her body and a space to move it in. The equipment she eventually added was there for the people who learned with their hands before they learned with their minds, and for the specific confidence that came from hitting something solid.

She ran the first session with seven women, ranging from fifteen to forty. She had not advertised it as being for anyone in particular. The word had spread the way useful things spread: she told two people, each of them told two people, and the seven who showed up were the ones who had decided to come.

She did not begin with technique.

"Tell me why you're here. Not the thing you said to the person you mentioned it to. The actual reason."

Not as a test, as a genuine question.

The answers were different from each other and the same as each other. Fear was in most of them. The specific fear of women who had learned to live with vulnerability they couldn't name and were now in a place where the possibility of changing it existed but felt fragile.

"You'll feel better after. Not safe, better. There's a difference. Safe is something other people tell you they'll provide. Better is something you make."

She taught them to fall without hurting themselves. This was the first lesson and it was always the first lesson because it was the most frightening thing and doing it first took the fear off the table. You could not learn to move well if you were still afraid of falling.

By the end of the first session all seven of them had fallen and gotten back up and fallen again and gotten back up again, and the specific lightness that this produced, the knowledge that falling was survivable, was visible in the way they walked back to their work for the afternoon.

Maxtla watched the first session from outside the boundary stones.

Maria did not notice her until it was over. When she did, she walked to the boundary edge and looked out.

"Well?" she said.

"It's what you said it would be," Maxtla said.

"Is it what you needed?"

Maxtla thought about this. The settlement had grown from six women to a population of several hundred, and the original understanding, that women who had escaped the Breeding should have the specific security of a place that would not reproduce the Breeding's power structure, was being tested by growth. The words in the charter were clear. The words could not be everywhere at once. What could be everywhere at once was people who had internalized the words and acted accordingly.

Maria's training ground was not the charter. It was the charter becoming physical, the principle translated into muscle memory, into the specific knowledge of a body that had been taught it could protect itself.

"Yes," Maxtla said. "It's what we needed."

"Good," Maria said, and went back to work.

Sael did not return after that first week. He had been given his one formal opportunity to misuse the mechanism and had taken it and lost, and the loss was thorough enough that attempting a second version would cost him more than staying quiet.

But he had people. Not followers, the settlement did not produce followers easily anymore, but people who thought the way he thought, who believed that founding status carried weight that the charter hadn't assigned to it.

They were not a threat. They were a friction, the specific slow friction of people who have decided an arrangement is unfair and will take every available small opportunity to demonstrate their dissatisfaction. It cost the settlement nothing decisive. It cost it something constant.

She walked past the training ground on her way back from the ridge that evening. The boundary stones were permanent now, set in the ground, weathered already to the specific aged quality of things that belong in their place.

Maria had named it the Listening Ground. Not the Fighting Ground or the Training Ground or anything to do with the obvious purpose.

"Why listening?" she had asked.

"Because the first thing you learn here is to listen to your body. The fighting comes after."

The name had spread without any announcement and was what people called it within the week.

Maria came back from the second expedition changed in a way she described to no one directly and that Maxtla understood without being told. The first trip she had been running from Sael. The second trip she had gone south knowing what she was going to. She had stood in the ball court at Yaxal Nah on the second day and understood, with the specific clarity of a person who has returned to a place they were once afraid, that she had not been afraid this time.

She came home to the training ground and the sound of it in the morning and the weight of work she had chosen.

There was a morning she didn't talk about.

Three weeks into the return from the second expedition, she woke before the camp and walked out to the edge of the desert and stood there. The sky was the gray-pink of a sky that has not decided what it is going to be. She stood in it and said nothing, because there was no one to say anything to, and she let herself be still in a way she had not been still for two years.

She had been moving since the night she packed. She had kept moving deliberately, because stopping meant the thing she was moving away from might catch up, and she had not known, when she left, whether it would catch up as memory or as the actual man and it had turned out to be memory and memory was survivable but only if you kept your hands busy and your body tired and your mind occupied with a specific forward problem.

She stood in the gray-pink morning and let the forward motion stop for a moment.

What was behind her: a man who had stood in her house and explained her future to her. The specific weight of that, not the fear, not the anger, which she had processed and filed and turned into useful fuel, but the other thing, the thing she had not named yet. The exhaustion of having had to be certain in front of him when she was not certain. The exhaustion of refusal when the structure around you is built to make refusal cost more than compliance.

What was in front of her: the training ground. The eight girls who were going to show up in the morning. Yeta, who already ran the circuit without being told, already arrived before the others and waited at the boundary stones with the patience of someone who has decided what they want and is prepared to wait for it. The work of teaching them not what she knew but what she had learned to become, which was not the same thing and was harder to transfer.

She stood there until the sun came up and showed her the desert in its actual colors, not the uncertain pre-dawn version but the real version: red rock, pale sand, the specific bright clarity of a sky that had decided to be blue.

She had run from something. That was true. It was also true that you could not stand where she was standing, having gone south twice, having trained seven women and eight girls, having built the thing she had built, without understanding that the running was not the whole story and had not been for a long time.

She was going somewhere. She had been going somewhere since before she knew where somewhere was.

She turned back to camp. The circuit wasn't going to run itself and Yeta would be at the boundary stones in an hour and she had a sequence to plan for the afternoon session that she hadn't finished thinking through yet.

She had not cried. She had considered it and decided against it, the same way she had considered the desert and decided she was done with the considering and it was time to go back.

"When you go back," Maxtla said to him one evening, "what will you tell your father?"

"That the north is real. That it's not a story. That there are people there who have built something he should be connected to."

"He already knows. He sent you."

"He suspected. There's a difference between suspecting a thing and having a son who was there."

She thought about this.

"Your brother. The succession."

He met her eyes. He was the second son. His mother's son. He had been watching the settlement's governance discussion with an attention that she now understood was not only academic.

"I'm not going home to be a player in that game. I'm going home to propose something different."

"The charter," she said.

"Not exactly ours. But based on ours. Based on the principle. A settlement that runs on written agreement and shared investment doesn't have a succession problem. It has an agreement about succession."

"That's harder than it sounds," she said.

"I know. I watched you do it. I'm going to need help."

"Ix Mam. Go to your mother first. She's been managing the informal version of this for twenty years. She knows where the resistance is and why."

He nodded. "You two are alike."

"She's smarter than me in her own territory. In mine, I'm smarter. That's how it should work."

He wrote this down. She let him, because she meant it.

Gedeon found her at the end of the day sitting at the edge of the trading post with Aki on her knee, watching the canyon shadows go long.

He sat beside her.

"The expedition will go well," he said.

————————

CHAPTER THIRTY-TWO

The Red Road

Three years later, the route had a name.

Not one anyone assigned deliberately. It grew up through use, the way real names do. They called it the Red Road, not because all of it was red, but because of where it started and who built it, and because the color attached itself to the route and stayed.

She had built two expeditions of her own, overseen three more, and was planning the sixth. The route had three reliable rest points and a reputation for consistency.

Parruk ran the mountain crossing. Teya's first instinct had been right about him, his understanding of terrain had become the route's insurance on the hardest section.

The canyon people's settlement on the outskirts of the Lowland, it had its own name now too, given by the people who lived there rather than by any authority, had four hundred and sixty people. It had the granary, the water system, a maintained road into the canyon from the south, a school of sorts where Peli and two colleagues taught notation to any child whose family wanted it, and a trading post that was beginning to look like a modest market.

The charter had been amended six times. Kael had died, and the settlement held the first deliberate civic ceremony to acknowledge his contribution. Lofn, at twenty-two, had organized it.

She had sent a letter south. She had a son who could already run fast and asked questions that stopped the room. She had Gedeon. She was not in a hurry.

She had a world.

On the morning of the sixth expedition's departure, she stood in the canyon mouth and watched Ixchel lead the column out, and felt the same pull she had felt at every departure, the road going somewhere she wasn't, and made the same choice.

She turned around.

Aki was running toward her from the granary, shouting something. He was three years old. He had her eyes, the specific quality of watching that she recognized as hers when she saw it in a face that looked nothing like her face.

She crouched down and opened her arms.

The canyon held them. The road went south without her. The first winter test came early.

Late in the season, earlier than the canyon's usual first frost, a cold front moved through from the north and sat on the settlement for eleven days. Not catastrophic cold, nothing that would kill the well-housed, nothing that the Lowland had not seen before in harder years, but cold enough that the harvest stores became the difference between eating and not eating for the settlement's most recent arrivals, who had come in the late season with little.

There were forty-three of them: a large family group from the plateau to the northeast, displaced by a territorial dispute that had turned violent and driven them south faster than they could plan for. They arrived in the second month after the expedition's return. They arrived thin and without sufficient provisions and with the careful hope of people who have been turned away before.

Kael brought the question to Maxtla. Peli reviewed the numbers. "The reserve exists for this," Peli said.

She smiled. Peli rarely spoke philosophically. "Good. Write the intake documentation. Start the contribution schedule in thirty days to give them time to find their footing."

The family group had been integrated with the friction that all integrations carried and none of the catastrophic friction that she had been watching for. There were personality conflicts. There were tensions around the contribution requirements that required two separate conversations with Kael and one formal mediation. There was a young man in the group, eighteen, with the aggressive energy of someone who had lost his standing in one world and was recalculating his position in a new one, who had to be managed with the same basic framework she had used with Sael: not punishment, not exclusion, but the patient reiteration of what the charter said was and wasn't available.

What they brought with them, beyond the bodies and the skills and the friction, was a ceremony. Seasonal, tied to the animal calendar, involving a single animal killed and burned at each seasonal turn in a specific sequence. The Tokosaj. They had been doing it since before their grandparents could remember, and they did not think of it as something that required permission. They did it at the first seasonal turn after their arrival, quietly, at the edge of the settlement's eastern boundary, and three of the canyon's founding members watched without being invited and had opinions about it afterward. The opinions varied. The ceremony had been done before anyone had formed an opinion, which was probably why it had been done at all.

By the time the cold front arrived, they were settled enough to weather it. The granary was open by the charter's terms during the provision period, not freely, not without accounting, but available. People ate.

It was the first time the granary had been tested against something real, and what the test revealed was that Eijá's original design was better than even she had argued for.

She had built it with more insulation than seemed necessary at the time, an extra layer of the packed-clay-and-fiber wall, a roof design that trapped air. The cold front that would have compromised a less careful structure left the stored grain unaffected. Temperature differential between inside and outside: measurable but not damaging. Moisture: controlled.

"You knew," Maxtla said, the seventh day of the cold, standing inside the granary with Eijá and watching Peli supervise the morning distribution.

"I modeled several scenarios," Eijá said. "The moderate cold scenario said the extra insulation paid for itself in the first winter."

"And the bad scenario?"

"The bad scenario said we'd really need it."

"Which scenario is this?"

"Moderate," Eijá said. "This is the scenario where we're glad we built what we built and the grain is fine and we have a good story to tell the new arrivals about why the granary is worth contributing to." She paused. "Wait for the bad scenario to see what the structure can really do."

Maxtla looked at the stored grain, the organized bins, the notation system, the record of every contribution and every withdrawal. All of it organized and legible and maintained by Peli, who was explaining the accounting to two of the newcomers who had asked to learn the ledger system.

Peli was explaining the notation: each family's contribution record, the credit system, the withdrawal limits. The newcomers paid attention the way people pay attention when the thing being explained is theirs to keep.

"Do you know what you've built?" Eijá said. "Not the whole settlement. The granary system. The combination of structure, accounting, and contribution model. People defend what they helped build, you gave everyone a stake in the ledger."

"Ixchel would say we invented banking," Maxtla said.

"We reinvented it," Eijá said. "A version that fits here."

The cold broke on the twelfth day.

The morning the cold broke, Maxtla walked the settlement's perimeter in the early hours. The settlement was three times the size of the original canyon community. It had 460 people. It had a granary and a water channel and eleven permanent structures and more in progress and a training ground that Maria had not only built but was already teaching from, six girls between ten and fourteen were running their morning circuit as she walked past, and Maria was running with them, not ahead and not behind but in the middle of the group, which was both a teaching position and a personal one.

It had a charter that Kael had written and Sael had signed and forty-three newcomers had been welcomed under.

It had Peli's ledger and Ahmik's notation system and Ix Mam's route documentation translated into the northern notation and the clay pots from Ix Chab sealed and stored with Lofn's careful labeling.

It had Gedeon, who was in the eastern field this morning with the new arrivals' eldest son, going over the spring planting schedule, because the eldest son had grown up farming a different soil and needed to understand the canyon's specific requirements before the first planting.

It had Aki, who was asleep in the structure that was theirs, hers and Gedeon's, and who would wake in an hour and require feeding and would be uninterested in the administrative concerns of the settlement's governance structure.

She stood at the north boundary marker and looked back at it.

Tested against actual winters and strangers arriving thin at the gate.

She had been thinking, since the night with Danijel by the fire, about the long view. About what persisted. About the specific question: is this enough?

She turned and walked back into the settlement.

CHAPTER THIRTY-THREE

Brea

The forty-three new arrivals were integrated now, their contribution records accumulating. But sixty-three new people in a single season had stretched the charter's informal mechanisms past what she had designed them for. The next hard question was already visible: not whether the charter would hold, but whether the people administering it understood what they were holding.

Across the clearing, Gedeon looked up from the field and saw her and raised one hand.

She raised one hand back.

The sun was warm on the cold ground.

The granary stood behind her, full, sealed, level. It would hold.

She talked with Ixchel. "Shared investment. Everyone who uses it."

"The first seasons are on us," Ixchel said.

"Ahmik's been sending condition reports on his own," she said.

"He's the network," Maxtla said.

A team walked the full route in spring. They documented damage: ordinary maintenance in most sections, but two significant problems, erased path markers in the sandstone approach, and rockfall in the canyon section.

"The rockfall section," Eijá said. "Two people and ten days."

"Take Maria," Maxtla said. "And two of the new arrivals."

"She'll see what I'll miss," Eijá said.

Eijá went, with a plan for repairs and a schedule for maintenance.

They left in the morning, four people with tools and supplies and the clay tablet, heading south on the route that would eventually bear a name, though the name had not been given yet.

Maxtla watched them go. She felt the trust that had become her most reliable operational tool: putting the right people into a problem and getting out of the way. She had needed to learn this. Her first instinct had always been to do the thing herself, it was faster, she knew what she wanted, the result was within her control. The year since the southern journey had been the year she had learned that the settlement was too large for any one person's hands and that her most important function was not doing but enabling.

Enabling was harder. Eijá's granary was better than Maxtla's design would have been. The charter was better for Kael's precision. Maria's training program was something Maxtla could not have built.

The thing she had built was too large for one person to hold.

She stood at the settlement's south edge until the team was out of sight, then turned back to the daily weight of the work.

Ahmik's quarterly dispatches were already threading information between nodes. The route was building its own intelligence network without being asked.

The first serious problem with the road was a rockfall.

A winter storm brought down a section of the western wall on the southern approach. Eijá saw a secondary fracture line that needed addressing first. She showed Maxtla the section the next morning. The secondary fracture was visible: a line running diagonally, wider at the top, the pattern of rock under freeze-thaw pressure.

"How long?" Maxtla asked.

"Could be this season. Could be ten years."

"What does addressing it take?"

"Four people and two days for the pinning work. Then the clear-out below, which is more people and more days. Then a retaining structure on the path edge to prevent future debris from reaching the path itself." She looked at the slope. "The retaining structure is the part that lasts. The rest is repair. The structure is prevention."

"What does the structure require?"

"The stone is here, the fall material is exactly the right size for dry-stacked retaining work. The knowledge is here. The labor is the question."

"How much labor?"

She said a number.

Maxtla sat with it. The labor was available. The question was the arrangement, the people who provided the labor needed to understand they were providing it for a thing that was collectively useful, not for Maxtla's expedition and not for the settlement alone. The route was used by Targat's people and Teya's people and the traders from three different territories. The repair should involve all of them, because the path was all of theirs.

"We write it into the route agreement," she said.

"The maintenance obligation."

"Yes. The protection agreement covers the traveling section. The maintenance obligation covers the fixed infrastructure. Each party with territory that includes route infrastructure is responsible for that infrastructure's upkeep." She paused. "Proportional to their use."

"We count. Ahmik has the numbers."

"The secondary fracture first," Eijá said. "Before anyone touches the lower material."

"Always fix the secondary fracture first," Maxtla said.

The repair took eleven days. Ahmik documented it. Two seasons later, Targat's people used the same technique.

"That's the point," Maxtla said.

Ixchel left on a Tuesday.

She left on the morning after the fifth rest day in the second moon of the third year, which the settlement's calendar had compressed into notation that everyone could read.

The departure was different from the first one.

The first had carried the weight of something attempted for the first time. This departure was known. The route was documented. The protection groups had been notified. The watching faces numbered over two hundred, most of them people who had arrived at the settlement afterward and had heard about the journey from the people who made it, the relationship of people who know something is possible because they have evidence rather than because they are betting on it.

"It feels different," Lofn said to Maxtla. They were standing at the south boundary, watching the expedition form up.

"It's not the first time," Maxtla said.

"That's the difference." Lofn paused. "The first time was, I didn't know if I could do it. I didn't know if any of us could. I kept waiting for the moment when it became clear that we couldn't." She looked at the expedition, sixty-five people, larger than the first, better equipped, with a route that had been walked and measured and documented. "Now I know we can. We did. The question is just, can we do it again, bigger, better."

"Can you?" Maxtla said.

"Yes," Lofn said. "Obviously." No hesitation. The certainty of someone who has evidence.

Ixchel was at the front of the expedition, going through the final checks with Sera, the route assessment woman who had become the expedition's lead navigator. Ixchel was not the fighter or the navigator; she was the trader, the reader of rooms, the person who understood what a thing was worth and who to say it to and how. She was also, for this expedition, the leader in the full sense, which was new: on the first expedition, Maxtla had been the center of gravity even in the moments when Ixchel's specific skills were doing the work. This time, it was Ixchel's expedition in the way the first one had been Maxtla's.

She moved through the pre-departure checks with the specific settled authority of someone who has accepted a responsibility fully and is not performing the acceptance. This was a thing Maxtla had watched her develop over the three years since the original journey: the quiet shift from someone brilliant and essential who deferred, to someone brilliant and essential who led.

"She's ready," Gedeon said. He had come up beside Maxtla without her noticing, he still did this sometimes, the quiet approach of a man who had learned to move through uncertain terrain.

"Yes," Maxtla said.

"So are you," he said. "Ready for her to go."

"I know," she said. "It's just." She stopped.

"Say it," he said. Not pressing. Just making space.

"It's just that the first time I was the one going," she said. "And the risk was mine to hold. I knew what I was doing, I was managing it, I was present for every decision." She paused. "This is different. The risk is hers and I'm standing here and the only thing I can do is watch."

"That's the trade," Gedeon said. "You built something big enough to send someone else to extend it. The trade is you don't get to hold all the risk anymore."

She looked at him. He was right. She knew he was right. The knowing did not make the watching easier.

"Aki's going to want to go south when he's old enough," she said.

Gedeon was quiet for a moment. "Yes," he said. "He is."

"I'll have to let him."

"Yes," Gedeon said. "You will."

They stood together, the three of them, Maxtla and Gedeon and the absent future of a seven-months-old boy asleep in a canyon settlement in the oldest part of his mother's world, and watched the expedition complete its formation.

Ixchel turned and looked back at the settlement crowd. She found Maxtla's face across the distance and held it for a moment. Her expression was the specific expression of someone who is about to do the thing they are most capable of doing: present, calm, slightly electric.

She raised one hand.

Maxtla raised one back.

Then Ixchel turned south and the expedition moved.

A clay tablet arrived eleven weeks after the departure, carried by one of Targat's route messengers, the first time a message had traveled the route in that direction, north rather than south, which was itself a proof of concept that Maxtla filed without ceremony.

It was Ixchel's hand, she had learned the notation more fluently than anyone in the original expedition except Lofn, and she used it the way she spoke: precise, with nothing she didn't intend.

The tablet said: we arrived on the fortieth day, which is eight days ahead of the first trip. The route holds. Ahmik was at the gate. He had been corresponding with the city for two years but he had not seen us since the first expedition and he stood there with his hands flat at his sides the way people stand when they have been waiting for something they were not certain would arrive. He is good. He is the best thing we put in that city.

The tablet said: Ix Mam received us the second morning. She looked at me the way she looked at you, the look of someone deciding whether you can be relied on to understand what she's telling you. I think I passed. She showed me the correspondence files. There are forty-seven letters between the settlement and Yaxal Nah in Ahmik's hand. They have a relationship. The route is not a route. It is a living thing that has been growing while we were at home planning to come back.

The tablet said: Ix Tunich is running the succession and winning. Tell Lofn: the medicine we brought will matter. I don't know how yet but I can see the shape of why it will.

The tablet said: we are going to the coast. Chalchih has a contact. The coastal route exists and Ix Mam has been trying to formalize it for ten years. I think we are the thing that makes it possible. I will write again from the coastal junction.

The tablet said: I understand now why you didn't describe this to me adequately. It is too large to describe in advance. You have to be in it.

Maxtla read it twice. Then she passed it to Lofn, who read it twice. Then she passed it to Gedeon, who read it once, slowly, and set it down and looked at the south edge of the canyon where the route began.

"The coastal route," he said.

"If it holds," Maxtla said.

"It will hold," Lofn said, without looking up from the tablet. "She found the junction. That's the hard part."

No second tablet came from the coastal junction. The route had no reliable messenger system below the mountain section, Targat's reach only extended so far. They waited without knowing if there was news, which was its own form of news: the world was now large enough that there were parts of it they were in and could not see.

They were gone for seven months.

In that time the settlement built four new structures and added eighty-one more residents and had two governance crises that the charter navigated cleanly and one that it navigated messily and one winter storm that tested the granary again and found it adequate.

Maria's training program graduated its first cohort: eight girls between twelve and sixteen who had completed six months of the full curriculum and who carried themselves, at the graduation ceremony that Maria had designed with the input of Lofn and Kael, with the specific physical vocabulary of people who know what they can do.

The graduation was not elaborate. There was food, there was always food, the canyon had learned to celebrate around food, which was both practically necessary and psychologically important. There was a formal acknowledgment by Kael on behalf of the settlement's governance structure, which was ceremonial in the way that all formal acknowledgment is ceremonial and substantive in that it said: the settlement sees this, the settlement values this, the settlement will defend the standing of these graduates.

And then each of the eight girls did something.

Maria had left this open: each of them chose what to demonstrate. There were no assigned demonstrations, no standardized performance. The point was the choice, that each of them had identified what they most wanted to show.

One showed the knife work. One showed the elbow strike chain. One showed the terrain-reading exercise, walking through the canyon in a way that made visible how she was reading it, where the shelter was, where the exits were, where the high ground sat. One showed the specific stillness that was the complement of the physical work: standing in a group of six people larger than herself and holding her position, making it clear with nothing but body language that this was not a person who needed to justify her presence.

Maxtla watched this last one, a twelve-year-old named Yeta who had arrived at the settlement nine months ago from the eastern plateau, thin and watchful and almost invisible in the settlement's social fabric, gradually becoming not-invisible, and now standing in the middle of six adults who were physically bigger in every dimension and holding her ground with a simplicity that made it look like nothing.

It was not nothing.

"That one," Maxtla said to Maria afterward, quietly.

"I know," Maria said.

"What do you see in her?"

"The thing you had when you left," Maria said. "Whatever that is. The part that doesn't ask whether you're allowed."

They looked at Yeta across the clearing, where she was now in an animated conversation with two of the other graduates, the stillness replaced by the ordinary animation of a twelve-year-old who had done a thing she was proud of.

"Teach her everything," Maxtla said.

"Already am," Maria said.

Ixchel came back in the deep autumn, loaded with goods and information and the specific expanded quality of someone who has been in the world and added to their internal map of it.

The copper. The coastal-dye samples. The fish preparations, dried and compressed, which Lofn immediately began analyzing for their medical applications. The seeds, more of them than the first expedition had brought back, twelve new varieties from the coastal lowland agriculture that the canyon country had never seen.

And the contacts: three coastal trading families who had agreed to the formal relationship with the settlement, whose tokens were sealed in clay alongside their written descriptions of what they traded and what they needed. Chalchih's letter, warm and specific and personal in the way that business letters from people who are also, carefully, friends are warm and specific and personal.

CHAPTER THIRTY-FOUR

Ixchel's road

A separate letter from Ix Mam, written in Ahmik's hand and notation, documenting eleven new route segments that had been added to the distribution network map since the last report. The map was growing. It was becoming, slowly, the thing Ix Mam had imagined and Maxtla had agreed to build: not a single route but a system.

And one more thing, which Ixchel delivered to Maxtla privately, in the planning room, before the full debrief.

A small clay cylinder, sealed with the mark of Ix Tunich's personal household, not the third wife's formal mark, but the personal one, the same seal that had been on the jade disc.

Inside: a pressed reed document in Ahmik's notation, covering a single subject.

Maxtla read it twice. The second time slowly.

"She found it," she said.

"She found it," Ixchel confirmed.

The document described a route to the east, not the existing route, which ran south and curved gently westward before the long southern approach to the Mayan cities. An eastern route. One that ran through the great river valleys that Ahmik had been hearing about secondhand, that connected to a network of settlements along the river that traded in things neither the canyon country nor the southern cities had seen.

"She's been working on this for two years," Ixchel said. "Since our first visit. She had her own people mapping the eastern approach."

"Why give it to us?"

"Because we're the northern node," Ixchel said. "We're the ones positioned to explore it from this end. The eastern route from here looks different than the eastern route from Yaxal Nah." She paused. "She's building the network, Maxtla. She's doing what she said she would do."

Maxtla rolled the reed document carefully and held it.

Twelve years Ix Mam had been working on this. Twelve years of documentation and relationship-building and patient argument to anyone who would listen, in the narrow formal margins of a second wife's authority in a city that made the informal work invisible.

And here it was.

The eastern route.

"When?" Ixchel said.

Maxtla looked at the reed. At the map it described. At the implication of it, not just trade, not just goods, but connection to the river valley civilizations that were, by all accounts, doing things neither of them had seen.

"Two years," she said. "Maybe three. We need to stabilize the southern route first. We need Aki a little older." She paused. "We need to know who goes."

"Not you," Ixchel said. "You stay here. You built the node. You maintain it."

"I know," Maxtla said.

"I can go," Ixchel said. "Or someone from the next generation. Yeta, in eight years."

"Yeta in eight years," Maxtla said.

She put the reed document in the planning chest, in the section reserved for future projects, the section that had been empty when she built the chest and was now, steadily, filling.

She went to find Aki, who was awake and requiring attention, which was the most immediate and most important fact of the afternoon.

The eastern route would wait.

It had waited twelve years already.

It could wait a little longer. The accusation came on the forty-third day, at the waystation south of the desert crossing.

A man from the waystation settlement, one of the permanent residents, not a trader, came to Ixchel's fire in the evening and said that a member of her party had stolen something. He said it loudly, with the specific volume of someone who has calculated that volume is itself a form of evidence.

Ixchel looked at him. She said nothing.

The something was a worked copper disc, he said. Small. Distinctive. His family's work. He had seen it in her party's camp that afternoon, in the pack of the man now sitting three feet to her left.

The man three feet to her left was named Pelo. He was twenty-two, from the northeast family, and had been on his first expedition. He was looking at the accuser with the frozen quality of someone who has been accused of something in a language they understand perfectly and still cannot process.

"Show me the disc," Ixchel said.

"It's in his pack," the accuser said.

"Then it will be easy to show me," she said. "Open the pack."

She said this to Pelo. He opened it himself, not defensively, not with the movements of someone trying to manage what was visible. He opened it the way someone opens a pack to find something. He removed everything. Item by item, in the firelight, before the accuser and the six traders from three different groups who had been at the waystation when the accusation was made.

There was no copper disc.

"The inner section," the accuser said.

Pelo showed the inner section. He turned the pack upside down. He handed it to Ixchel, who ran her hands along the seams.

Nothing.

"He moved it," the accuser said, with less volume now, the calculation not having produced the expected result.

Ixchel was quiet for a moment.

She looked at the six traders. She looked at the accuser. She looked at Pelo, who had the look of someone still waiting to understand what was happening.

"Sit down," she told Pelo. To the accuser: "Walk with me."

She took him fifteen feet from the fire. Far enough to be private. Close enough to be visible.

"I don't know if you lost your disc or never had your disc or invented your disc," she said. "I don't know if someone else in this camp took it, or if you mistook another disc for yours, or if you're making a claim you know is false." She paused. "What I know is that you made it loudly, in front of traders who are deciding whether this waystation is safe to use."

He said nothing.

"This is the thirty-second party to use this waystation this season," she said. "I've counted. The notation goes south with the quarterly dispatch, and it says this waystation is a reliable rest point on the northern route." She looked at him steadily. "An accusation of theft against a northern party, documented, unresolved, unproven, gets entered in the same dispatch. Every party deciding whether to use this route reads the dispatch."

He was quiet.

"Is there a disc?" she asked.

A long pause. Then: "I may have misremembered where I last saw it."

She went back to the fire. She sat down beside Pelo.

"It's resolved," she said.

Pelo looked at her. "How?"

"He looked again and remembered it differently," she said.

She did not explain. Pelo was twenty-two and would eventually understand, or would ask her about it later and she would explain then, but right now what he needed was to eat his dinner and have a night's sleep before the morning's walking.

The six traders from three different groups went back to their fires.

She thought about it later that night, in the sleepless hour when the camp was quiet and her mind would not be quiet with it.

Maxtla would have argued the principle, the accusation requires evidence, the charter protects expedition members, here are the specific provisions. She would have been right, and the accuser would have backed down.

Ixchel was not Maxtla.

She had forty-three people, six weeks from home, seven more weeks of walking through territory where the route's reputation was still being built. The argument from principle would have been right and would have made an enemy. The man at the waystation had people, family, permanent residents, local relationships. An enemy there would compound for the remaining forty-nine days.

She had used the route's principle instead: you are part of this network, the network depends on the traders who use it, and I have more ways to damage your standing than you have to damage mine.

She was not certain Maxtla would have approved.

She was not certain it mattered.

What mattered was that Pelo had eaten his dinner and the traders had stayed and the morning walk would happen without yesterday's problem attached to it. What mattered was that the accuser understood, without it being said directly, without a scene, without a record that showed the settlement in conflict with the waystation's residents, that false accusations against expedition members were expensive.

This was the thing she had learned in the trading stalls. You could win a specific confrontation and lose the relationship, or you could end the specific confrontation and keep the relationship available for the next time you needed it. Maxtla won confrontations. Ixchel kept relationships available.

Both were necessary. She had known this since she was seventeen, watching Maxtla in the canyon's trading stall, the way certain problems bent to Maxtla's direct approach and others required a different angle. She had filed it then and had been practicing it since.

The expedition was hers. She was not Maxtla's instrument. She was not Maxtla at all. She was Ixchel, and she had her own methods.

The hardest decision came on the sixty-first day.

Three days past the southern jungle section, one of the expedition's traders, a woman named Dara, solid and reliable through two months of travel, came to Ixchel before dawn and said she was not going on.

Not injured. Not sick. Finished.

Ixchel looked at her. The light was still gray. The camp was asleep.

"What happened," she said. Not a question. An opening.

Dara described the last four days in the flat voice of someone reporting events they have decided they are done having feelings about. A trader picked up at the desert junction had been persistent in a specific way, and the handling of it had required daily management she had done without complaint because he had goods they needed and she had decided it was her problem.

"It's not your problem to manage," Ixchel said.

"I know," Dara said. "I managed it anyway. And now I'm done."

The desert junction trader had the coastal-dye samples and the contacts they had been working toward for two months. She looked at Dara, who was waiting with the patience of someone who has already made the decision and is watching someone else arrive at the same calculation.

"I'll handle him," Ixchel said. "Not directly. What he did is in the record now, I'm making it right now, and the record goes back to the settlement and from there to every trading partner on the network. A man whose behavior is in that record does not have a long career as a route trader."

Dara was quiet.

"He won't know I've done it until the doors stop opening the way they used to," Ixchel said. "It's not enough. It's what I have."

"Do I have to be near him for two more days?"

"No. You're at the front with Sera."

Dara nodded once and went back to her bedroll.

Ixchel made the note. Name, date, behavior, Dara's words. Sealed it with the other documentation for the next dispatch.

She sat with it. The record was real. It would travel south. But no word she put in it would give Dara back the four days. The record was the most she had. The most she had was not enough, and the distance between those two facts was not going to close.

She went to find the desert junction trader, to review the day's travel plan, to be entirely pleasant to him, to do the work for two more days without letting him see any of it.

She came back to the canyon with the copper samples and the dye contacts and the coastal family's tokens and Chalchih's letter and Ix Tunich's sealed cylinder and Dara, who had come the whole way and delivered a full account to the governance record and had asked, before the formal debrief, if the dispatch had been sent.

It had been sent the week after the event.

"Good," Dara said.

That was all she said about it.

Ixchel watched her walk across the settlement on the day of their return, Dara moving through the people who had come to meet the expedition, finding the family she'd left behind seven months earlier, the specific quality of a person arriving in the place where they are most themselves. Not a person who had been through a difficult thing. A person who had come back with what they went for.

That was what it meant to run an expedition. Not that nothing went wrong. That you came back with what you went for.

Maxtla was across the clearing. She raised one hand. Ixchel raised one back.

Later, in the planning room, she would give the full debrief. She would explain the Pelo incident and the Dara documentation and every decision she had made that Maxtla might have made differently. She would explain her reasoning. She was not going to present it as the right approach. She was going to present it as her approach, and Maxtla would have things to say about it, and those things would be useful.

She had run the expedition the way she ran things. Not the way Maxtla ran things. Not trying to approximate Maxtla at all.

It had worked because it was hers.

CHAPTER THIRTY-FIVE

Three departures

He found her the evening before he left, at the south boundary marker in the last of the light.

She was not doing anything. He knew, after years, that this was not the same as resting, Maxtla not-doing had the quality of a tool between uses: present, ready, pointed somewhere you couldn't see yet.

He stood beside her. He did not begin immediately. The pause before speech had always been part of his speech.

"The direction," he said.

She had not known she was waiting for this until he said it.

"Yes," she said.

"It's holding." He looked out over the canyon. "Not finished, it won't be finished in any timeline that matters to me. But it has weight now. It will be harder to undo than to continue. That's the threshold."

"How often does it reach the threshold?"

He considered this honestly. "Not often," he said.

A silence. The last light went off the upper walls.

"Where do you go?" she asked.

"North first. Then." He stopped. "I don't plan well at distance."

She understood this about him. Three hundred years of the next thing followed by the next, no address to return to, no way to plan for distance when the distance itself was what changed the plan.

"You're going to be fine," he said. Not as encouragement. As a finding, after sufficient evidence.

"I know," she said.

"Yes," he said. "That's why I can go."

He did not say goodbye. She did not expect it. Goodbye was for people with a fixed direction to come back from. He had not had one for longer than she could hold in her mind.

She stayed at the marker until the canyon went dark.

Lofn and the thing she kept The medicines arrived from the south in small quantities and Lofn worked through them the way she worked through all technical problems: systematically, with documentation, with a patience that surprised people who had only seen her grief and not the competent efficiency on the other side of it.

She documented everything, Ahmik's notation with her own modifications for precision. She transcribed the knowledge from Ix Chab twice, checking for discrepancies. One was significant: a plant's harvest timing that the translation had compressed.

She wrote to Ix Chab. Not directly, she couldn't, but through Ahmik, who passed the question south. The answer came back in the spring report, three months later: clear, specific, the timing restored.

She updated the records.

She had been doing this for two years: the slow, methodical work of building a medical knowledge base that was not dependent on memory. That did not die when its holder died. That could be read by the next person who needed it without requiring the original teacher to still be alive and available and willing.

Dewii's death had taught her: the window for passing on knowledge is not guaranteed. She taught everything she knew to at least two people. She documented everything. She documented the gaps too.

This had produced the settlement's first recognizable medical training.

Five people could now handle the most common medical problems: wound care, fever management, the specific childhood illnesses, plant preparations.

She had not set out to build a training. She had set out to solve the death problem, and the training was what the solution looked like.

"You're building a training," Maxtla said, watching Lofn with a student.

Dewii would have been good at this, he liked being helpful quietly. That's exactly what Lofn was doing now.

She was not over Dewii. She had not told anyone she was over him, she had been careful about that, because saying it would make it a claim she didn't want to defend and because it wasn't precisely true. She was past the acute phase. She was in the long phase, which was different: a Dewii-shaped space in her life that she had built around rather than through. The building had produced things, the training, the archive, the specific competence of someone who has converted grief into work, which was not the same as happiness but was real and useful and, on most days, sufficient.

She had told Maxtla about the device. Danijel had come to her, on the day before his departure, and told her. She had been angry, she had sat with the anger for two days, the anger of someone who has been given something without being asked. She had wanted the asking. She would have said yes if asked.

She had told Maxtla about this because she told Maxtla most things and because she wanted Maxtla to understand the distinction.

Maxtla had said: you're right. And: he was wrong not to ask. And: do you still want it removed?

She had thought about it. Honestly, with the specific honesty she applied to herself when no one else was watching.

"No," she had said. "I want to keep it. I just wanted to be asked first."

"He knew you'd say yes," Maxtla said.

"That's exactly the problem," Lofn said. "The people who make decisions for other people because they know what the other person would decide if asked, that's the same logic. Smaller stakes, benign intent, same structure."

Maxtla had looked at her for a long time. "You're going to teach that," she said.

"I'm going to teach that," Lofn confirmed. "In the women's sessions. The difference between benign intent and consent. Why it's not enough to mean well."

It was now part of the women's sessions that she ran twice in the moon cycle, in the building the community had designated for it after the sixth consecutive session exceeded the space in her own quarters.

The sessions covered: what the body needs and how to maintain it. What medical help is available and how to access it. The specific practical knowledge that had been kept in relationships between women and was now also kept in writing. And the harder things: what you are owed and what you are not. The difference between what the charter says and what the people around you say. How to hold your position when the pressure to yield is sustained and quiet rather than sudden and loud.

The quiet pressure was the one Lofn knew best.

She taught it like someone who had lived it.

The women who came to the sessions learned.

The hardest session was the one she had not planned for.

A woman named Sura had been coming to the sessions for four months. She had arrived at the settlement nine months before that, from a plateau settlement two weeks' walk to the east, and she had come alone, which was unusual, most arrivals came with family groups or in the company of traders. She had come alone and she had not explained why and in the settlement's early months no one had pressed her, which was the charter's provision in practice: you did not have to be anyone's history before you were this community's member.

She had found work in the granary administration, which suited her, she had a precise mind and a tolerance for the granary's specific routines. She had learned the notation quickly. She had been, by any visible measure, building a life.

She came to Lofn's session on a Tuesday and at the end of it, after the other women had left, she stayed.

"I need to tell you something," she said.

"Tell me," Lofn said.

"I'm going back."

Lofn held very still.

"To the settlement I came from," Sura said. "To my husband. My children are there." She paused. "I came here because I needed to leave for a while. To think. To understand what I was choosing." She looked at her hands. "I understand now."

"What do you understand?" Lofn asked. Carefully. The specific carefulness of someone holding a response she hadn't yet decided to offer.

"That I chose a hard thing," she said. "Not that I was wrong to leave. I wasn't wrong to leave. But I can go back knowing that now, knowing I chose it, not that it just happened to me." She looked up. "Does that make sense?"

It made sense. Lofn had spent four months in these sessions with Sura and had understood, without being told, that the departure had been sudden and driven by something she hadn't spoken about. She had understood it was her business and not Lofn's.

"Your husband," Lofn said.

"Is not a good man," Sura said. "But he is the father of my children, and my children are small, and the conditions of the settlement I left." She stopped. "You can't help me with the conditions of the settlement I left. No one here can. The only thing that can change them is my presence in them, over time."

Lofn wanted to argue. She had the arguments: that presence in a bad situation was not the same as changing it, that her children might be served better by a mother who had left than a mother who had returned to a lesser version of herself, that the charter had a provision for children in disputed custody situations.

She did not say any of it.

The cost of the principle was that sometimes the principle ran in a direction you would not have chosen for the person standing in front of you.

"Are you sure?" she asked.

"Yes," Sura said. "I've been sure for two months. I stayed to finish the sessions." She paused. "I wanted to know what I was walking away from. So I would know if I needed to come back."

"You can always come back," Lofn said.

"I know," Sura said. "That's also why I can go."

She left three days later. Lofn walked with her to the canyon's south edge.

"What you taught me," Sura said, at the edge. "The part about knowing the difference between the charter and the people around you. About holding your position when the pressure is quiet."

"Yes," Lofn said.

"I'll teach it to my daughters," she said. "Informally. The way things get passed."

Lofn looked at her. "Write it down," she said. "If you can. In any notation. Even rough."

"The Mayan notation?"

"Or your own. Something that exists outside you." She paused. "So it doesn't die if you do."

It was the harshest thing she could have said. She meant every word of it.

Sura nodded once. She turned and walked south.

Lofn went back to the settlement. She sat with it for two days, the specific discomfort of a person who has taught something and been required to live it in a direction they would not have chosen. She thought about Dewii, who had made no decision about his own departure, who had not been given the opportunity to choose. She thought about what it meant that Sura had chosen, clearly and with full information, and how that was different from what had been done to Dewii and what had been done to every woman in the settlement before the charter existed.

She could not know if Sura would be all right.

She could know that Sura had left with her own authority intact.

She went back to teaching.

She was still technically angry with him. She had decided the anger was appropriate and worth maintaining as a principle even after she had understood and accepted the decision. So she sat with him in the precise way of someone who is choosing to be present despite an ongoing grievance.

"I know you're angry," he said.

"Yes," she said.

"You're right to be."

"Yes," she said again.

A silence.

"You do the same thing sometimes," he said.

She looked at him. "What thing?"

"Make decisions for people because you know what they'd decide." He paused. "The woman who arrived in the autumn, the one I'm thinking you told about the southern medicines before she asked."

"She needed to know," Lofn said.

"Yes," he agreed. "And she would have said yes if asked. The same structure." He paused. "I'm not saying you're wrong. I'm saying the structure recurs."

The specific discomfort of being right about something and being the example of it.

"I'll ask first," she said.

"So will I," he said. "Next time." His expression said clearly that there would not be a next time, but the saying of it mattered.

"Where do you go?" she asked.

"North first," he said. "Into the upper plateau country and beyond. I want to see the northern routes before." He stopped. "Before."

"Before you leave the world," she said.

"Yes."

"Is there anyone else up there? People like you?"

"Not that I know of," he said. "Ohad was the last." He paused. "I have been alone here for longer than you would find comprehensible."

"Three hundred years," she said.

"Three hundred years," he agreed. "Without anyone who understands the full picture. Without anyone to tell."

"You've been telling us," she said.

He looked at her.

"Maxtla, and Eijá, and Ixchel," she said. "And me." She paused. "You've been telling us for years. Not everything, not the big things until recently. But the way you talk. The way you answer questions. You've been." She searched for the right word. "Teaching."

"Yes," he said.

"That's not nothing either," she said. "Three hundred years and you made it count at the end."

He was quiet for a long time.

"Thank you," he said.

"I'm still angry about the device," she said.

"I know," he said.

"But not only angry," she said.

"I know," he said again. "That's enough."

He left before dawn.

She had heard him go, the specific nothing-sound of someone who had spent three centuries learning to move without disturbance.

She had stayed in her bed and held the knowledge of the small device in her neck, the thing she hadn't consented to and had chosen to keep, and she thought about Dewii in the way she thought about him late at night: directly, without the buffer she maintained during the day. She told him about the device. She told him about Ix Chab and the knowledge archive. She told him about Yeta, who was twelve and extraordinary.

She told him about the rain in Yaxal Nah, and sitting in it with Eijá, and the moment she had understood that sitting was not the absence of useful activity.

She told him she was building the thing he would have built if he'd had the time.

Then she slept.

In the morning she taught. The test came from Brea, an original member who had developed gravitational pull in the settlement's social fabric. The problem was land allocation.

Brea had been assigned a good plot but wanted the one given to the new-arrival family from the northeast. Kael reviewed it and confirmed the allocation. Brea did not accept it. She had proposed a formal vote to revise the allocation criteria, a founding-member preference that would give early arrivals structural priority over later ones regardless of contribution record. The charter required a full moon cycle before any such vote could be held. The argument spread through the settlement the way all arguments spread: quickly, incompletely, and with the specific momentum of a concern that sounded reasonable.

Two women she had worked with since the founding period came to her. Women she trusted. Whose judgment she had relied on throughout the southern journey.

"We're not going to vote for the change," the first one said. Her name was Torva, and she had been the settlement's primary bread-baker since before the charter existed. "But we want you to understand what she's tapping."

"Tell me," Maxtla said.

"We were afraid in those years," Torva said. "Not the way the men were afraid, the men were afraid of the obvious things. We were afraid of something else. Whether what we were building was real. Whether it would hold." She paused. "Brea was there. She saw the same things we saw. The charter is real to you because you built it and you can see the whole shape of it. It's less real to the people who lived through the years before it existed and weren't sure it was going to."

"What does she want?" Maxtla asked. Not about the land plot.

"She wants to believe the thing she risked matters," Torva said. "She wants the charter to say so."

Maxtla let this land.

The charter said contribution matters. Earned standing. What it did not say, what she had chosen not to put in it, because the principle was clean and exceptions corroded principles, it did not say: the people who were afraid first, who built this with their hands when they didn't know if it was going to work, are owed something specific for that fear.

Brea was not wrong that she was owed something.

She could see the problem clearly.

The vote was eighteen days away.

She called an open meeting. Brea came. Everyone came.

She did not argue her position first. She asked Brea to explain the proposal.

Brea explained it well. She was articulate and the framing was sympathetic, she spoke about the founding members' risk, about the specific losses some of them had taken in the early period, about the reasonable expectation that early investment would be recognized.

People listened. Some of them nodded.

Then she asked the question that was harder to answer.

"Who built the route they traveled?" Brea said. She was looking at Maxtla directly now, not performing for the room. "The family that arrived in the autumn, the forty-three. They came south on a route that exists because of who was in this settlement before the charter. Before the granary. Before any of it." She paused. "You're telling me that the people who built the foundation that made their arrival possible compete equally with the people who arrived on that foundation. And your answer is that the record accounts for it." A beat. "The record is numbers. What I'm talking about is something the numbers don't hold."

Maxtla understood: Brea was pointing at the fear the record doesn't capture. She had an answer she believed in, but wasn't certain it was clean. She asked questions.

"If founding membership is the criterion, how do we define it?"

The questions went to the core of the proposal's logic.

"Not under the founding-member preference," Brea said.

"So a family that has been here eight months and has contributed, Peli, what are their contribution credits?"

Peli looked at his ledger. "One hundred and fourteen credits. Above average for the period."

"A hundred and fourteen credits," Maxtla said. "More contribution than several founding members in their first eight months. But under the proposed change, their contribution record would not be enough to override the founding-member preference of someone who has been here longer but contributed less."

A silence.

"That is a different settlement than the one the charter describes," she said. Not to Brea specifically. To the room. "The charter says standing is earned through contribution. The proposed change says standing is also inherited through arrival order." She paused. "These are two different principles. They can't both be true at the same time without producing outcomes like the one I just described."

She looked at Brea.

"Your contribution is real," she said. "Your risk during the founding period is real. The charter honors it, your contribution record honors it, your seniority weighting honors it. What the charter does not do is give you permanent structural advantage over people who are doing the same work you did, because doing the same work is what the system rewards."

Brea was quiet. She was not a stupid woman, she had heard the argument and understood where it led.

"What would you take to the vote?" Maxtla asked her. Genuinely. "Not to persuade you to withdraw it, if you want to vote, we vote. But: what is the actual thing you want? If it's recognition of founding-period contribution, the charter already has it. If it's something else, tell me what it is and we'll see if there's a way to address it that doesn't undermine the contribution principle."

A very long silence.

"I want people to remember," Brea said. "The founding members. What it cost to be here first."

"Yes," Maxtla said. "So do I." She looked at the room. "What the founding members built is the foundation that every person in this settlement is standing on. That's what we commemorate. Not as a claim, as a history." She paused. "What if we built the commemoration formally? A record of who was here from the beginning and what they contributed. Permanent. In the archive. Not a preference in the land allocation, but a real record of the real history."

Brea was quiet.

The vote took the full day.

Not because the mechanics were slow, the process Kael had designed was clear, each full member recording their choice in the contribution ledger, witnessed and dated. It took the full day because nobody left. They voted and then they stayed, moving around the edges of the clearing in the specific pattern of people who have committed to something and are now watching what they committed to land.

Fifty-one in favor of the proposed change. One hundred and four against.

The archive record was created the following month. Kael drafted it. Brea was listed first.

She never challenged an allocation again.

Fifty-one. Roughly one in three, and not just the men who had always been waiting for it to fail. People she had worked beside for years. The charter had held. That was true. Believing in the process and being easy about the outcome were not the same thing.

Gedeon found her that evening at the water channel.

Not to discuss the vote. He had been in the settlement long enough to know when she needed the problem named and when she needed the problem set down. He sat beside her and looked at the water moving. Eijá's slope calculations working in the quiet way of things that had been designed correctly and then left alone.

They sat for a while.

"The granary roof," he said. "I noticed a sag in the third beam."

"Eijá knows," she said.

"I thought she would." He paused. "I wanted to tell you something you didn't have to worry about."

She looked at him. He met her eyes briefly, his way of saying the thing underneath the thing, and then looked back at the water.

The channel ran. The canyon held the last of the light. She was not easy about the outcome. She was not going to be easy about the outcome. That was not the same as not being able to continue.

"The spring planting," she said.

"Tomorrow," he agreed.

They went back inside.

But more importantly: the forty-three people who had arrived hungry and displaced learned what had happened. They had not been in the meeting, they were still in the contribution period, not yet full members. But news traveled in the settlement the way it traveled everywhere, quickly and imperfectly and on the whole more accurately than official channels suggested.

What they learned was: the charter held. What they learned was: the governance structure was not managed by whoever was loudest or oldest or most connected. What they learned was: this place was what it said it was. The gate was never empty now. The drought came in the fifth year. Not catastrophic, but the care was the problem.

In a drought year, every allocation decision required explicit justification. The hard questions had nowhere to hide.

Forty-one people arrived in the drought season, farmers whose settlement had failed, three bad harvests and a declining water source.

Kael brought the numbers. Forty-one people would reduce reserves from twelve percent above minimum to four percent. Risk: twelve to fifteen percent chance of falling below minimum if spring planting underperforms.

Maxtla sat with this. Twelve to fifteen percent was not nothing. It was also not a reason to close the gate on forty-one people who had arrived hungry and exhausted and hoping.

She went through the numbers alone the night before.

She wrote the number down and looked at it.

Twelve to fifteen percent. Roughly one chance in seven.

The forty-one people outside the gate were farmers. She could see this in how they had organized their camp, the arrangement of a group accustomed to managing resources carefully, that had made rationing decisions before, that had the discipline of people who had lived close to the margin for three years without collapsing. They had held together through three bad harvests and a failing water source. They had made the decision to leave while the decision was still available, which was the hardest version of the decision.

One chance in seven that taking them in put the settlement below minimum threshold.

Six chances in seven that it didn't.

She thought about the woman at the gate who had asked about the charter, a woman in her thirties, precise and tired, who had asked whether the provision guarantee extended to contribution-period members or only to full members. She had asked it the way someone asks a question they already know might have a bad answer, because the alternative to asking was assuming, and she was too careful to assume.

Maxtla had told her it extended to everyone. This was what the charter said.

She went to sleep. In the morning she told Kael.

"We take them in," she said.

"Yes," Kael agreed. He had not been presenting it as a question.

Pela, the eldest, noticed the soil in the third terrace was losing water too fast. The drainage slope was off. The correction took three people one afternoon and yielded measurable improvement.

Sael came to the meeting with a proposal Kael had helped draft. This made it dangerous.

"A mature governance structure has emergency provisions," Sael said. "Not to abandon the principle. To protect it."

Emergency clause: two-thirds vote modifications in drought, never below subsistence, always documented.

"It's a door," Maxtla said.

"With a combination lock," Kael said. "Two-thirds majority. Documented. Time-limited."

"You helped draft this," she said.

"I helped draft it well," he said. "Because if it was going to be proposed, I wanted it drafted as contained as possible."

"You should have told me first," she said.

"Yes," he agreed. "I should have. I'm telling you now."

Lofn argued the forty-one couldn't vote on an amendment affecting them. The response: the language prevented this. The vote was called.

Eighty-nine in favor. Eighty-six against.

The amendment passed.

She didn't move. Around her, the room began to move, people coming and going, the normal social reconfiguration that followed a close vote, small conversations forming and dispersing. She did not move for several minutes.

Kael came and sat across from her.

"You're angry," he said.

"I'm not angry," she said. "I'm worried."

"About which use?"

"About the use I can't anticipate," she said. "The one that looks like the specific protection language and turns out to be its opposite." She paused. "History is full of provisions that said exactly the right things and were used for exactly the wrong things and the drafters couldn't explain how it happened because the language was so clear."

"The language is clear," Kael said.

"Yes," she said. "And the people applying it will be human, in a crisis, under pressure, and the record will show what they did but the record doesn't prevent the doing."

Kael was quiet for a moment. "I thought about not helping draft it," he said. "I thought about letting Sael bring it unpolished and fighting the unpolished version on the obvious grounds."

"Why didn't you?"

"Because the unpolished version would have passed too. The votes were there, I could see it before the meeting. And the unpolished version would have been dangerous." He looked at his hands. "I made a calculation. Maybe I made the wrong one."

"You made the calculation you thought was right," she said. "That's what we do here."

"That's what you do," he said. "That's what you built."

The amendment was invoked for the first time seven months later.

A severe late-spring frost had reduced the planting season yield by eleven percent, which was slightly below Eijá's conservative threshold. The reserve fell to three percent above minimum. The governance council convened and invoked the emergency provision.

The modifications they implemented reduced the allocation for the top forty percent of contribution-record holders by eight percent for a period of six weeks. The bottom sixty percent, including all members currently in their contribution period, received full standard allocation. The modification was documented in the archive. At the end of six weeks, with the summer stores partially in, the emergency was lifted and allocations returned to standard.

Maxtla had voted against invoking it.

She had been outvoted eleven to four.

The emergency resolved. The reduced allocation had been inconvenient and not catastrophic for the people it affected. Two people came to her during the six weeks to complain about the reduction, both full standing members with high contribution records, both aware that the high contribution record was specifically why they were in the affected group.

"The charter says I contributed," one of them said. A man in his late thirties, originally from Sael's informal faction, who had been converted by three years of the granary's actual function into someone she would have described as a genuine believer. He was genuinely angry, which meant he genuinely believed.

"The charter says you contributed," she agreed. "And the charter also says that in a declared emergency, the governance council can implement temporary modifications that protect the settlement's minimum threshold. You voted for the amendment."

"I voted for the amendment as a protection against catastrophe," he said. "Not for routine reduction."

"Yes," she said. "So did most of the people who voted for it. And the council invoked it, and it was invoked within the terms of the amendment, and it worked. The reserve held. No one went below subsistence." She paused. "The amendment did what Kael said it would do."

He looked at her. He understood what she was saying.

"You didn't want it," he said.

"No," she said. "I voted against it."

"But you're defending it."

"I'm administering it," she said. "The vote was legitimate. The invocation was within the charter's terms. My job is to run the structure, not to run the version of the structure I preferred when the vote went the other way." She looked at him steadily. "That's what the charter means. Not that the right side always wins. That the process is real. Both when I win and when I don't."

He was quiet for a long time.

"I still think the reduction was wrong," he said.

"Maybe," she said. "Write it in the archive. Put your name on it. That's what the record is for."

He did.

Torva did not come to her.

This was the thing Maxtla noticed on the twenty-third day of the six weeks, watching the morning bread distribution from the south side of the clearing. Torva was there, as she was every morning, doing the work she had done since before the charter existed. She was the settlement's bread-baker by practice if not by title, the person who knew every oven, who had trained six apprentices, who arrived before first light on cold mornings to start the fires that would warm the loaves that would feed everyone else.

She was thinner.

Not dramatically. The kind of thin that comes from managing carefully over weeks rather than days, the quality of a woman who has been making small decisions about her own portion for long enough that the decisions had accumulated into something visible.

Maxtla did the calculation in her head. Torva's contribution record: founding member, continuous high-level contribution, never a gap. She was in the top forty percent, well into it. The eight percent reduction applied to her. By the charter's subsistence definition, she was above threshold.

She watched Torva work for another few minutes. Torva moved with the efficiency of someone who had done this ten thousand times, which was probably close to accurate. She was not slow. She was not incapacitated. She was managing.

Maxtla went to find her that afternoon.

Torva was at the secondary oven, cleaning the racks, the end-of-day task that nobody else wanted. She did not look surprised to see Maxtla. She looked like a woman who had expected this conversation and had been deciding what to say.

"You managed," Maxtla said.

"I managed," Torva said.

"Tell me what that means."

Torva was quiet for a moment. She set down the rack brush and looked at her hands.

"The subsistence number is written for a working adult," she said. "I know what it is, I was in the room when Kael drafted it. We used the standard daily requirement and built the threshold from there." She paused. "It's correct for a working adult of average age."

"You're not an average age."

"I'm sixty-one," Torva said. "My body runs at a different rate than it did when I was forty. I need less than I did then, but I need it more consistently, and the eight percent matters more to me than it would matter to someone younger." She said this without complaint. As a technical observation. "Also I kept the informal allocation."

Maxtla was quiet.

"I didn't stop," Torva said. "There are three families in the settlement who I've been feeding informally for two years. Not from the granary, from my own supply, the supplemental work I do above the standard baking. Nobody records it. It's not in Peli's ledger." She met Maxtla's eyes. "I didn't stop during the six weeks because stopping would have meant telling them why, and telling them why would have meant."

"Admitting you had less," Maxtla said.

"Yes."

The light was going. Somewhere in the settlement, children were being called in for the evening. The sound of it, ordinary, made the clearing feel large and the conversation feel small.

"The subsistence definition is wrong," Maxtla said. "Not for everyone. For you. For people your age with your kind of contribution pattern."

"I know," Torva said. "I knew when we wrote it. I thought: I'm fifty-five, I'll probably not see the thing invoked, it's not worth complicating the language."

A silence.

"I was wrong," Torva said. "You should revise it."

"I will," Maxtla said. "This week."

She looked at Torva carefully. The thinness. The diminishment of a woman who had done everything correctly, had applied the charter's own logic to herself, had decided that someone else needed the resource more, and had been right, and had paid for being right.

"What do you need now?" Maxtla asked.

"I'm fine," Torva said.

"That's not what I asked."

A long pause.

"Extra oil," Torva said. "For the next month. The supplemental ration, not from the standard allocation. I know there's a process."

"There's a process," Maxtla agreed. "Come to me in the morning. We'll document it correctly."

Torva nodded. She picked up the rack brush. She was not angry, she was practical in the way she had always been practical.

"You should put it in the charter," Torva said, not looking up from the rack. "The age provision. Specifically. Not just a revision to the definition. A named provision."

"Why named?"

"Because in twenty years, someone is going to face the same situation and they're going to want to know whether the charter saw them coming." Torva set the rack in its slot. "I would have wanted to know."

Maxtla revised the subsistence definition that week, as she had said she would. She added a tiered provision, age-adjusted thresholds, a separate category for contribution patterns with informal community components that didn't appear in the ledger. Kael helped draft it. He was careful with the language. He had been, she noticed, careful about every provision since the amendment.

The provision was named. In the archive, it was called the founding-period provision. Torva's name was not attached to it.

Torva died in the winter of the seventh year. Not from the six weeks, not from that specifically. From the accumulation of years and from the specific diminishment of a woman who had managed carefully through one winter and come out the other side lighter than she went in and never quite recovered the weight. The settlement held a ceremony at the central clearing. The bread-bakers came. So did the three families she had fed informally for years, they knew what she had done, they had always known, they had not been in a position to say so while she was alive.

Kael noted the death in the archive with the detail he gave to founding members: name, contribution period, founding designation, cause as known. He wrote one additional line, which was not standard format.

"She managed."

The amendment did what Kael said it would do.

Maxtla held the full weight of that for a long time.

The amendment was invoked for the second time in the following year.

The northeast family, now forty-three strong, fully integrated, past their contribution period, part of the settlement's fabric in the way that families who have been somewhere long enough become part of it, brought the invocation. Their seasonal ceremony, the Tokosaj, had been challenged by a newer group of arrivals who had come from a tradition that considered the ceremony's animal component offensive. The challenge had moved through the governance structure and had reached, with genuine disagreement on both sides, the point where the council needed to decide.

The northeast family invoked the emergency provision. Not for resource allocation, for the ceremony itself. They argued that the challenge to their recognized ceremony, which had been in the settlement's calendar for three years, constituted an emergency to their community's cohesive functioning.

It was a creative interpretation of the amendment's language.

Maxtla read their argument three times.

The language said: temporary modifications to protect the settlement's minimum threshold. The northeast family's argument was that a community's ability to practice its recognized traditions was part of the settlement's minimum threshold, that cohesion was a resource like grain, that you could run below safe threshold on it, and that the challenge to the Tokosaj ceremony had taken them below.

It was an argument she would not have made. It was an argument Sael's faction would definitely not have made three years earlier. It was an argument that used the provision she had opposed to protect exactly the people she had built the charter to protect.

The council voted to recognize the invocation. Nine to six.

She voted yes.

Kael sat with her afterward.

"You were wrong," he said.

"About what specifically," she said.

"About the door," he said. "You said it wouldn't close easily once opened. But look who's opened it."

She thought about this.

"I was right about the danger," she said. "The first invocation, the reduction, I still think that was the wrong call. The mechanism was used for something it shouldn't have been used for. The protection held and no one was hurt, but the principle bent."

"And the second?"

"The second is what I hoped the charter would produce," she said. "People who had been afraid the system would be used against them using it for themselves. Properly. Within the terms." She paused. "I don't know which of those is what the amendment meant. Maybe both. Maybe neither."

"You're not building the charter you planned," Kael said. "You're building the charter the settlement is making."

She held it.

"Next time someone brings an amendment," she said, "I want to see the draft before the meeting."

"Yes," Kael said. "I know."

"And I want to be part of the drafting."

"Yes," he said again. "I know. I should have brought you in."

"You should have," she said. "Not because I'm in charge. Because the thing you're drafting affects everyone and the more people thinking about how it can be used wrongly before it passes, the better."

He nodded. He wrote it down.

Outside, the canyon held the last of the afternoon light in its specific way, the red walls going deeper red, the shadow creeping up from the canyon floor. Somewhere in the settlement, someone was beginning to prepare the fire for the Tokosaj ceremony. The northeast family had been preparing for a week. The sound of it was already present in the settlement's texture.

The charter had changed.

She was not sure it had changed for the better or for the worse. She would not know for years. Maybe decades.

She went to find Gedeon, and Aki, and the weight of a day that had produced more questions than answers. Gedeon had come from a people who measured time in seasons. The settlement's notation system tracked granularity he had to learn. He learned it by watching Maxtla, who moved through fine time as naturally as she moved through the canyon.

He was good at raising Aki. He had the patience for questions and the gift for explanation.

"He's going to ask you hard questions," Maxtla had told him, when Aki was old enough to be asking questions.

"Yes," Gedeon had agreed.

"You'll need to answer hard questions," Maxtla said.

"I know how to sit with a question," Gedeon said. "Sometimes that's more useful than the answer."

She had looked at him, precise and present and saying nothing.

He taught Aki the land. How to read the soil, track water, understand plants. He taught the older histories, the stories of the people he came from, passed on the way they had been passed to him.

"Are they true?" Aki asked.

"All of them have truth," Gedeon said. "You'll need both kinds."

In the fourth year, a party heading north stopped at the settlement for two days. Seven people. Three of them were from the hill country east of where Gedeon had grown up, not his people exactly, but close enough that he knew the specific way they moved, the specific way they held their loads, the habit of walking with the hands slightly open that came from years on terrain where you needed to be ready to catch yourself.

He sat with them at the communal fire on the second evening. They were heading into the northern high country, routes he had traveled before the canyon, territory he knew as well as he knew anything. Moving with the easy confidence of people who had not stayed anywhere long enough to know what they were leaving behind.

"Come north," the leader said. Not quite an invitation.

Gedeon looked at the fire. He knew that pull.

Inside the settlement, Aki was asleep the way young children sleep, completely absent from the world. Maxtla was in the planning room, working on something that would bear fruit in two years.

"Not this time," he said.

The leader nodded, the look of a man who had maybe made his own version of that answer somewhere and still felt the shape of the choice when the weather changed.

They left in the morning. Gedeon turned back and went inside.

CHAPTER THIRTY-SIX

The calendar

There was a day in the third year when Gedeon came to Maxtla with a specific problem.

The northeast family, the forty-three who had arrived hungry and become, over two years, an integrated and contributing part of the settlement, had a practice that was creating friction. A ritual, seasonal, that involved a kind of animal sacrifice. Not elaborate, not large, a single animal at the turn of each season, killed and burned in a specific ceremony that had been part of their tradition for as long as any of them could remember.

The friction was not about the ceremony. No one in the settlement was particularly opposed to the ceremony, the canyon country's relationship with animals was pragmatic enough that the act of killing did not itself disturb anyone. The friction was about where the ceremony was being performed: in the central clearing, which had become the settlement's shared space, the space where communal events happened and where the daily life of a larger and more heterogeneous community intersected.

The issue, as Kael had phrased it, was: whose clearing is it?

Gedeon had come to Maxtla because he had been sitting with the northeast family, he was the one who had built the relationship with them, through the farming work, and he understood what the ceremony meant to them in a way the governance problem couldn't contain.

"It's not the ceremony," he said. "It's the visibility. Performing it in the clearing is the announcement: we are here, we belong here, this is our community too."

"I know," Maxtla said. "And they do belong here. The charter says so."

"The charter doesn't say where they can perform their ceremonies," Gedeon said. "Which means the default applies, and the default is the clearing is shared space and shared space requires consensus."

"What do they need?"

"They need the ceremony to be visible," he said. "Not to everyone, not a spectacle. They need to be able to do it without hiding it. The doing-it-in-the-open is the statement: this is real here. This is recognized here."

She thought about this.

"It's the same thing Brea wanted," she said. "Recognition. Different form."

"Different form," Gedeon agreed. "But not the same solution."

"What's the solution?"

He had thought about it. He was not a governance person, he did not think in terms of charters and provisions. He thought in terms of relationships and what people needed from them.

"A ceremony calendar," he said. "In the shared space. Anyone who wants to use the clearing for a ceremony registers it, time, duration, nature. The clearing is available on a scheduled basis for exactly this kind of use." He paused. "It solves the consensus problem because the calendar process is the consensus. And it makes the ceremonies visible in the communal record, which is the recognition."

She looked at him.

"That's elegant," she said.

"I talked to the northeast family about it," he said. "They'd accept it. They'd want their ceremony listed by their name for it, not just by the date."

"Of course," Maxtla said. "Kael will build it into the archive format. We'll give each ceremony a name entry. Their ceremony. Whatever they call it."

"Tokosaj," Gedeon said.

"Write it that way in the archive," she said. "The Tokosaj ceremony, northeast family, quarterly, central clearing." She paused. "And anyone else who wants to perform a ceremony has the same access."

"How many do you think will use it?"

She thought about the settlement's composition, the range of origins, the range of traditions. "All of them, eventually," she said. "Once it exists as a practice."

He nodded. Then: "You know what you've built." He looked at the ceremony entry in the calendar. The Tokosaj. Northeast family. Quarterly. Central clearing.

She did not answer. The entry said what needed to be said.

"Thank you," she said.

"Thank you," he said. He meant: for the life. For the boy. For the work. For letting him be what he was and not what the center of gravity needed.

They went back to the work.

Outside, Aki was running the perimeter with the older children, a game, or training, or both, the line unclear at his age. He ran with the specific unconscious ease of a child who has grown up physically capable, who has Maria's training in his body and Gedeon's land knowledge in his mind and his mother's way of seeing in his eyes.

Not yet ten.

Somewhere to the east, a route waited.

He would find it when he was ready. The name came from a trader.

The trader was from the coastal network, Chalchih's connection to the Jalisco family, who moved goods between the lowland cities and the dry north. He had been using the route for one season when he referred to it, in a letter to Chalchih that Chalchih forwarded to the settlement through the quarterly dispatch, as the Red Road.

He had explained why: the canyon walls in the northern section were red, and the specific color of them, the deep iron-red of canyon sandstone at low sun, was the visual memory he carried from the route. He had never seen canyon country before. The red walls were the thing his mind kept returning to.

It spread through the trading network faster than any official naming would have. Within six months, Ahmik's correspondence was using it. Within a year, it was the name in the city's records.

The Red Road.

Maxtla heard it the first time in Ixchel's report from the second expedition, and she felt the satisfaction of a thing being named by the people who used it rather than by the people who built it.

"It's right," she told Ixchel.

"The color is right," Ixchel agreed. "The first time you see the canyon from the south, coming up, the walls in the evening, that color, it's the thing you remember."

"Did you remember it? Coming home?"

"I remembered it the whole way north," Ixchel said. "The last month, the walls getting higher and redder, and knowing you were getting close." She paused. "It's like a signal. The road tells you where you're going."

Maxtla lived to see it become natural.

The third generation, the children of the first children, born into the settlement as an ongoing fact, began asking questions about the early years with the distance of historical interest rather than living memory. A girl named Palik, twelve, Brea's granddaughter, asked what it was like before the route. She genuinely could not imagine the canyon country without it.

"Slower," Maxtla said. "Everything south of the desert was story."

"Did you believe the stories?"

"It was much larger than I expected. More similar too. The same argument about surplus and granaries, just further along."

Palik understood instantly, the same quality Eijá had, the mind that went straight to the structural implication. "The route changed what you could do about the problems."

"Yes. It's a granary for the region."

"And the eastern route would be." Palik looked east.

"For a much larger region," Maxtla said.

"Who's going?"

"Yeta. When she says she's ready."

Palik thought about this with the urgent calculation of a twelve-year-old mapping future possibilities against her own timeline.

"What do I need to know?" she asked. "To go on a route."

"Everything," Maxtla said.

Palik nodded, as if this was the obvious answer and she was glad it had been confirmed. "I'll start," she said.

She stood at the south boundary marker one morning, a different marker now, the settlement's south edge having moved twice as the community expanded, and let it arrive the way things arrived when you had been building them long enough to forget you were building.

Coming up the southern approach was a caravan she didn't recognize. Ten horses, heavily loaded, four people she'd never seen, and in the lead a young man from Teya's lineage who knew the canyon approach the way she knew it, without thinking, by the light. Behind the caravan, two hundred yards back, a second group was visible in the morning dust. The route was carrying traffic she hadn't sent and didn't need to manage.

That was what twenty years looked like.

At the morning market, Ixchel's daughter was handling a price dispute between a canyon trader and a coastal man, the same low patient voice, the same way of making both parties feel they had arrived at the conclusion themselves. Maria's girls were running their circuit. The granary roof, Eijá's design, had been standing for eighteen years. Lofn's students were teaching Lofn's students. Ahmik's notation was in use from the canyon to the sea, which meant a message written here could be read there and answered back in a hand Maxtla had never met and could still read.

She had walked the full route six times. Young and uncertain, experienced, old enough to know what it meant to have made a route your own.

She would walk it once more.

Not south to the city. South to the desert crossing and back, three weeks, on the section she had walked first and knew the way she knew her son's face: by feel, in the dark, without needing to see it.

She told no one except Gedeon. He said: when do you leave? She said: tomorrow morning. He said: I'll be at the gate.

She went in at dawn. The gate was open. Gedeon was at it.

"One more," she said.

"One more," he agreed.

He walked with her to the first southern marker and stopped there. She kept walking. The canyon walls were red in the first light. They were always red. She walked south on the Red Road. Eijá kept a list.

She kept a list: Technical Problems Observed and Partially Solved. Partial solutions were more useful than full ones, a place to start rather than stop.

The problems on the list:

The rockfall section of the Red Road, which she had solved twice and which required a third pass after the earthquake in the sixth year loosened the cliff face above it again. Her solution evolved each time, the first was a workaround, the second was a repair, the third was a structural redesign that moved the route thirty feet south and eliminated the exposure entirely. She wrote this up as a methodology: three-pass problem solving. You work around it, then you fix it, then you redesign so fixing is no longer required.

The granary roof, which had been adequate until the seventh winter's snow load, heavier than any year she had modeled, put a visible sag in the central beam. She had been there before the sag became a crack. She rebuilt the beam with a design that Maxtla had called over-engineered and she had called calibrated to the actual range of conditions rather than the expected range. The next three winters had proved her right.

The water channel extension, which she had designed in the third year, built in the fourth, and had been modifying continuously since. The channel was the settlement's single most important piece of infrastructure, more important than the granary in the sense that you could survive without the granary if you had water, but you could not survive without the water regardless. She had revised it six times. Each revision improved flow rate and reduced the maintenance burden. The sixth version was, she believed, close to optimal for the canyon's specific conditions.

"Close to optimal," Maxtla had said, when she used this phrase.

"There's always a better solution," Eijá said. "The question is whether the improvement justifies the cost. At revision six, the answer is probably no for a while."

"You'll revise it again," Maxtla said.

"When the settlement gets big enough," Eijá said. "Or when there's a drought bad enough that the current flow rate isn't adequate." She paused. "Probably both at once."

The settlement's size required the seventh revision. The drought happened two years after, and the seventh revision's capacity proved adequate.

The bridge problem. Seasonal streams blocked wheeled transport. She'd spent three winters on the problem. She had a design, but it required materials and infrastructure that didn't yet exist.

"Convince them by showing it," Maxtla had said, when she explained the problem.

"I need to show it before I can convince them," Eijá said.

"So show it small," Maxtla said. "Not a bridge for the route. A demonstration. Something that exists in the settlement, that people see working, that proves the principle."

"What do you want to move on wheels in the settlement?" Eijá asked.

"Grain," Maxtla said. "From the field to the granary."

She thought about this. The distance was short. The terrain was relatively flat. The weight was significant, heavy enough to prove the load-bearing but manageable enough to test safely. The proof of principle, demonstrated in the settlement's daily operations, would be more convincing than any argument.

"I need two people with stone skills," she said. "And two with wood skills. And six weeks."

"You have them," Maxtla said.

The demonstration vehicle was smaller than she had imagined in the large version. Two wheels, a flat bed, a simple axle design that she had refined from first principles. It moved a load of grain in one trip that would have required three pack animal loads. The friction was not solved, wood on wood was a significant limitation, but the principle was proven.

Kael watched the demonstration. He was quiet for a long time afterward.

"The southern route," he said.

"The bridge sections first," she said. "Once the bridge sections are crossed, the load capacity changes everything."

"How many seasons to build the bridges?" he asked.

"Two," she said. "If we have the labor." She paused. "The labor is the investment. The bridges pay for themselves in the third season if the load increase is what I think it will be."

"Convince Peli," Kael said. "If Peli says the math works, we build the bridges."

Peli looked at the numbers for two days and said the math worked.

They built the bridges.

The third season, the load increase was larger than she had projected.

Peli wrote a note in his ledger: "Eijá's estimates are conservative."

He showed it to her.

She said: "They're calibrated to the actual range of conditions."

He said: "Yes. Which turns out to be better than actual."

She looked at him for a moment.

"Next time I estimate, add twenty percent," she said.

"You could just estimate twenty percent higher," he said.

"I could," she agreed. "But then my estimates would no longer be accurate. They'd be already-adjusted estimates, which is a different thing." She paused. "The accuracy matters more than the convenience."

He absorbed this. He added a second note in his ledger: "Eijá's estimates are accurate. The conditions exceed them."

The last item on the list was not a technical problem. She had added it in the fifteenth year, in the section she had started calling future problems, which was problems she anticipated but hadn't encountered yet.

The future problem was: what happens when we have more than one route and more than one city and more than one network, and the networks need to coordinate?

The Red Road worked because it was organized. The organization worked because everyone who used it understood the rules and the rules were consistent and the enforcement of the rules was known. One route, one set of rules, one enforcement structure.

When there were three routes, the rules might diverge. Different enforcement. Different contribution requirements. Different protection arrangements. Different pricing conventions.

The divergence would be invisible at first, small differences, easily bridged case by case. Over time, the small differences would compound. A trader moving goods between two routes would find the transition point a friction. A settlement at the junction of two routes would have to navigate two sets of rules. The friction would be small, then large, then a genuine problem.

She had written this out in the archive as a problem to anticipate.

Maxtla had read it and said: "You're right."

"You'd thought of it," Eijá said.

"I'd thought of something like it," Maxtla said. "Not this specifically." She looked at the entry. "What's the solution?"

"I don't know yet," Eijá said. "Which is why it's in the unsolved section."

Maxtla had looked at the list, the columns of solved and partial and unsolved, and been quiet for a long moment.

"This is the most useful document in the settlement," she said.

"The charter is more useful," Eijá said.

"The charter says what we value," Maxtla said. "This says what we still need to build." She paused. "Both are necessary. Neither is more important." She looked at Eijá. "You've been keeping this since the beginning?"

"Since the journey south," Eijá said.

"Will you keep it?"

"Yes," Eijá said.

"Until?"

Eijá thought about this. "Until someone takes it from me," she said. "Not takes it away, takes it over. A successor. Someone who sees the problems the way I see them and wants the job."

"Is there anyone?"

Eijá thought about the settlement's young people, the ones who had Maria's quality of watching the physical world, who lingered near building projects and asked the right questions about why rather than just how.

"Maybe," she said. "One of the northeast family's younger people. The one who helped with the bridge."

"The tall one?"

"She's not tall," Eijá said. "She's exactly the right height for her center of gravity." She paused, aware that this was a distinction most people would not make. "Yes. That one."

"Talk to her," Maxtla said.

"I will," Eijá said.

She didn't say: I already have. Just: inviting. Letting the interest grow in its own direction. Providing access to the problems and watching what the young person did with the access.

The girl had, last week, identified an inefficiency in the water channel's third juncture that Eijá had noted six months ago and had been watching to see if anyone else noticed.

She had.

Eijá had not told her she'd seen it first.

She had said: what do you think the solution is?

The girl had three ideas. One of them was better than Eijá's.

She had added it to the list.

Revised: water channel third juncture. Solution: the girl's version.

Under that, in the fine notation of someone who documents carefully:

Name of solution contributor: Nena.

CHAPTER THIRTY-SEVEN

What Aki brought back

It was the best entry in the list. At eighteen, Aki went east on a newly mapped route. The eastern route dropped into a river valley system, green, wet, complex with seasonal flooding. The river settlements were old and large.

"Understanding takes more time than trading," Maxtla had said.

"Yes," Yeta had agreed. "But the trade that comes after is more durable."

He went east with eight people: Yeta, two fighters, a healer, Palik, a translator, and Suri.

Maxtla stood at the gate. "Come back different," she said. "That's the whole point." He walked east without looking back. Gedeon stood beside her. They stood at the gate together until there was nothing left to see.

He returned after eleven months changed. The confidence he had was deeper, tested against unknown conditions and found real.

He debriefed the governance council and his family. The river settlements were old and large, their governance structures tired.

"The high-ground families control the surplus. They see it as flood insurance, not just advantage," he said.

"That's legitimate," Lofn said. "So the granary model needs modification. Not just storage of surplus for bad years, specifically storage that addresses the asymmetric flood risk. The high-ground families contribute more in good years. In flood years, the first allocation goes to flood victims." He paused. "I proposed this. In the third month, to the family council."

The room was quiet.

"What happened?" Maxtla asked.

"They talked about it for two weeks," he said. "The high-ground families needed to believe that the flood-year priority allocation wouldn't be gamed, that low-ground families wouldn't claim flood damage they hadn't suffered. I suggested what Peli built here: the contribution record. If you can see who contributed what, you can see who the system should prioritize."

"Did they go for it?" Kael asked.

"They're considering it," he said. "I left documentation. The formal proposal, written in their notation, they use a different system but it's compatible with ours, which is one of the first things I checked." He looked at Maxtla. "I think they'll do it. Not because I convinced them, but because the logic is clear and the river valley is entering a period where the flood variability is increasing and the old system's weaknesses are becoming more expensive."

"Climate," Eijá said, with the precision of someone who had been tracking the canyon country's own weather patterns for fifteen years and had noted the drift.

"The floods are getting less predictable," he confirmed. "The first-deposit soil is moving. The high-ground families who relied on the pattern are beginning to understand the pattern is no longer reliable." He paused. "Change sometimes needs the thing it's replacing to fail."

Maxtla looked at him.

"You learned that there," she said.

"I already knew it," he said. "You taught it to me."

"I taught you the idea," she said. "You learned it there. There's a difference." She looked at him steadily. "Come back different. That's the whole point."

He smiled at her.

"Yes," he said.

In the morning, he started writing the full report. It took three weeks. When it was finished, Peli bound it and it went into the archive next to the documentation of the first southern expedition, Maxtla's original route, the mother route, the one the settlement was built on.

The eastern route documentation went in beside it.

Two routes now.

The beginning of the system.

The written report had a section she hadn't expected.

He had titled it: What I Got Wrong.

The section described a community in the river valley, not one of the three he had negotiated with, but a fourth, smaller one, that Sera had taken him to visit in the third month. He had read the community as ready for the granary model. He had spent two days making the case. They had listened and thanked him and he had left believing he had planted something that would take root.

What he had not known, what Sera had not told him, he wrote, though he had come to believe she knew, was that this community had a long-standing dispute with one of the three communities he had already made agreements with. By building relationships with both sides of a conflict he hadn't understood, he had placed the settlement in the middle of it. The three-community agreement was now complicated by a fourth party with reason to be suspicious of anyone connected to their longtime adversary.

He wrote: I built the relationship before I understood the context. The relationship was genuine. The context made it costly.

He wrote: Sera didn't tell me because I didn't ask the right questions. I asked what do these communities trade. I should have asked what do they remember.

He wrote: I am including this because the report is most useful if it is accurate. The accurate version includes this.

Maxtla read the section twice.

She found him at the eastern field, where he was walking the perimeter with the same attention to drainage and soil quality that Gedeon had walked it with for twenty years.

"You knew when you were writing it," she said.

"Yes," he said.

"The report is better for it."

"The report is accurate," he said. "Whether it's better is a different question."

She looked at him. He had her way of making distinctions. Gedeon's patience with himself when the distinction didn't resolve cleanly.

"How do you repair it?" she asked.

He had been thinking about it for three weeks. "Slowly," he said. "The relationship with the fourth community is real. The dispute between them and the third is real. They're not going to resolve on our timeline." He paused. "We send someone back in two years. Not me, someone they haven't met yet. Someone who can build the relationship with the fourth community without carrying what I carried."

"Someone who asks what they remember before asking what they trade," she said.

"Yes."

She thought about it. "Yeta," she said.

He considered this. "She'd need to be older."

"In two years she will be," Maxtla said.

He looked at her steadily, with the specific look he had inherited directly and she recognized as her own: not asking for reassurance, not asking for absolution, just checking whether the direction he'd identified was the right one.

"Put it in the archive," she said. "The section. As a methodology note. What to ask before you build the relationship."

"I already did," he said.

"I know," she said. "I'm telling you it was right."

She walked back to the settlement. He returned to the field.

The granary stood at the canyon's center, expanded twice now, the second expansion his design built in his absence. A structure that had started as one person's solution to the death problem and had become, over two decades, the settlement's trust mechanism, its proof of principle, the thing that said: we are what we say we are.

Its grain didn't care who built it.

Neither did the archive.

Neither did the road.

"When I'm home long enough to learn what I missed," he said, "I want to plan the third."

She looked at him.

"Not yet," he said. "I know. But eventually."

"Eventually," she said. "Yes."

The fire was warm. The settlement moved around them, going about its midday, a hundred small transactions and decisions happening in the ordinary way of a place that had enough practice at existing to make existence look easy.

It was not easy. It had never been easy.

TWENTY-THREE YEARS

The original fire

The settlement had the feel of something that would continue, which was not a small thing. In the twenty-third year, the settlement held a ceremony for the five original travelers still living. Lofn organized it. She had learned to mark moments without making them heavier than they were.

The five: Maxtla, Ixchel, Lofn, Eijá, Maria. Teya sent a message: I remember the first pass. I remember thinking you might not make it. I was wrong.

Targat came himself, with two of his grandchildren, more than any message could have said about what he thought.

He sat with her before the ceremony. "The route runs clean," he said. "I didn't believe the plan when you were standing in the desert. But talking was worth trying." She understood: he had watched her from the ridge for a very long time.

They held the ceremony in the late afternoon, when the canyon walls were at their reddest. The settlement gathered, not everyone, the settlement was now large enough that everyone in one place required deliberate planning, but the people who wanted to come, which was most of them.

Maxtla spoke last.

She was forty-seven. Lean, precise, carrying decades without visible damage. She had found, in the last few years, that she was beginning to feel like the canyon walls, something that had been here long enough to be part of the landscape, that the new arrivals oriented themselves by without necessarily knowing its history.

She stood in front of the settlement and let herself be in it, the full weight of twenty-three years, her son across the clearing and Gedeon beside her and the canyon walls still red.

She had not looked at him before she spoke. She looked at him now, briefly. He met her eyes and looked away, how Gedeon expressed things too large for acknowledgment.

She looked back at the settlement.

"I didn't know if this would work," she said. "I want to say that clearly. I left because I needed to, because staying was not survivable, and I came back because what I found made coming back worth the difficulty. But I did not know, when we left with sixty people and what we could carry, if any of this would be here."

She looked at the settlement.

"It's here," she said. "That's the whole thing. All the governance structure and the granary and the route and the archive, all of it is downstream of that one fact. The thing we built is still standing. It works. The people who built it are still here, and the people who came after us built on what we made and took it further."

She paused.

"Aki came back from the east with a proposal for how to apply the granary model to a river valley settlement that has different problems than we had," she said. "He modified the model. He improved it." She looked at her son across the clearing. "That is the whole point. Not that the model stays the same, but that what we learned is in his hands now and he can do more with it than we could."

She looked at the five of them, her four, the women who had walked the road south and back.

"What we did," she said, "is we went somewhere and we came back different, and the difference was useful." She paused. "I don't know a better description of a good life."

The canyon walls were very red.

The settlement was quiet in the way that large groups of people are quiet when they are fully present.

Somewhere in the crowd, Palik was writing everything down.

After the ceremony, people stayed for a long time.

This was the thing about the settlement at this stage: it had the specific social gravity of a place that had been somewhere long enough that people wanted to be in it, not because they needed to be but because they chose to be. The canyon held light well in the late afternoons of this season, the walls catching the last gold and holding it while the floor below moved into shadow. People stayed in the warmth at the canyon's edge and talked, and the talking continued after the light went.

Maxtla moved through the edges of it, not leading anything, not managing anything. This was Lofn's day in that sense, the ceremony had been Lofn's work and the gathering was its continuation, and Maxtla's job was to be present rather than useful. She had not gotten good at this. She was better at it than she had been at thirty, which was not a high bar.

Eijá found her by the archive building.

"I've been thinking about the next version of the granary design," she said, by way of greeting.

Maxtla looked at her.

"I know," Eijá said. "Not today."

"Not today."

"I just wanted to tell you I've been thinking about it." She paused. "It helps to say it out loud."

"Tell me what you're thinking."

"The orientation problem. We built ours for this canyon's specific temperature patterns. Aki's modified version works for the river valley's flood risk. Neither design works for the coastal settlements, the salt air gets into the sealed materials differently than dry air or flood water. I've been working on a coastal variant for three seasons and I think I have the exterior sheathing solved." She looked at the archive building. "I wrote it up last month. I wanted your opinion before I sent it to the coastal families."

"Show me tomorrow," Maxtla said.

"Tomorrow," Eijá agreed. She did not move. "It's a good day," she said, after a moment.

"Yes."

"I didn't expect to make it to forty-five," Eijá said. Not dramatically. As information. "When I was twenty-two, I thought I would die on the road or in a season with bad harvest or in a situation I didn't have enough fighters for. I had a specific picture of how it would go." She looked at her hands, the hands that had been building and adapting and documenting for twenty-three years. "I was wrong about the picture."

"What does forty-five look like?" Maxtla asked.

“Like there’s more to do than there was at twenty-two.” She paused. “Which is not what I expected. I thought it would look like less.” She looked at the archive. “The archive has forty-seven tablets. In five years it will have a hundred. The knowledge is accumulating faster than I can document it, which means the documentation problem is getting bigger, not smaller.” She looked back at Maxtla. “It’s an engineering problem I can’t solve by building faster.”

"What solves it?"

"Training more people to document," she said. "Which is Lofn's method, not mine. But I'm starting to think she's right."

"She usually is," Maxtla said.

"Yes," Eijá said. "I know." A pause. "Don't tell her I said that."

"Why not?"

"Because then she'll know I think she's right, and she'll start applying it to situations where she's not right, and I'll have to argue with her twice as much."

"Eijá."

"What?"

"Go enjoy the ceremony."

She went.

The canyon was dark by the time most people had gone. The five of them were at the original fire, not the largest fire in the settlement now, not the most central, but the one that had not gone out since the beginning, the one they built every evening out of a habit that had outlasted the need for it.

It was Lofn who said what the day was.

"Twenty-three years," she said.

Not as a weight. As a fact she was still finding the dimensions of.

"Dewii would be forty-six," she said. "He would have been in charge of the ceremony. He would have made it better." She paused. "And worse. He would have added three things that didn't need to be there and one that did, and you would have had to talk him out of two of them."

Maria, across the fire: "Which one would you have kept?"

"The music," Lofn said. "He always wanted more music." She looked into the fire. "I still sleep on his side of the bed. I don't mean to. I just wake up there."

No one said anything.

"Danijel would have counted the people," Ixchel said. "To assess attendance. He would have identified the three most important conversations happening in the crowd and positioned himself to overhear at least two of them." She paused. "He would have called it observation. We would have called it exactly what it was."

"He would have watched from a distance and then found each of us separately afterward," Maxtla said. "And said the thing he thought we needed to hear. Which would have been the right thing. Which would also have been slightly annoying."

"What would he have said to you?" Maria asked.

Maxtla thought about it honestly. "He would have said: the interesting part is what happens next." She paused. "He always said the interesting part was what happens next."

"Was he right?"

"Usually."

She stopped. She had not let herself think past that point, what it had cost him to argue for the interference, whether the argument had prevailed, whether he was still an observer at all or something else now. She would never know. She had decided, sometime in the third year, that the not-knowing was the correct weight to carry. That making it certain, even in her imagination, would be a smaller thing than the actual open question of a man three hundred years old who had chosen a canyon over his protocols and disappeared into the distance with nothing but his record and his argument.

Eijá had been quiet through most of it. She was sitting slightly apart from the others in the way she sat when she was thinking about something that had nothing to do with the conversation. Now she looked up.

"The granary," she said. "The third expansion. I've been going over the eastern wall. There's a load distribution problem that's going to show up in two or three winters when we fill the upper bins." She paused. "I wanted someone to know I'm aware of it."

Maria looked at her.

"Not tonight," Eijá said. "I know. Just, someone should know I'm aware of it."

"I know," Maxtla said. "Now we both know."

"Good." Eijá looked back at the fire. "Good day," she said, after a moment. It came out like a structural assessment, not sentiment exactly, more the conclusion of a calculation she had been running since morning. "Better than I expected, when I was twenty-two."

The fire held. The canyon held. Somewhere in the middle of the settlement, someone was doing what Dewii had wanted, there was music, thin and real, the kind that started at the edges of gatherings and grew when no one was managing it.

Gedeon appeared at the edge of the firelight. He looked at the five of them and the fire and the canyon above them, and then he sat down at the fire's edge without being asked, which was not something he did often.

He did not say anything for a while. He had brought two cups of the drink from somewhere and passed one to Maxtla, and she took it.

"Twenty-three years," she said.

"Twenty-one for me," he said. "I was late."

"You were here when it mattered."

"Yes," he said. He looked into the fire. He was fifty-one years old and the firelight did what firelight does to a face after fifty, showed the structure of it, the accumulated weight. He did not look unhappy. He looked finished in the way that good work looks finished, the way a wall looks after the last stone has been set and the mortar has cured. "I've been thinking about the eastern route. The extension beyond Aki's reach. The settlements at the high plateau."

"I know you have."

"I think." He paused. "I think next spring."

She looked at him.

"I'm not done," he said. "There's more to map."

"I know," she said. "Go when you're ready."

"I'll come back," he said.

"I know that too."

He raised his cup. She raised hers. It was not a formal gesture. It was the gesture of two people who had been in the same story for twenty-nine years and were acknowledging it without making it into a thing it didn't need to be. She felt, briefly, the weight of twenty-nine years of him being there, not all of it good, not all of it easy, but all of it his and real and chosen. She did not say this. Neither did he. They had never been people who said the large things out loud, and they were too old to start now.

Maxtla was forty-seven years old.

She had come from the canyon and come back to it and built a thing in it that was larger than what any of them had planned, and the thing was running without her driving it, and her son was across the clearing with his own plans and her friends were at this fire and the knowledge was in the archive and the route was on the map.

She did not have a word for what this felt like. True was the closest.

"What does Palik do with the record?" Maria asked. "The one she was writing."

"Puts it in the archive," Lofn said. "With everything else."

"And then?"

"Someone reads it," Maxtla said. "Fifty years from now, a hundred. Someone who wants to know how it started reads it." She paused. "And gets it wrong in some ways and right in others, and adds what they know to what we knew, and the record gets longer."

The music from the settlement's center had picked up a second voice. A third.

"That's enough," Ixchel said. Not a verdict. A recognition.

"Yes," Maxtla said.

She had left this canyon because staying was not survivable and she had come back to it with what she found in the going, and the canyon had held all of it, the medicine and the route and the knowledge and the people and the grief and the three hundred and fourteen marks on the charter and the twenty-nine years of him beside her in the dark. She did not have a word for the accounting of that. She had not had one at twenty-two and she did not have one now. Some things came before their names.

The floor was up.

Don't miss out!

Visit the website below and you can sign up to receive emails whenever Joe Zeigler publishes a new book. There's no charge and no obligation.

https://books2read.com/r/B-A-NTPQE-JMMCJ

BOOKS 2 READ

Connecting independent readers to independent writers.

Did you love *The Journey*? Then you should read *The Breeding*[1] by Joe Zeigler!

[2]

The Breeding (2025, formerly *The Gorge*) follows the migratory Cliff Dwellers, whose survival hinges on a sacred ritual: the "Breeding of the Virgins." Young women are offered to elders, told it is their duty.

When Maxtla is chosen, she expects honor but finds exploitation. Her resistance challenges the sanctified lies underpinning their culture. A visceral study of power and obedience for readers of Atwood and Butler, *The Breeding* warns that traditions can hide violence.

1. https://books2read.com/u/mqJMj8
2. https://books2read.com/u/mqJMj8

www.ingramcontent.com/pod-product-compliance
Lightning Source LLC
LaVergne TN
LVHW090552110826
845146LV00001B/108

* 9 7 9 8 9 9 5 2 5 3 9 0 7 *